DATE DUE

JAMES BRANCH CABELL
The Dream and the Reality

JAMES BRANCH CABELL

THE DREAM
AND THE
REALITY

BY DESMOND TARRANT

UNIVERSITY OF OKLAHOMA PRESS
NORMAN

Library of Congress Catalog Card Number: 67-15595

Copyright 1967 by the University of Oklahoma Press, Publishing Division of the University. Composed and printed at Norman, Oklahoma, U. S. A., by the University of Oklahoma Press. First edition.

To Dorrie
For coming Home with me and
For giving me access to the Maker

INTRODUCTION

The work of James Branch Cabell is one of the most ambitious attempts in twentieth-century art to renovate an age-old medium —the myth. Real mythologies are not very popular at the moment, possibly because:

> We have lost our immediate feeling for the great realities of the spirit—and to this world all true mythology belongs—lost it precisely because of our all-too-willing, helpful and efficient science. . . . We have to ask ourselves: is an immediate experience and enjoyment of mythology still in any sense possible?[1]

Before examining Cabell's art itself it may be useful to glance at certain aspects of the development and nature of myths. Only in this way does it seem possible to do any justice to what is virtually a unique addition to the realm of mythology, an addition which seems to give a most definite "yes" to the above question.

It has been said that as soon as an Englishman realizes that he is enjoying himself, he feels guilty. This statement may apply to all practical people, and it is therefore tempting to take as sufficient evidence of the enjoyment to be derived from Cabell's works the fact that he was censored. And perhaps it is this enjoyment or "immediate experience" undergone by the spirit, through both the heart and the head, that is of most importance. For, as with all mythologies, the consequence of this experience is, if anything at all, a form of revelation. Cabell's powerful mind has observed his universe imaginatively; he reflects selected expe-

[1] C. G. Jung and C. Kerenyi, *Introduction to a Science of Mythology* (Routledge & Keegan Paul, Ltd., London, 1951).

riences in a host of specially contrived symbols; he juxtaposes and manipulates these to take us to the heart of the intangible mystery of creation, of life and death, of the past, and of the future.

Great insight, great feeling, great craftsmanship—these are the prime requisites for great art. And Cabell had them all. But to appreciate him needs imaginative understanding, and we seem to be content, at least for the present, to dispense with the imagination. Even before this trend had really begun Carlyle stated:

> Were we required to characterise this age of ours by a single epithet, we should be tempted to call it, not an Heroical, Devotional, Philosophic or Moral Age, but the Mechanical Age. . . . Not the external and physical alone is now managed by machinery but the internal and spiritual also. . . . Men are grown mechanical in head and heart, as well as in hand.[2]

Or, a little later in the process, Thomas Wolfe illustrated:

> . . . an America that had been lost beneath the savage roar of its machinery, the brutal stupefaction of its days, the huge disease of its furious, ever-quickening and incurable unrest, its flood-tide horror of gray, driven faces, starved, brutal eyes and dull, dead flesh.[3]

And thus Judge Charles C. Nott, when advising the jury to acquit the defendants of *Jurgen*, was able to say, "It is doubtful if the book could be read or understood at all by more than a very limited number of readers." What a pity! For the Virginian opens the door of this mechanical madhouse into a world entirely more magnificent, more profound, and infinitely less limited in spirit.

The following study is an attempt to examine certain aspects of Cabell's thought and art in the hope that there may be a greater understanding of Vernon Louis Parrington's description of him:

> A self-reliant intellectual, rich in the spoils of all literatures, one of the great masters of English prose, the supreme comic figure thus far granted us, he stands apart from the throng of lesser American novelists, as Mark Twain stood apart, individual and incomparable.[4]

[2] "Sign of the Times," *Edinburgh Review* (June, 1829).
[3] *Of Time and the River.*
[4] *The Pacific Review* (1921).

As Cabell himself observed frequently, the true and mature romanticist begins where the realist leaves off. In other words when the finished work is carried out of the workshops of the realists, who "represent" photographically, it is just ready to be carried into the workshop of Cabell, who "reveals" like an oil painter. In doing so he makes much modern fiction seem puerile in the inadequacy of its thought and expression.

Cabell's work is unlike that of his major contemporaries in that his setting is not national but cosmic, as was Milton's in *Paradise Lost*. His work is likely to wear better than theirs, because it is less likely to lose meaning with the passing of the topical in language and situation. Like his contemporaries he descends into the depths of life's meanings, but unlike them, he refuses to stay there for his mode of expression, preferring to ascend to the heights again, to the cloud-encircled summit of Olympus, to create his own special medium of distilled beauty and truth.

The final impression of Cabell's work is very different from that of much of his contemporaries. In reading the fiction of the Plebs and even of many of the Patricians (of Faulkner and Hemingway for example), the almost uniform impression is that of man's insignificance, his impotence in the face of devastating odds. Life dwarfs man, who is but another "chemism" turned up for a moment by a cruelly jesting Nature and shortly to be thrown aside. Cabell's work, while reflecting current trends of disillusion and pessimistic determinism, makes of these things something more positive. The collapse of one set of "illusions" or beliefs only sets man free to go in search of better ones. If matters are predetermined there must be something which has done the predetermining and which therefore has an interest in man; this itself is positive and indicates positive ends. If the means (i.e., man and his actions) are predetermined, the chances are that so are the ends. These considerations began the evolution of Cabell's "philosophy of life" which is the mainspring of his art. This philosophy renders him unique in his time and place; ultimately it sets his work not only against but beyond most of that of his contemporaries.

The nearest figure comparable to Cabell in stature and outlook is Theodore Dreiser. No one can say that the final impression of Dreiser's work is that of unmitigated cheerfulness. Neither is that of Cabell's. Yet, where Dreiser's pageant is akin to a funeral march on a downward slope, there is another unmistakable symbol dominating the work of Cabell. It bears a remarkable resemblance to Jacob's ladder, even if we climb it in the dark and there are numerous rungs missing.

Cabell is almost alone in twentieth-century literature in presenting man as, if not master of his fate, at least equal to it. For one glorious moment, to the crescendo of the Deems Taylor symphony inspired by him, a mere mortal once again moves with ease among the gods to re-create from American life a mythologem of all life.

Desmond Tarrant

Nightingales, Hook, Hants, England
May, 1967

CONTENTS

xi

PART ONE

THE ARTISTIC VALIDITY OF MYTHS AS A MEANS OF COMMUNICATION

Bring me my bow of burning gold,
Bring me my arrows of desire . . .
                                    —Blake

1: Some Historical Comments

Perhaps it is advisable to give some brief definitions of certain words which will be used frequently in the following study. By "image" is meant the shape, created in the understanding, of anything tangible. The image is the inner reflection of the outward appearance of something seen. Thus the image of a hammer or a sickle conveys the shapes and substances of these things but nothing more. A "symbol" is an image with a significance over and beyond its shape and substance: the images of a hammer and sickle juxtoposed in a certain way "symbolize" initially the Communist world and additionally, perhaps, concepts of fear and horror. "Imagination" is understood in its twofold nature as illustrated by Coleridge: having a primary quality which selects experiences most relevant for intelligibility, and a secondary quality which remakes or re-creates the selected data into a new combination that more adequately or emphatically communicates this intelligibility. Imagination involves both the intellect and the feelings in a kind of chemical fusion which can produce greater understanding of matters fundamental and eternal to all departments of man's living. "Fancy," which also involves the intellect and feelings, combines selected data, but not in such a way as to create a final significance distinct from any of its individual parts. For example:

> *I put my hat upon my head*
> *And walked into the Strand;*
> *And there I met another man*
> *Whose hat was in his hand.*

3

This combination of selected data produces a notion of the ludicrous and so, quite legitimately, can produce a comic catharsis; but the selected data, the images, remain themselves and merely add up cumulatively for the final effect. There is no profound involvement of intellect or feeling—it is fanciful, not imaginative. Whereas the process and effect in the following is somewhat different:

> ... *Who would fardels bear*
> *To grunt and sweat under a weary life,*
> *But that the dread of something after death,—*
> *The undiscovered country from whose bourn*
> *No traveller returns—puzzles the will,*
> *And makes us bear rather those ills we have*
> *Than fly to others that we know not of?*

These images are all concrete enough, but they are so juxtaposed as to fuse together to produce a final significance which is quite different from any of the images regarded individually. Something new has been created—in this case a vision of all human life. Mind and heart have been profoundly involved: the imagination has been at work. Perhaps the difference between fancy and imagination is largely one of degree, but when the problem at issue is the evaluation of art, the difference is an important one. It is measurable most directly by the extent of the catharsis produced. Catharsis is regarded as the purging of the emotions to regain tranquillity, or, as Dylan Thomas regarded it, a moment's peace.

It may be valuable to note now the romantic extension of these conceptions of imagination. Coleridge, in Chapter 13 of his *Biographia Literaria*, states:

> I hold [the imagination] to be the living Power and prime Agent of all human Perception, and as a repetition in the finite mind of the eternal act of creation in the infinite I AM.

Thus the imagination is regarded as participating, by imitation and within the limits of the human mind, in the forces of creation at work throughout the whole universe. In this treatment of myths we shall repeatedly return to this conception of the oneness of all created things, to the view of a prime spirit permeating everything. Note also Shelley's remark in his *Defence* that "A poet participates in the eternal, the infinite, and the one." And Shelley, in what is perhaps the most outstanding or complete expression of his ideas, was obliged, in *Prometheus Unbound*, to resort to myth. By "myth" is meant the interaction of symbols and images to reveal an inner or spiritual significance. An allegory explains (usually, if not always) men's follies and crimes; it is a kind of simplified or partially rationalized version of a myth. Sometimes there is a combination of allegory and myth, as perhaps in *Pilgrim's Progress* or *Prometheus Unbound*. Langland's *Piers Plowman* is virtually entirely allegory while *Beowulf* is myth. Myth reveals; allegory explains. In modern myth the intellect balances feeling; in allegory it dominates feeling.

Perhaps these theories of the imagination amount to no more than working hypotheses which cannot be completely verified; on the other hand, their validity is attested to by the degree of comprehension they produce when applied. As Carlyle observes in *On History:*

> . . . there are Artists and Artisans; men who labour mechanically in a department, without eye for the Whole, not feeling that there is a Whole; and men who inform and ennoble the humblest department with an Idea of the Whole and habitually know that only in the Whole is the Partial to be truly discerned.

As T. E. Huxley says, "Those who refuse to go beyond the facts rarely get as far as the facts." It seems to have been a conception of "the Whole," used imaginatively upon the data of a falling apple and a blow on the head, which produced the Law of Gravity. The truest scientists are always artists. The poet is the most, not the least, objective of men. The person using his imagination thus tunes in to the harmony moving through all things; he becomes "divine." His divinations add to human understanding and, eventually, may become rationally comprehensible as well. Whereupon later artists must penetrate, on the basis of the fullest data, even further into that oneness, the infinite "I am," using the medium of all too feeble consciousness, the finite "I am." As Sir Philip Sidney says in his Defence, the *Apologie*, only the poet delivers a golden world. His compatriots may mock and persecute but, willy-nilly, they follow after.

Man, in the earliest stages of his development, seems to have reacted to life almost entirely through a primitive imagination. He felt or imagined forces at work all round him. By examining existing primitive peoples an idea can be obtained of the stages through which mythical thinking has developed. Initially, man felt that he was part of the world around him and that he was subject equally with the rest of nature to the forces in nature. Gradually he evolved a society; he developed rituals and magic in an attempt to gain control over these forces for his own benefit. But even at this stage, man's magic derived from actual experience; he did not live in confusion and create magic haphazardly. His rituals and magic were constructed deliberately for definite ends which had their beginnings in his social life—a social life which very closely involved nature.

> To us the most essential point about magic and religious ritual is that it steps in only where knowledge fails . . . man attempts to enact miracles, not because he ignores the limitations of his mental powers, but . . . because he is fully cognisant of them.[1]

So, even here, right at the beginning, man enters the unknown armed as much as possible with the known. He had reasons for his rituals, his taboos, his religions and his myths as these things developed in the course of time. But he "felt" his reasons; they were forms of intuition which enabled him to build up a conception of his universe. "Myth and primitive religion are by no means entirely incoherent, they are not bereft of sense or reason. But their coherence depends much more upon unity of feeling than upon logic," writes Cassirer,[2] who adds that primitive man's view of nature was "sympathetic." It seems to be this ability to feel in tune with, or sympathetic to, nature that holds the key to the long

[1] Malinowski, *The Foundations of Faith and Morals* (London, Oxford University Press, 1936).

[2] *An Essay on Man* (Yale University Press, 1944).

6

development of myths, religion, and poetry, all of which attempt, wittingly or otherwise, to cross from the known into the unknown. The ability to feel is the fundamental necessity; as time passed, the ability to think commensurate with feeling became increasingly necessary. The problem for the modern myth-maker is that his feelings, to be justified or to be truthfully expressed, must be matched by consummate logic and objective analysis if they are to be accepted as anything more than fanciful fairy stories. But that the process is essentially only a development of that which has led man on from the beginning may be seen from Wordsworth's poem on Tintern Abbey, the corner stone of the *Lyrical Ballads*. Speaking of the 'beauteous forms' of nature, he writes of the mood induced by them until,

> *. . . we are laid asleep*
> *In body, and become a living soul:*
> *While with an eye made quiet by the power*
> *Of harmony, and the deep power of joy,*
> *We see into the life of things.*

This close identification of man with all other forms of life was a paramount feature of man's early development. (It is seen at its later stage in Carlyle's statement.) Closely akin to that attitude was man's conception of immortality. He did not at first conceive of dying but of passing on in endless reincarnations, the grandfather being rejuvenated in the child and grandchild. This became fundamental to the creative mind. It is the foundation of Cabell's mythology, which represents the perpetuated spirits of Manuel and Jurgen from the thirteenth century to the twentieth century. The idea is well treated in Cabell's *The Silver Stallion* (Chapter 35). In this conception of immortality, myth merges with religion. As Cassirer observes,

> In the development of human culture we cannot fix a point where myth ends or religion begins. . . . Myth is from its very beginning potential religion.

Consequently the next stage in the development is the transition from magic and taboo (taboo represents one of the earliest forms of discrimination) to religious awareness. This was expressed first through functional gods who helped with the crops and all practical needs (cf. *Beowulf* for the interaction of the functional with the personal gods). The personal gods mark a major development. With them man has distinguished himself from the rest of nature and animal life and acquired a sense, through his own creators, of his ideal or spiritual self. In the development of Greek religion, Gilbert Murray calls this phase the "Olympian conquest," in which,

> The world was conceived . . . as governed by an organised body of personal and reasoning rulers, wise and bountiful fathers, like man in mind and shape, only unspeakably higher.[3]

Now this development embodies a paradox which is at the heart of both modern experience and Cabell's writings as they reflect an age-old predicament. For in the earliest stage man was at one with nature; he constructed, for example, his taboos which were intended to keep him in tune with the benevolent forces around him. But in constructing his taboos he was, in fact, also surrounding himself with a barrier of "thou shalt not's" which, in effect, stunted or frustrated his sympathetic sense of the unity of all life. What was initially a dynamic development became static; this seems to be a recurrent aspect of all human activity and is paralleled later by Bergson's conception of static and dynamic religion. Static religion expresses itself through the weekly mouthings of prayers, often unintelligible, accompanied by a glance at a watch. Dynamic religion is that force which refuses to be hedged in by taboos and strives for individuality. The struggle for individuality usually involves a return to the harmony of the oneness of nature. Emerson wrote:

> There is a correspondence between the human soul and everything that exists in the world; more properly, everything that is known to man. Instead of studying things without, the principles of all of them may be penetrated into within him. . . . The purpose of life

[3] *Five Stages of Greek Religion*, (New York, Columbia University Press, 1930).

seems to be to acquaint man with himself. . . . The highest revelation is that God is within every man.

But to pursue this individuality Emerson had to break with his Church. Similarly Tolstoy, on pursuing his religious thinking actively, caused himself to be excommunicated. This relationship of the artist to his society goes back to the very beginnings perhaps: Cassirer writes,

> . . . the great religious teachers of mankind found a new impulse by which, henceforward, the whole life of man was led to a new direction. They discovered in themselves a positive power . . . not of inhibition but of inspiration and aspiration. They turned passive obedience into an active religious feeling.

Thus the negative prohibitions of taboo were shattered. Functional gods yielded to personal gods, contemplative and rational for the Greeks, practical and domestic for the Romans; yet magic remains if not integral yet important. Today, in Cabell, it still expresses freedom from physical limitations and is a means of communicating essential reality while dispensing with the merely mundane: a supernatural summer can equal a natural lifetime (as in *Something About Eve*) or Jurgen can don the shirt of Nessus and, in regaining his physical youth, enable Cabell to review life retrospectively without loss of the wisdom of his maturity.

From the functional and personal gods, particularly of the Greek and Roman, the next step was a concentration of force within one single godhead with the emergence of the monotheistic religions. But though moving from the earliest stage, in which all life was seen as one force embodying man with everything else, man, even in distinguishing himself and striving for individuality, still returned to nature and to oneness with it. The chief of the personal gods of the Greeks was Zeus, a god of nature, controlling the clouds, rain, and thunder. To be in harmony with these personal gods still meant to be in harmony with the forces of nature personified by them. But now these forces had their ideal significance as well. With the Greeks this ideal significance was complicated, taking into account the ambiguities and contradictions of motive and deed. The Greek gods emphasized the ideal of Beauty as expressed in harmony of design, physical, spiritual, and intellectual. In so far as Beauty is Truth, it may have embodied moral considerations, but these did not receive the direct emphasis given them in the monotheistic religions. These, Zoroastrian and Christian for example, concentrate directly upon the problems of good and evil. With the single godheads, the rational elements of the mind expressed themselves along with the earlier imaginative and "felt" sympathy with nature. A new strand had to be woven into the tapestry of mythical representation.

With ritual magic there were functional gods expressed through the symbols from which they originally derived and with which they were originally associated; these gods tended to be local, to have descriptive names, to be concrete in their acts but not in their appearances, and they oversaw all practical departments of life. In addition were the personal gods, like those of the Greeks, who had human shapes but, who also, could change at will either into whatever aspect of nature they personified or into whatever animal or combination of animals most expressed their significance. 'To the myth-maker as to the poet nearnesses were probably less fertile than likenesses; fusions depending upon resemblance are then the most numerous and important."[4] Combinations were endless and the medium for representing man's associations with the gods became a vast one. Then with the monotheistic religions came additional deities and celestial hierarchies from civilizations in West and East. But the central significances seem remarkably akin and even the differences each contain their truths; hence it is easy to understand the amalgamations that went on where cultures overlapped or intermingled, the absorption into one heritage of the chief contributions of an earlier or another one. Thus Keats, Shelley, Arnold, and Swinburne preferred to express themselves through the mythology of the Greeks while Cabell needed just about all of man's mythologies plus a new one of his own.

[4] F. C. Prescott, *Poetry and Myth* (New York, Macmillan, 1927), 27.

In this brief glance, we can see how man, since his first days on this earth, has attempted to express his relation with his makers, with forces which he has felt to be influencing his destinies. In the beginning he had much feeling but little discrimination; he evolved to functional and personal gods which represented not only strange and arbitrary powers but also those aspects of his experience which seemed most to improve the quality of his existence. Through an understanding of the quality of his living he evolved ideal versions of himself and distinguished the "divine" from the "devilish" and forces making for harmony from those making for chaos. Thus religions emerged, initially because of the prophets who opened the way into the golden west of the unknown, only to have their territory occupied, staked, and fenced so that ever new (or renewed) prophets, merging into poets, were obliged to break fences and thrust ahead again, often, it seems, stoned and alone. With the personal deities came the beginnings of rationalization, continued more directly in the monotheistic religions, expressed in considerations of good and evil and their consequences. The source of life now was seen in a single god opposed by a single personified force of evil, each struggling either directly or through ambiguity for mastery of the individual and of his habitat. Man has been regarded to varying degrees as having some personal say in his individual relationship with these forces, but from the beginning to the present he has been felt or consciously regarded as also being subject to them beyond his own power. Many imaginative leaders, if not all, have continued, from one stage to the next, to see an advantage in tuning in to the creative forces of nature, to submit to the powers producing order, harmony and balance, to achieve these within themselves as the best hope of a tranquil state of mind or happiness. "In thy service is perfect freedom," said, in effect, blind Samson for blind Milton, revealing perhaps more vision than most.

Up to the present, these developments have shown increasing proportions of the intellect in that fusion of thought with feeling that makes the imagination. Mediocrity has become mechanized: the poets tend to be lost in thought.

Yet ultimately, true science cannot really be detrimental, and with at least something of the scientific attitude, perhaps we can now examine the nature and significance of the myths produced in various world stages together with Cabell's use of them.

2: On the Nature and Significance of Myths and Cabell's Use of Them

A modern scientist, Bronislaw Malinowski, who has made an extensive and empirical study of myths, observes in *Myth in Primitive Psychology:*

> The myth . . . in its original living form, is not a mere tale told but a reality lived. It is not in the nature of an invention such as we read in our novels today . . . [but] the assertion of an original, greater and more important reality through which the present life, fate and work of mankind are governed.[1]

This comment seems to have a most direct relevance to the myths of Cabell, and it is possible to examine more closely the organic origin of his mythology, as it has evolved from the living tissues of his immediate experience, by looking at the origin and nature of mythology in general.

Myths do not explain; they reveal. They do not deal with causes but with origins or first principles, as is clearly illustrated in the thorough and detailed exposition in the *Introduction To A Science of Mythology* by Jung and Kerenyi. This book establishes the foundations of behavior by tracing happenings back to their origins or motives, to those forces within man which most move him to his beliefs and conscious deeds. And those forces appear to be spiritual forces; indeed Kerenyi traces them back to within the very organic germ of life itself: ". . . it seems as if there already were in the human plasm . . . something spiritual, a compulsion towards the spiritual." And he adds:

> What grows out of this compulsion is . . . exposed to its environment—and woe to anything that wants to grow when there is nothing in the environment to correspond with it.

[1] Keegan Paul, London, 1926.

12

The earlier myth-makers expressed, in a form of narrative, their fundamental experience as the inner spiritual forces interacted with their environment, which either assisted or impeded their growth. Magic could be invoked in myth to facilitate this figurative growth and convey the notion of freedom and power to bring about the aid of catharsis. The insuperable sword is one of the oldest and most universal mythological symbols used to augment man's power by the power of magic. And Cabell's heroes have such an aid—the sword Flamberge:

> This is Flamberge . . . the weapon which was the pride and bane of my father, famed Miramon Lluagor, because it was the sword which Galas made, in the old time's heyday, for unconquerable Charlemaigne. Clerks declare it is a magic weapon and that the man who wields it is always unconquerable. I do not know. I think it is as difficult to believe in sorcery as it is to be entirely sure that all we know is not the sorcery of a drunken wizard . . .[2]

Yes—with Cabell we have rationalization and paradox every inch of the way as his self-conscious intellect persistently checks on his intuitions. Myth has been brought up to date and what a magnificent medium it makes. The primordial relationships are retained: spiritual growth is not frustrated but, accompanied by the ever solicitous and questioning (or pestering) intellect, its substance is rendered all the more marvellous by the complications of reason.

The very fine but anonymous thirteenth-century poet of *Gawain and the Green Knight* would have appreciated this development, for whereas in his case the irony enveloped simply the objects, in Cabell's case the ironical perception of dualities not only envelops the symbols but, as it spirals back to examine the origins of motive, it queries the germ of the life force itself. At the same time, this ironical perception represents the spirit's state of being as it attempts to grow. All things move through dualities to paradox. In the realm of ideas it is necessary to see double to see straight. It is the poet's or myth-maker's burden to create that dual tension which is inherent in growth and, by his own creation, to resolve

[2] *Domnei.*

13

it for the reward of a moment's peace—only to have to begin the process again.

"Going back into ourselves in this way and rendering an account of it we experience and proclaim the very foundations of our being," states Kerenyi. The myth-maker establishes that line of most relevant experiences which constitutes his real inner life from birth until—by anticipation—death. He takes these two ends and bends them into as near perfect a circle as possible so that the end must ever be a fresh beginning as generation follows generation. This is a paramount and consistent feature in Cabell's structural technique, which is not an explanation but a revelation of Cabell's fusion of observed and consciously selected experience (using the primary imagination). His real inner life is rendered symbolically to achieve unity of feeling in the expression of himself and his experiences. The result is mythology because it does not represent merely man's relations with his society but something ultimately far greater—man's relations with his Creator. Although, as is made apparent in all first-rate novelists (who must always tend toward myth), even man's dealings with his society can reflect his relationship with his gods—as in Dreiser's determinism, or Tolstoy's conception of men as unwitting instruments of supernatural forces, or Hardy's version of hostile gods, or D. H. Lawrence's liking for the personal gods of Greece. Lawrence was most viciously stoned by his own countrymen, particularly at the beginning of the first world war, and he described America as "The land of Thou shalt not." The breaking of taboos is dangerous as well as rewarding.

Kerenyi observes:

> A particular kind of material determines the art of mythology, an immemorial and traditional body of material contained in tales about gods and god-like beings, heroic battles and journeys to the underworld—Mythology is the movement of this material: it is something solid and yet mobile, substantial and yet not static, capable of transformation.

What Cabell has done is, in effect, to take immemorial and traditional bodies of materials and transform and add to them so that they represent a mythologem of the American way of life. The skyscrapers are the functional gods, and his mythological land, Poictesme, has its tall towers; the business titans (Carnegie, Ford, Rockefeller, Yerkes alias Dreiser's Algernon Cowperwood) are the personal gods, the men of great action, and Manuel is the original of these in the Biography;[3] the American hierarchies are administering salesmen and bank managers—Jurgen is a Pawnbroker;[4] the subsidiary or affiliated hierarchies are in the government, churches, and Universities, which tend to represent static religion and thought as opposed to the dynamic artists who provide them with food for their initial thinking; representatives of static religion permeate nearly all Cabell's works. For example, Kerin, in *The Silver Stallion*, is one of a number of notable scholars in Cabell's books, all portrayed with ironic perception. The man in the street is the Tumblebug in *Jurgen*. The American temples are not only the profitable churches but also the tall-columned railway stations, show rooms, and banks; and revolving on a specially built altar is—the automobile. The symbol of Poictesme is a silver stallion, as befits an age of rapid motion, disintegration, and increasing functional complexity.

Cabell, though, takes it much farther than the realist. Round it all he spins ever-enlarging concentric circles of the gods taking us out from observed facts to revealed significance and indicating the unknown that extends to star-spangled infinity. Today we are entering it faster technically than spiritually.

Perhaps it is in order to try to justify the validity of Cabell's myths as a means of communication. What it really amounts to is that if the artist has enough to say he *must* use myth. Previously mythology has taken the form of a more or less unconscious or intuitive expression of the inner self through the appropriate sym-

[3] Cabell arranged all his books in the Storisende Edition to illustrate in historical chronology the descendants of Manuel the Redeemer, the founder, so that the books represent Manuel's biography as his life reappears in the lives of his descendants.

[4] Cf. T. Roosevelt's description of his wealthy countrymen as "glorified pawnbrokers," A. M. Schlesinger, Jr., *The Crisis of the Old Order* (Boston, Houghton Mifflin Co., 1957), 19.

bols of supernatural significance. But the modern artist is obliged to think as well as to feel. Much modern art is very unfeeling, even as, quite accurately, it may be expressing its age. Carl Jung, in a recent article entitled "God, The Devil and The Human Soul,"[5] went to the heart of man's modern situation (an intensification of his eternal situation), and fully justified mythology. After noting the manner in which most art today deals not with beauty but with the "dark chaos of subjectivisms," he observes:

> Certainly art . . . has not yet discovered in this darkness what it is that holds all men together and could give expression to their psychic wholeness.

Nature has always been niggardly in producing humans whose thought and feeling are equally powerful. Even that finest of novels, *War and Peace*, is built around a philosophical vacuum at its heart, which Tolstoy attempted to fill with more than one bucket of patriotism. As his philosophy improved in quality his art diminished in quantity. And yet, all the time, for half a century now, an American has been persistently and—except for a farcical interruption early in the 'twenties—quietly giving expression to man's psychic wholeness. And hardly anyone has seen his work for what it is. This is because, by using an eternal form which is temporarily out of fashion, Cabell was too far ahead of his time. Jung states in his article:

> Great art till now has always derived its fruitfulness from the myth, from the unconscious process of symbolisation which continues through the ages and, as the primordial manifestation of the human spirit, will continue to be the root of all creation in the future. The development of modern art with its seemingly nihilistic trend toward disintegration must be understood as the symptom and symbol of a mood of world destruction and world renewal that has set its mark on our age. . . . We are living in what the Greeks called the "right time" for a metamorphosis of the gods.

Herein lies the uniqueness of Cabell's achievement: *he has created this metamorphosis.* He has taken the primordial myths

[5] *The Atlantic Monthly* (November, 1957).

16

and all they represent, and by the addition of his own he has absorbed the disintegrating factors and rewoven them into wholeness. If we recognize this achievement, if we cease most shamefully to ignore it, this wholeness may be ours also. We are very much in need of it. Jung observes of modern man:

> Does he know that he is on the point of losing the life-preserving myth of the inner man which Christianity has treasured up for him? Does he realise what lies in store should this catastrophe ever befall him?

As we glance back into the mad house, into that corner in which they are stacking the hydrogen bombs, we seem to see man advancing creatively to self-destruction, the ultimate paradox. There are only two possibilities—destruction or construction. Self-knowledge is the key to the latter. Cabell's stature derives from his refusal to wallow in the lush lowlands of self-deception, from his determination to climb through the bleak and misty uplands of self-perception to the very summit. At the summit he found "distinction and clarity, and beauty and symmetry, and tenderness and truth and urbanity." He found, in fact, everything we most lack and most need. It is well worth following him, for the atmosphere at the summit of Olympus is most exhilarating, probably more so than that at the summit of Everest, where we were again technically ahead of ourselves.

The means by which Cabell has achieved this triumph marks him out as a modern myth-maker because they require the most profound and astute application of the intellect. Previous myth-makers unconsciously expressed their origins; the images and symbols flowered up spontaneously like a plant growing—if they had roots and the right soil. But in this complicated age, a great effort of introspection was needed before Cabell could lay his own foundation, before he could see what made him tick, before he could establish the essence of his being and the factors conditioning it. Kerenyi observes:

> The mythological "fundamentalist" who, by immersion in the self, dives down to his own foundations, founds his world. He builds it

up for himself on a foundation where everything is an outflowing, a sprouting and springing up.

This is where Cabell's mythology differs from and is more adequate than most modern novels. This modern myth-maker, with superb reason and discipline, journeys consciously toward the essence of his own psyche to explore and annotate the contents of his being, or state of mind, and all that produced it; then he re-moulds, in an imaginative, symmetrical and ordered re-creation, the images and symbols which seem most to express this essence. He re-creates his cosmos and peoples it with the creatures who most represent, in dynamic poetry, himself as he strives for spiritual growth. He imitates the Creator and directly reveals Him for us through the interplay of his ingredients. If the intellect and feeling are strong then the symbolism is capable of endless implications and interpretations: they will accrue significance as the future joins the past because the origin from which they derive is that of the whole race as expressed in the individual.

Cabell undertakes this introspective grounding twice, in his prose essays *Beyond Life* (1919) and in *Straws and Prayer Books* (1924); the first of these flowers out directly into the novels *Jurgen* (1919) and *Figures of Earth* (1921), while the second influences and is expressed in the novels *The Silver Stallion* (1926) and *Something About Eve* (1927); later revision of these works complicate but do not distort this picture.

It seems advisable to transfer one more working hypothesis from the realm of science to offer what seems like verification from the field of Cabell's myths. Kerenyi states,

> Mythology provides a foundation insofar as the teller of myths, by living out his story, finds his way back to primitive times.

Cabell's earliest works, such as *The Eagle's Shadow* (1904) and *The Cords of Vanity* (1909), deal with contemporary life, while the earliest short stories take us back first to the seventeenth and eighteenth centuries or, as in *Chivalry* (1909), to the semihistorical treatment of the period of the twelfth to the fourteenth centuries. It is not until *The Soul of Melicent* (1913, revised and renamed *Domnei* in 1920) that we enter more thoroughly into myth and the recognizable background of Poictesme. We do not move back into Poictesme proper until *Jurgen* (1919), *Figures of Earth* (1921)—the real foundation of it—and *The Silver Stallion* (1926). And in *Something About Eve* (1927), Cabell combines his own cosmos and mythology, more directly perhaps than in any of his other works, with preceding mythologies, to take us much farther back in time to Prometheus. He does this in one of the finest passages of fictional synthesis in the whole canon of the Biography, in Chapter XII, entitled "Confusions of the Golden Travel":

> All arts that were among the human race had come from Prometheus, and all these benefits were now preserved for his so inadequate, dear puppets, through the nineteen books in which Prometheus had set down the secrets of all knowledge and all beauty and all contentment.

There could hardly be clearer evidence, it seems, of a genuine myth-maker travelling back to that primordiality which is his authenticity; the pattern of universal or eternal life unfolds itself through paradox but in complete unity right from the beginning. The beginning—"the first principles"—is the same in its general origin as it is in the individual psychic origin of Cabell himself. Thus Cabell really does illustrate, through revelation, what it is that "holds all men together"; he gives "expression to their psychic wholeness."

Beware of thinking that Cabell's mythical symbols lack the punch or immediacy of the topical. Discussing the idea of American civilization,[6] Max Lerner notes the various mythical means of labelling civilizations, recorded by Charles W. Morris (*Six Ways of Life*). These include the Dionysian (surrender to instinct—cf. D. H. Lawrence), the Buddhist (annihilation of self for serenity —applies also to the Hindu), the Christian (self-purification according to spiritual values), the Apollonion (conserving of traditional values), and the Promethean (conquest and organization through science and technology). The significance of Cabell's

[6] *America as a Civilization* (New York, Simon and Schuster, 1957), 70.

reference to Prometheus may be seen when Max Lerner's observation is noted:

> He [Charles W. Morris] sees American civilization as primarily Promethean but with elements of the Christian and the Apollonion pointing out that the Apollonion has hardened into a Toryism of the spirit which could mean a static civilization, and that the Christian strain has had to be subordinated when it has conflicted with the more dominant elements of the civilization. I cite this suggestive scheme to illustrate how the study of the great world myths can shed light on what Americans are like and what they live by.

This could be taken as a summary of the Biography. But there is still further evidence of Cabell's relevance. As will be seen, a figure central to Cabell's thinking and art is Christopher Marlowe, together with Helen and Faustus. Cabell closely identified his own Biography with the necromancy of Faustus in that same Chapter XII of *Something About Eve*. Max Lerner, in describing the emergent American, gives as accurate a description as one could wish for, first of Manuel and then of the essence of all Cabell's heroes. The "new" man is:

> . . . not too finicky in his sexual life . . . or about rigid standards of virtue. Hungering for a sense of personal worth, he is torn between the materialism he can achieve and the feeling of wholeness which eludes him. . . . He is an amoral man of energy, mastery and power. . . . He is the double figure in Marlowe, of Tamurlane and Dr. Faustus, the one sweeping like a footloose barbarian across the plains . . . the other breaking the taboos against knowledge and experience, even at the cost of his soul.[7]

Cabell sees all this and absorbes this "new" man into the old myths, making his material universal and eternal in its appeal and significance. As we come to comprehend his imagination he may well emerge as the literary giant of his era.

3: Cabell Himself

Cabell was born on April 14, 1879, in Richmond, Virginia,

[7] *Ibid.*, 63.

Richmond being the Lichfield of the novels. The following year saw Lowell appointed ambassador to England and the birth of H. L. Mencken and Joseph Hergesheimer. In 1879, Stalin and Einstein were born; Jack London, Sherwood Anderson, and Willa Cather were three years old. Upton Sinclair was aged one as was Henry James's *Daisy Miller*. Emerson and Longfellow had three years to live. Mark Twain was just approaching his best work as embodied in *Life on the Mississippi* (1883) and *Huckleberry Finn* (1884).

In Europe, Matthew Arnold was preparing for his famous American lecture tour; Hardy the year before had published *The Return of the Native*. In the year that came forth with Cabell, George Meredith came forth with *The Egoist*, and Ibsen with *The Doll's House*. Horse-drawn carriages seemed permanent possessions of both Russell and Washington squares.

Cabell is directly descended from two distinguished Southern families and connected with the group of leading Southern families through the Ballards and Waddils, the Majers and the Branches. Being unable to obtain the necessary references from two London householders, he had the greatest difficulty in obtaining a ticket for the Reading Room of the British Museum. He married Priscilla, daughter of William Joseph Bradley of Auburn, in old Charles City County, and for many years inhabited Dumbarton Grange,[1] Dumbarton, Virginia, although he later moved to Monument Avenue, Richmond. Dumbarton Grange appears as Willoughby Hall in *Beyond Life*. Willoughby Hall, "an eighteenth century house," is complete to the "last mullion and gable."

> Fairhaven itself, I find, has in the matter of "atmosphere" deteriorated rather appallingly since the town's northern out-skirt was disfigured by a powder mill. . . . But Willoughby Hall had remained unchanged since my last visit save for the installation of electric light . . . in his determined retention of "atmosphere."

[1] Which seems to have provided the setting, described in detail, for the library scenes in *Beyond Life*, *Straws and Prayer Books*, and the general setting in such works as *The Cream of the Jest* and *Something about Eve*.

Priscilla Bradley has been described by Roy L. McCardell[2] as "fair, energetic and charming." As Cabell's autobiography, *As I Remember It* (1955), makes clear, Priscilla Bradley Cabell was integral to her husband's spiritual development and appears in most of his writings. Cabell married twice and was the father of one son.

Thus the setting appears to have been fully in keeping with the creator of the beautiful sun-dappled lands of Poictesme. Yet, as ever, the reality appears to have been a little more difficult, a little more concerned with suffering and hardship than the above may at first sight suggest.

Cabell attended the old Virginia college of William and Mary, and at the age of nineteen, he received his degree of A.B. in 1898, having achieved "a high scholastic record" and written many of the verses included in *From the Hidden Way*. He also taught Greek and French at William and Mary and it is presumably this experience which gave him something of his very substantial learning in the Classics and French, and in European history and literature. No mistake should be made about this. Cabell's ironical comments about false scholarship should not conceal the fact that his knowledge became extensive and exhaustive in his own special fields. That, in his day and place, these fields were unusual is another matter: he is a most learned author, one of the most learned authors that America has produced—even more so than the New Englanders, including the Transcendentalists.

After he left college in 1898, Cabell entered the wilderness by way of the press room of the Richmond *Times*, Richmond, Virginia. He moved fairly quickly on to New York, where he became a reporter on the staff of the New York *Herald* (which had had Karl Marx as a foreign correspondent). Then, amidst the laughter of diabolic gods, Cabell, author-to-be of *Jurgen*, was assigned to the Sunday society page with the task of reporting the social activities of the inhabitants of Harlem. It was presumably at this time that Cabell's sense of humour began to develop rapidly as a lifebelt for the preservation of sanity.

[2] *The Morning Telegraph* (Sunday, August 21, 1921), 4.

His personal appearance at this time has been described by Roy L. McCardell:

> His air of innocence and modesty is so childlike and he looks upon the world with such an inquiring "can-such-things-be" expression . . . that the most taciturn and suspicious persons . . . tell him all about themselves.
>
> In his conversation there is astonishingly little he will say concerning himself, but his reserve is never ungracious. His smile is whimsical and, when occasion presents, sardonic. But he seldom laughs. . . . He is married but knows nothing of husbandry as it pertains to anything around the place, from the farm to the Ford. . . . His dominant characteristic is that he constantly presents the picture of pure innocence.[3]

Or, again, from H. L. Mencken's description in his introduction to the revised version of *The Line of Love* (1905, revised 1921):

> When he does bad work, he suffers for it as no holy clerk ever suffered from a gnawing conscience or Freudian suppressions; when he does good work he gets his pay in a form of joy that only artists know . . . he is a man of agreeable exterior with handsome manners and an eye for this and that . . . forever fussing over his books, trying to make them one degree better. He rewrites almost as pertinaciously as Joseph Conrad, Henry James or Brahms.

In other words, Cabell, "a young man of middle height," appears to have had in his appearance and temperament much in common with the slight figure of Chaucer (whose language Cabell used frequently, for instance, to preface *Jurgen* and for dedications such as that for *The Line of Love*), who described himself in the words of the Host of the Tabard:

> *Thou lookest as thou woldest find an hare,*
> *For ever upon the ground I see thee stare . . .*

---

[3] Cf. Oscar Wilde's observation in *De Profundis* (another handbook to Cabell's work) that to be impractical is the great thing; in view of the necessity for roads and bridges, not to mention such things as tin-openers, this presumably refers mainly, if not only, to the unacknowledged legislators.

He seemeth elvish by his contenaunce,
For unto no wight doth he daliaunce.

And Chaucer's description of himself in *The House of Fame* parallels that of Cabell's picture of himself in *Beyond Life* and *Straws and Prayer Books* in his cloistered hermitage with his neighbors:

> *But of thy verray neighebores,*
> *That dwellen almost at thy dores,*
> *Thou herest neither that ne this;*
> *. . . dumb as any stoon,*
> *Thou sittest at another boke*
> *Til fully daswed is thy loke,*
> *And livest thus as an hermyte—*
> *Although thyn abstinence is lyte.*

Cabell's views on Prohibition add to the similarity as well as linking him to Dr. Middleton in *The Egoist,* who was modelled on the English novelist Peacock.

Because of the inartistic societies that man has so far produced, the artist must contend against very great odds to follow his bent to fulfillment. In some ways these odds were greater against Cabell because the whole climate of thought and feeling of his time was devoid of those things which he regarded as essential to "the good life," whatever that was to be. To find these things required outstanding independence, for it meant a quest to other places and bygone times to a greater extent than it did even for such as Shelley or Browning. It was not as if the expatriates offered a solution. For Cabell it had to be not merely across the Atlantic, like Dreiser, Hemingway, and Wolfe, but back in time as well. If Cabell, like most of the others, came home again, he did so only within the protective suiting of his own imaginative worlds, suiting woven of ancient cultural textures unobtainable as yet in the largest of home supermarkets.

Cabell next devoted himself to writing verses, which he had done from his teens, some of them appearing in the collection of his poetry entitled *From the Hidden Way* (1916, revised 1924). Magazine stories, translations, and essays provided other literary outlets. Yet, as McCardell observed, "He was too highly educated to make any great success at the time." He returned to Richmond and worked in the editorial department of the Richmond *News*.

Between 1901 and 1910, Cabell wrote many short stories and articles and contributed to national magazines such as *Harper's*, *The Smart Set*, and *Argosy*. He also indulged in genealogical research which, in Cabell's case, had major results for his own creations, turning him to those searches into the past which were to make acceptable the present.

His first novel appeared in 1904 when he was aged twenty-five. This was *The Eagle's Shadow*, and it appeared as a serial in the *Saturday Evening Post*. He was encouraged and praised by his contemporaries H. L. Mencken, Joseph Hergesheimer, and Sinclair Lewis. In 1909 followed another prentice novel of contemporary life called *The Cords of Vanity*.

Cabell traveled in Europe, delving into the background of his learning in Provençal, early Italian, and medieval lore; in England he had difficulty in gaining access to old family records in a little church near Abingdon as well as difficulty in entering the British Museum. These little obstacles appear only to have supplied him with a respect for the importance of the trivial in this life and (once it had been rendered a little less incredible) with further material for fiction. England also confirmed the background for his stories of medieval England and Wales, Restoration England, and eighteenth-century England.

Yet it was in his continental travels that Cabell discovered his real home—in those parts of France and Italy which bask in the sunshine of the Mediterranean and in the reflected spiritual inheritance of Greece and Rome. These lands, with their ancient cultural heritage, were the only ones capable of supplying the material for the intricate, richly woven texture of Cabell's imaginative tapestries. If the modern world had lost its sanity, its poise, balance, and harmony, what cared he when they were here, ready and waiting, centuries of accumulated beauty, of wisdom, and of the questing spirit?

Yet the trials and tribulations were not ended. Between 1901 and 1909, Cabell's art was gathering strength in spite of, or because of, personal vicissitudes. In 1907, Howard Pyle dealt him a blow that could have been fatal to a young writer by refusing to illustrate any more of his stories in *Harper's Magazine* because they were "neither exactly true to history nor exactly fanciful." Cabell's art was already moving beyond the confines of his era.

There is a gap in Cabell's productive output between 1909 and 1913 (excluding a piece of family history entitled *Branch of Abingdon* in 1911); during this time Cabell worked in, although not down, the coal mines of West Virginia and on *The Soul of Melicent*. No biography of this writer has yet been written but it seems clear that, as with all creators of literature, Cabell lived what he wrote. Whereas so many popularized their work for easy money, Cabell listened faithfully to his muse. If the going was hard, the scenery was good, but the marks of sadness and the hints of bitterness which, kept in place by rigid artistic discipline, were to give his work its stature and its universal implications may well have been derived from the experience of these years, even if a further turn of the screw was to be given in the years following the publication of *Jurgen*.

In 1913—the year of Lawrence's *Sons and Lovers* and the year following Dreiser's *The Financier*—came the novel *The Soul of Melicent*, which was revised in 1920 and renamed *Domnei*. In its earlier form this book attracted the attention of Mark Twain.[4]

Mark Twain continued to acknowledge and encourage the art of Cabell, and in Mark Twain's final sad years Cabell's books constituted his chief reading. Along with "Walt" and "Edgar," "Mark" was represented in *Jurgen* as being one of the three chief American literary figures hounded to miserable ends by uncomprehending tumblebugs. The philosophical attitudes of both these authors provide their common link and both were equally misunderstood; Mark Twain was regarded as the great clown or public jester while Cabell was retained as the lewd mountebank.

---

[4] According to Burton Rascoe (to whom Cabell dedicated *Jurgen*) in his introduction to *Chivalry*, "Mr. Cabell wrote *The Soul of Melicent* . . . at the great humorist's request."

Prayer Books (1924), together with historical studies, interpreta-

The Rivet in Grandfather's Neck (1915) was another and final novel of contemporary life; from this time on the output was fairly consistent. *The Cream of the Jest* (1917, revised 1922) fully launched the Biography. Just as Meredith sorted out his mass of ideas in the "Essay on Comedy" to produce the disciplined clarity and symmetry of his masterpiece *The Egoist*, so did Cabell sort out his ideas in 1918 for *Beyond Life* and write *Jurgen* immediately afterwards.

Jurgen was labeled "vicious and indecent" by a group of tumblebugs calling themselves a society for the prevention of vice. H. L. Mencken wrote in his introduction to *The Line of Love:*

> The Cabell case belongs to comedy in the grand manner. For fifteen years or more the man wrote—good stuff, sound stuff, extremely original stuff, often superbly fine stuff—and yet no-one in the whole of this vast and incomparable Republic arose to his merit. . . . The newspapers, reviewing him, dismissed him with a sort of inspired ill-nature; the critics of a more austere kidney—the Paul Elmer Mores, Brander Matthewses, Hamilton Wright Mabies, and other such brummagem dons—were utterly unaware of him. Then, of a sudden, the imbeciles who operate the Comstock Society raided and suppressed his *Jurgen* and at once he was a made man.

Thus was Cabell launched into nationwide notoriety and presented with an extensive reading public. This was a twist in the author's plot ironical enough for Cabell's own auctorial use. This episode marked the peak of Cabell's fame and fortune. *Jurgen* is a unique achievement of the English-speaking peoples. For writing it, Cabell was placed in the dock and, with spotlights well focused and to catcalls from the gallery, commanded to convey the meaning of color to people who had been color-blind from birth.

These were hectic years indeed. *Main Street* by Sinclair Lewis, *The Age of Innocence* by Edith Wharton, and *This Side of Paradise* came out in 1920, all reflecting America as it was, as it had been, and as it wanted to be. Then followed Cabell's second masterpiece, *Figures of Earth*, in 1921 (with Prohibition two years old), to be followed in turn by Lewis's *Babbitt* and T. S. Eliot's *The Waste Land* the following year.

Cabell himself was at the center of the storm, with bootlegged copies of *Jurgen* selling for up to fifty dollars each. He brought out further highlights in *The High Place* (1923) and *Straws and Prayer Books* (1924), together with historical studies, interpretative essays (for example, one on his friend and aid Joseph Hergesheimer), and a one act play. In addition, he heard *Jurgen* transposed into a symphony by Deems Taylor in 1925 for the New York Philharmonic Orchestra.

He had attributed some of his stories to a fictitious Nicolas of Caen—the stories were reputed to be translations of medieval verses and prose—and received apt confirmation of his philosophies when a leading American anthologist hinted familiarity with the originals and when the citizens of Caen, having searched their libraries in vain, wrote for further information concerning their ancestor to enable them to erect a tablet to Nicolas and to commemorate the fame he had brought them. In the abstract it could no doubt be made humorous enough.

With *Straws and Prayer Books* we come to the epilogue of that bulk of his work which Cabell called the Biography with *Beyond Life* as the prologue.

While his output continued and in some respects, particularly in pungency of treatment, improved, Cabell refused to add to the Biography after he reached the age of fifty; thereafter he dealt more directly with America.

The tempo of Cabell's life inevitably slackened in the 1930's, and eventually his reputation sank quietly to the level of the pre-*Jurgen* period. Yet Cabell himself, older and with more bitterness in his acquiescence, became increasingly pungent rather than docile in his writings. Wintering in Florida, he kept close to the picturesque and colorful in St. Augustine (with its fort and memories of Drake, the Elizabethans, and the Spaniards) and Tampa, on the warmly lapped beaches of the Gulf of Mexico. He summed up, finally, his conception of America in *The First American Gentleman* (London, 1942; American title, *The First*

Gentleman of America). There are suggestions that Cabell, like Thomas Wolfe, had gone home again: European Christian civilization is analogous to the Spanish Inquisition. Yet as far as Cabell was concerned, the real spirit of America seemed to have departed long ago with the Indians into "a hollowed-out crevice in the Alleghanies."

Leading, as far as possible, a retired life of work and research, he was for many years a genealogist for various colonial societies in Virginia and editor of the Virginian War History Commission from 1919 until 1926. From 1932 to 1935 he edited the *American Spectator*. He became a director of the Edgar Allan Poe Shrine and—final accolade of respectability—a member of the National Institute of Art and Letters. Cabell died, intellectually alert to the last, in Richmond in 1958.

For *Jurgen*, Cabell was suppressed for what he did not say and exalted for what he did not mean. Over one quarter of a century has passed since all that tumult and confusion. The mud has settled and the pool is again clear. Cabell is a neglected classic much overdue his rightful place and interpretation. As Edward Wagenknecht observes,[5] "Is it too much to hope that a highly controversial figure may now be reasonably assessed and at least tentatively assigned to what one may hope will be his permanent place in our literature?"

[5] *Cavalcade of the American Novel* (New York, Henry Holt & Co., 1952), 340.

PART TWO

EARLY WORK AND THE EMERGENCE OF A PATTERN

4: The Period of Apprenticeship

Cabell's earliest novels attempt to deal with contemporary life. They do not show him at his best any more than the *Two Gentlemen of Verona* does justice to Shakespeare. In *Straws and Prayer Books*, Cabell himself referred to the "facile, false inspiration of *The Eagle's Shadow*." The early novels include *The Eagle's Shadow* (1904), *The Cords of Vanity* (1909), and *The Rivet in Grandfather's Neck* (1915). Yet they are noteworthy for several reasons. Already we meet several characters who are to walk in and out of Cabell's work throughout the whole cycle of the Biography, and they quite clearly speak individually for various aspects of Cabell himself. Thus, from the beginning, we have personal spokesmen holding forth concerning Cabell's philosophy and his deepest thoughts concerning his own art, that of other people, and art in general.

In *The Eagle's Shadow* we meet Felix Kennaston, who has the central role in *The Cream of the Jest*; he speaks here with the rather bored cynicism of fashion rather than of feeling. *The Eagle's Shadow* is about a very nice young man and a very nice young girl who become, not surprisingly, mutually infatuated in an atmosphere of great wealth, a large house, beautiful lawns, and all the paraphernalia of youthful misunderstanding of motives in a welter of emotion.

The plot is reminiscent of P. G. Wodehouse as is, for that matter, the characterization. Cabell, very much an artist of the abstract, became interested primarily in myths, which even when embodying allegory, obviate the necessity for fully drawn, individually complicated characters. The use of myth enables him to exploit himself as the source of his figments, rather as Virginia Woolf personifies various aspects of herself in *The Waves*. Yet, as his short stories show, he can create individual characters who are lifelike people displaying individual natures in spheres almost entirely of action. However, *The Eagle's Shadow* and *The Cords of Vanity* display him still unaware of his true bent, and he relies heavily on characterization. A group of "hangers-on"—there is a rather self-conscious note of the condescending—gathers around the heroine Margaret Hugonin, who is "young and beautiful," in the hope of living on her wealth. Most of the accusations concerning Cabell's style are true enough if applied to these early novels. He indulges in a pseudo-intimate relationship with the reader, couched in flowery self-conscious language which eventually clogs in its abundance of adjectives and qualifying redundancies. It is what one would expect of a young writer moving with pleasure among words and concerned more with ornament than with solid meaning. It is a pretty world of youthful daydreams in which all problems are solved by the advent of great wealth easily achieved. In the words of Richard Harrowby—another spokesman who reappears in later works—this is "a comedy of that Golden Age which has always been chronologically located about twenty years ago."

As the news of death is introduced so incongruously into *Love's Labour's Lost* so, here, the possibility of death enters into this golden comedy of prose with equally embarrassing consequences. But there is a hint of something else apparent in the treatment of the characters during this "accident" which itself is contrived so obviously. There is already an insight into the motivating causes of human behaviour which is intellectually ruthless. This intellectual quality later matures not to the exclusion of feeling but to complete control over it.

The Cords of Vanity was written in 1909 and revised in 1920. In it we meet more of Cabell's spokesmen—Robert Etheridge Townsend, who has much of the Restoration Etheridge in him, and Charteris. It is almost possible to select the revised passages, yet the novel is a much better affair than *The Eagle's Shadow*. Again there is flamboyant prose; the preciosity smacks very much of glossy women's magazines; much of the dialogue is false and the situations still too contrived and improbable—such as the nice boy in pyjamas and the nice girl in nightgown discussing Greek poetry while trapped on the roof of a blazing hotel. Promiscuous wealthy Americans, at home and abroad, provide the characters, and the hero is portrayed rather confusingly as a selfish young lout, completely devoid of any sense of consideration, who is nevertheless likeable. Yet there are flashes now of real art. They appear in moments of genuinely moving relationships between the sexes and in the insight into the double nature of youth's aspiration interwoven with dangerous self-love or conceit. On the whole, though, the relationships have the shallow glibness, the hard superficial glitter of Fitzgerald's society in *The Great Gatsby*. Again, death intrudes, but this time it is not so embarrassingly incongruous and supplies depth and substance. On the whole, while the maturity of the revision gives the impression at times of old wine in a new bottle, there are definite signs now of potential worth. And another feature worth noting is the nature of the title and its attached quotation. Beneath the title, *The Cords of Vanity*, is the biblical quotation:

> Woe unto them that draw iniquity with cords of vanity! . . . their root shall be as rottenness and their blossoms shall go up as dust.

This is perhaps the first indication in Cabell's work of his attraction to Biblical concepts, an attraction which, with the passing years, becomes an important influence on his thinking and art.

The object of the book is very ambitious and already reveals American insight untrammelled by sentimentality. It points out the incipient dangers of youthful self-love—that narcissism which is unwittingly a common feature of much youthful American literature as it appears, for example, in the work of Jack London. Here Cabell reveals in action American youth impelled not by aspiring integrity, as it was known in nineteenth-century England, but by the cords of vanity—all is vanity. Cabell later wonders if vanity is all.

In *The Cords of Vanity* the artistic bull is missed but the target itself is considerably chipped and the aim was to be much surer as the sights became adjusted.

Hugh Walpole wrote of these books on contemporary life[1] (*The Eagle's Shadow*, *The Cords of Vanity* and *The Rivet in Grandfather's Neck*):

> These three of all the books are the most vulnerable to attack. They must seem . . . confused, unpleasant, and uncompleted. . . . Mr. Cabell is always more deeply interested in the stream of life that flows beneath his characters than in the characters themselves.

5: The Poetry

The period of apprenticeship must include most of Cabell's verse. Much verse, as with Meredith, is scattered throughout the whole of Cabell's work. Yet the bulk is contained in the volume entitled *From the Hidden Way* (1916, revised 1924). *From the Hidden Way* contains an "Apologia Auctoris" written under the name of one of Cabell's favorite fictitious spokesmen, Robert Etheridge Townshend of Lichfield in 1926. It may be wise at this point to examine this matter of Cabell's spokesmen.

The chief of these are Townshend; John Charteris of Willoughby Hall, Lichfield, Fairhaven—perhaps the most important; Richard Fentnor Harrowby, whose questions bait the traps of discourse; and Felix Kennaston. They speak almost directly for various aspects of Cabell's views. In addition to these are characters who act out Cabell's views in the course of the action, such as the commentator and guide Horvendile and the protagonist John Bulmer, Duke of Ormskirk. Cousins at second remove are real-life people who further reveal Cabell's own sympathies and interests in fictionalized episodes. The chief examples of such figures are Christopher Marlowe, François Villon and Alexander Pope.

Cabell has frequently been accused of affectation, of hiding behind a screen of encircling imaginery characters in order to be

---

[1] Walpole, Hugh, "The Art of James Branch Cabell," *Yale Review* (July, 1920), 684-99.

perversely obscure and difficult and to cloud issues unnecessarily. This is very far from the real truth. There are valid reasons for these spokesmen and for such as Nicolas de Caen and a host of other medieval and renaissance "authorities" reputed to be responsible for the originals of verse and prose "translations" and "adaptations" which are in fact the original creations of Cabell himself. We can see the validity of Cabell's method by comparing it to the conception of life as a complicated trickster who, like a woman, often apparently unwittingly delights in surrounding the heart of beauty (or truth) in veils of ambiguity—real truth can be captured only by fiction while factual truth must be sent "skulking into the footnotes." J. B. Priestley, estimating new writers in 1954 in *The New Statesman and Nation*, was of the opinion that they were not rebels any longer—there was a much sadder and more pathetic element in their literary and facial expressions which, as they looked at modern life, amounted to "count us out"; there was not the desire to rebel—things have gone too far, the odds are too great—but to ignore. In his choice of material, Cabell anticipates this attitude. If the hollow men in wastelands have lost the truth, then a restatement of it can be only in terms of the past. In this age, when the ends of learning are often being subordinated to the means, when abundant new evidence gives priority to analysis, it is merely incidental irony to couch these ancient truths in such modern "scholarly" terms. Hence Nicolas de Caen and the "scholar" who was familiar with his originals.[1]

The role of the spokesman is equally important as if not more important than that of the numerous "authorities." It is a matter of structural convenience as well as of intellectual integrity and can be seen most clearly in *Beyond Life* and *Straws and Prayer Books*. Yet we can see one aspect of the role in the introductory "Apologia Auctoris" of *From the Hidden Way*. In this, Cabell, who in his subtitle, "Dizain des Echos," makes a direct implication, immediately covers himself with, not qualifications, but further implications that point out that he is aware of the possibility of aspects of the truth over and beyond those which he has implied

---

[1] Including, for example, an erudite reviewer for *The Boston Transcript*.

directly. In his major work the technique involving spokesmen is of fundamental importance. It enables Cabell to convey meanings all around his subject and to capture a far wider significance; it enables him to express his own central belief through the chief spokesman (e.g., Charteris in *Beyond Life*) and yet to give credit also to the weaknesses in the central belief by expressing these in the form of arguments raised by secondary spokesmen. In this way is achieved the twofold nature, the extra depth of the work of Dreiser and E. M. Forster. At one point in *A Traveller at Forty*, Dreiser was to say:

> ... I accept no creed. I do not know what truth is, what beauty is, what love is, and what hope is. I do not believe anyone absolutely and I do not doubt anyone absolutely. I think people are both evil and well-intentioned.

For both Dreiser and Cabell, this attitude, representing American lack of sentimentality, American intellectual realism at its best, is a starting point rather than a culmination. It means, however, that, when dealing with a thing so large as "life," at no time is it safe to state a single, or narrow, point of view (or line of propaganda), failing to acknowledge other possibilities. Herein lies much of the greatness of their work. The introduction of numerous spokesmen helps Cabell to solve his constructional problems more artistically than does Dreiser; while filling in all aspects of his picture he can nevertheless remain as detached as were the creators of Lambert Strether and Mme Bovary.

In addition, there have always been uncomprehending critics and Cabell could always shrug and refer them to the spokesmen:

> This book's sub-title appears to me a bit affected. But Mr. Cabell believes that it will please reviewers, by enabling them to start off with a smart witticism about its applicability to other books: and so I yield ...

So writes Robert Etheridge Townshend from Lichfield in the introductory "Apologia Auctoris" to *From the Hidden Way*, the book of verses in the preparation of which he "collaborated" with Mr. Cabell.

In this introduction, Cabell separates, at once and quite clearly, his own poetry from that of his contemporaries. His own verses are "based upon pre-Renaissance formulae" and quite devoid of any influences from the Imagists, creators of the "new poetry of hitherto unknown directness and simplicity." This is largely because he considers it a fallacy that poetry "should deal with workaday life," which lacks the "fore-ordained and uncontrollable, or the beauty of fatality . . . and human inefficiency thereunder, such as the Greeks knew was necessary to art's highest strivings." This statement was written in 1924, and is thus a reiteration of the views which governed the choice of the mediums of the novels and not an early indication of his philosophy-in-embryo. Nevertheless, the ideas set forth apply directly to his poetry, much of which was created between 1895 and 1900 (some while Cabell was still at William & Mary) but continually revised until 1912; hence, it is fairly safe to assume that the statement is a retrospective glance at his cultural tendencies which must have been in existence, and possibly consciously so, at eighteen or nineteen and which seem to have governed Cabell for the rest of his life.

In Cabell's time, most modern poetry was aiming at expressing in striking individual images the nuances of complicated modern life. As did Matthew Arnold, Cabell insisted that the best subject for poetry (or, at any rate, his poetry) was the deified familiar, the eternal experiences which recur generation after generation. These universal experiences eventually form deep instinctual reservoirs of feeling which, for Cabell, could not be tapped by topical subtleties. Cabell was taking his stand on simplicity of feeling and complexity of medieval form; his contemporaries were taking theirs on complexity of feeling and simplicity of form. This relationship between Cabell's art and that of his contemporaries was to remain a constant one, providing one of the reasons for his neglect by the public. Cabell's work is in direct contradiction to Tolstoy's conception of art, which maintained that art should speak directly for its age. But then, so was Shakespeare's whose admiration for aristocracy Tolstoy regarded as provincial.

In his introduction to his poetry Cabell writes:

... these medieval rhymesters wrote by choice of what seems to us prosaic because to them it was throughout heart-shakingly strange. Their more alert perceptions were aware of a continuous wonderfulness, on every side, which we have learned to overlook. . . . Life affords nothing more remarkable than its truisms.

These mature observations were written more than twenty years after some of the poetry to which they refer. It becomes clear that the intentions were—inevitably and understandably—better in some cases than the performance. Much of the verse is slight in impact and as artificial and contrived as the early novels. Yet some of this poetry deals with Cabell's deepest themes.

FALSE DAWN IN TROY

Helenam omnes amant; invidia semper movente."
Allexandro de Medici.

There is no man but loves her, I well know;
Yet mutinous women, muttering with pinched lips,
Cast side-long glances always when—unvexed—
Queen Helen passes; for she is very fair,
And they have only right and truth with them.

Helen, the Marlovian symbol, is recurrent throughout Cabell's work and is a primary concern of Jurgen, whose behavior toward her was to be as revealing in one sense as it was not revealing in another. Some poems illustrate a youthful tendency to sentimentality, like that of Dickens; others reveal the genuine emotions of rationalized compassion which, in the novels, is sometimes concealed by barbed bitterness.

There is a short cycle of poems which deals directly with what is the heart of much of the prose:

OF ANNUAL MAGIC: AT TWENTY

Somewhere—impressively,—people are saying
Intelligent things (which their grandmothers said),
While I loiter, and dream to the branches' swaying
In furtive conference, high overhead.

The Poetry

... AT TWENTY FIVE

April wakes;—it were good to live
(Yet April passes), though April give
No other gift for our pleasuring
Than the old, old burden of burgeoning.

... AT TWENTY EIGHT

Thus all we laud May's sowing,
Nor heed how harvests please
When nowhere grain worth growing
Greets autumn's questing breeze.
And garnerers garner these—
Vain words and wasted breath—
And spilth and tasteless lees—
Until released by death.

... AT THIRTY

Now I in part forget . . . recall
In part . . . how yonder throstle's call
Inveigles whither mirth is,—
Because so many lips have told
The tale I told, once, who am old,
However young the earth is.

THE DOTARD CONJURER

Spring is become a dotard conjurer,
And his old magic words not any more!
No more avails the whisper of friendly leaves;
And now the forest is undenizened
Of daydreams, which, like elfin outlaws, once
Lay hid in wait for every passer-by
And pilfered all his sorrows; dawn abates
In wonder and tells flatly, *It is day,*
And tells no more than that now . . .

. . . And there is nothing hidden in the woods
Save birds, and trees, and flowers, and ravenous gnats,
And, under all, dead and decaying leaves.

Nay, under all, dead and decaying leaves
Enrich that mould which bred them, and whereby
The tree is nourished and new leaves put forth.

Was age, then, to be no more than the anticlimax to youth? Cabell's story—which is much that of a Hamlet who lived on —echoes round and round this theme in the novels.

The place of nature in Cabell's novels can be seen very clearly in the poetry. He views nature more as did Browning and Tennyson than Wordsworth or Emerson. With Browning he regards it as the frame to man, not as the medium through which spoke directly the still sad music of humanity. Emerson's conception of nature is virtually a rationalization of Wordsworth's emotional or poetic interpretation; Emerson regarded nature as a medium which received a power of good directly from God; this power then passed into the sympathetic, sensitive observer to strengthen him for his battle against ugliness and destruction. Thus the natural beauty of mountains and woods was man's direct link with God and a major medium through which he drew his divine sustenance—nature was a key link in the cycle between the creator and the created. The good works of the man who was in tune with nature completed God's circle of influence, creating the love which returned to the Father. Wordsworth's well-known little verse "The Tables Turned" speaks of this:

> One impulse from a vernal wood
> May teach you more of man,
> Of moral evil and of good,
> Than all the sages can.

At first sight, Cabell's series "Of Annual Magic" bears some resemblance to a Wordsworthian theme—as the inherent meaning echoes that of Wordsworth's Immortality Ode:

> Whither is fled the visionary gleam?
> Where is it now, the glory and the dream?

These lines formed the end of the "Ode on the Intimations of Immortality," in 1802, although Wordsworth was in the following four years to add answers to his own questions. Moral considerations, and not, as in the poem on Tintern Abbey, joyous moments of sensual recollection, came to supply the guiding light.

Both Cabell and Wordsworth show an awareness of departing youth, but the resemblance ends there. Cabell's interests are dominated intellectually rather than emotionally. He turns to the forces at work in humanity itself. Nature is admittedly one of these forces and a powerful one—especially in the spring of the year. But his awareness of nature's beauty is, like Tennyson's, that of the inspired scientist, pinpointing precise details and distilling them into a cultivated beauty. Cabell's version smacks something of the eighteenth-century hothouse and the formal gardens, in other words, of nature assisted and controlled by the civilized mind.

Cabell's conception of the spirit of nature is essentially Greek; again, his poetry indicates the direction his prose is to take. He takes two lines from Wordsworth and, for a chapter heading, adapts them thus.

> One impulse from a vernal wood
> May teach you more of Pan . . .

Pan, renamed Janicot in Cabell's mythology, was to have a predominating role in the novels. According to Cabell, in *Straws and Prayer Books*, Pan was the chief of the Greek gods to live on as sacred to the poet even in a "Christian" civilization. In this, Cabell is more in tune with Keats and Shelley; also with Spenser, whose allegory was as close to Cabell's as the widely differing tempers of their times would allow. The sunlit vistas of Poictesme are identical to those in *The Faerie Queene*, with good positive colors, clear natural greens and reds and yellows predominating over the half tones of decadence with which Cabell has been associated—the mauves, purples, golds and crimsons; nevertheless, these latter colors *do* appear and have their due significance in Cabell's works.

On the whole, then, Cabell's poetry, like that of Meredith, is secondary to the poetic prose of the novels. While much of it is intrinsically good and quite able to stand on its own merits, in general it is more valuable for its indications of the mind and temperament which were to harness this same poetic impulse to a far-reaching intellectual quest. The poetic impulse was to create the medium and the objective intellect was to govern the actions in that medium.

Cabell's medium leads him to Poictesme, and with luggage labeled accordingly, it is to this legendary land that we must now travel.

6: Poictesme

While Jurgen travels to numerous regions, including Hell, where he does very well, and Heaven, where he climbs upon the lap of the Almighty Himself to pull his beard (so difficult it is, these days, to distinguish between the true and the false), his permanent place of residence is Poictesme.

Quinquiremes of Nineveh yielded to dirty British coasters. Yet the hardships of the crews were much the same in either case. Truths concerning the former can at least be presented in an aura of beauty while applying none the less to the latter. Instead of the filthy back streets of American (or European) slums, Cabell decided to create his own worlds which would be more palatable for the imaginative artist, more civilized in the true sense of the word, than those around him.

To begin with (in 1905), the odds were in favour of Kent for the setting of Cabell's imaginative world, with Tunbridge Wells as its center. But this was not to be, mainly because of local geographical difficulties. Yet, as Edward Wagenknecht pointed out, "The wheel came full circle when, many years later, Frank C. Papé drew pictures of Poictesme for the illustrated editions of Cabell's books, in his studio in Tunbridge Wells [in Kent]."

With Poictesme, Cabell has given the atmosphere of Arcadia the substance of Hardy's Wessex. Poictesme[1] itself is situated in that part of the south of France which borders on the Gulf of

---

[1] A map appears on page 245 of Volume 18 of the Storisende Edition, with "A Note upon Poictesme" as the preface to the illustrated edition (1928) of *The Silver Stallion*.

Lions in the Mediterranean. It approximates the district of Gard overlapping into the Bouches-du-Rhône and Hérault. The mountains of the Cévennes form the northwestern boundary—containing the Vaidrex of *Figures of Earth*, where nightly dreams are made and through whose valleys they wend to the sleeping minds of mortals. To the east lies Provence and the barrier of mighty Alps; to the southwest lie Montpelier, the Carcassonne, Castile, and greater Spain.

On its eastern side is Storisende, the capital of Poictesme, which approximates Arles. A major road runs north from Storisende to Paris via Lyons and south to the coast and thence east to Provence. Another major road runs due east from Storisende to Bellegarde and near to Bellegarde is the very important Cistercian Abbey. This road linking Storisende to Bellegarde runs through the district of Amneran with its ominous heath; south of this road and parallel with it is the partly cleared Forest of Acaire, containing, in that corner of it nearest Storisende, Brunbelois. North of this major road is the district of Piemontain and another range of mountains parallel with the road.

As the road from Storisende south to the coast and north to Paris forms the eastern boundary of Poictesme, so the road north from Bellegarde to Naimes and south to the coast forms the western boundary. Naimes approximates Nimes; a branch road runs northeast from Naimes also to Paris. On the road running north from Bellegarde and nearer Bellegarde than Naimes is the home of Jurgen. South of Bellegarde, toward the Gulf of Lions is another branch road southwestward to Montepelier while at the coast itself the main road follows the shore west to Villeneuve and Castile.

As Sir Hugh Walpole observed,[2] "for those who have the key to Jurgen's world here is a world indeed!" In the Forest of Acaire are many strange creatures. There are catoblepas, mantichora, bleps, strycophanes, and calcars (especially the grey one), and they all wear fangs and scales as do the tawny eale and the leucrocotta, with its golden mane and whiskers and the opal-colored

[2] Introduction to *Jurgen* (English edition, The Bodley Head, London, 1921).

tarandas. These "have to be handled in just the right way . . . for each is unique, and in consequence lonely." The hatred felt for these monsters is due to the fact that their apparel, fangs and scales, is "not quite the sort of thing to which men are accustomed: whereas people were wholly used to having soldiers and prelates and statesmen ramping about in droves." However, as discovers Florian, Prince de Lisuarte, guided by Melusine through the Forest of Acaire towards *The High Place*, if these monsters are given a little confidence and the "admiration which men everywhere else accorded to the destroyers of mankind," they become "a great deal nicer to look at than the most courted and run-after people, and much less apt to destroy anybody outside of their meal hours."

In Poictesme we meet again the sunbathed innocence of Alfred's translation of Orpheus and Euridice, *Sir Orfeo*; the green glory of *Gawain and the Green Knight* and Chaucer's Gallic and Italian gardens; the corveting cavalcade of Spenser and the voluptuous luxuriance of Milton's Paradise here regained; the Grecian wood nymphs of Keats and Shelley; the cloying dangers of Circé set against the ennervating purples and crimsons of Yeats' *Wanderings of Oisin*, Tennyson's *The Lotus Eaters*, Pater's *Marius the Epicurean*, and Oscar Wilde's *A House of Pomegranates*.

This, then, indicates the geography of Poictesme, the kind of thing one might meet there and its varying atmospheres and climates. But this is not all. Many of Cabell's characters move from fable into history, and some are historically true. Most of this movement—either wholly in the real lands of France and England, or between these and Poictesme (where traditional mythology combines with Cabell's own)—takes place in the short stories. The books of short stories representing this are *The Line of Love* (1905 revised 1921), *Gallantry*, (1907 revised 1922), *Chivalry* (1909 revised 1921) and *The Certain Hour* (1916). Most of the action in these four books of stories takes place in England and France between 1265 and 1805. One story, "The Lady of all our Dreams," features, with great significance, John Charteris, the chief spokesman for Cabell himself; this takes place in Lichfield, Farehaven, in the twentieth century. It is the last story in the volume entitled *The Certain Hour,* and it requires individual attention, for it appears to be Cabell's only short story set in his own time. It has special significance for the interpretation of his artistic impulse.

7: The Framework of the Biography

The vast majority of Cabell's characters, ancient or modern, in or out of Poictesme, are represented as being the descendants of Dom Manuel of Poictesme. The first date to be established is that of 1234, when Dom Manuel the Redeemer and Miraman Lluagor meet at the famed Pool of Haranton. Melicent of *Domnei,* Dorothy la Desirée of *Jurgen,* and Ettarre of *The Cream of the Jest,* are all daughters of Manuel. Count Emmerick, who succeeded Manuel as ruler of Poictesme, is Manuel's son. Jurgen is joint founder with Manuel, the date of his retrospective travels being 1277. Jurgen unites with the line of Manuel through his association with Manuel's second daughter, Dorothy la Desirée. Florian, hero of *The High Place* and a Puysange, is a French Regency descendant of Manuel and Jurgen.[1]

Manuel represents the Achilles of Poictesme while Jurgen is its Ulysses. Their descendants are men either of action or of contemplation according to their proportions of the blood of Manuel or of Jurgen.

In his revisions Cabell brings even his own spokesmen of Lichfield, the characters of his early novels of contemporary life, into the Biography. For example, in *The Cords of Vanity* the "hero," Robert Townshend, speaking to Stella, tells the story of Ole-Luk-Oie and of how he, Robert Townshend, was once allowed entry into the illustrations of the *Popular Tales of Poictesme,* where "we met my great-grandfather Jurgen."

[1] Cabell has drawn up a genealogy of Manuel and his descendants in *The Lineage of Lichfield* (1922), in which all the relationships are traced in detail. There is also a detailed account of Poictesme and its inhabitants and associates in Edward Wagenknecht's study of Cabell (340–44) in his *Cavalcade of the American Novel.*

In *The Certain Hour* the episode concerning John Charteris in effect makes Cabell himself a descendant of these "Figures of Earth" moulded by Manuel and inspired by the "Sparkes and smalle Flamings" of the artistic impulse inherited from Queen Freydis of Poictesme. These figures include Shakespeare, Herrick, Wycherley, Pope, and Sheridan.

The actual order in which Cabell wrote his books must be re-arranged if the "historical" sequence of the generations of the Biography is to be unfolded in logical order. For example, *Figures of Earth* was not written until 1921. This was some considerable time after *The Cords of Vanity*—twelve years after; yet when all are brought into the Biography, *Figures of Earth* must come first, as it is the story of the founder Manuel and the first generation of the Biography in thirteenth-century Poictesme; the characters of Robert Townshend and John Charteris in the early novel, *The Cords of Vanity*, represent the descendants twenty generations later in twentieth-century Lichfield, Fairhaven, U.S.A.

For the order required for the Biography and not the actual order in which the books were written,[2] *Beyond Life* (1919) is the natural prologue to the history of Manuel's perpetuated life, and *Figures of Earth* is the opening chapter, followed by *The Silver Stallion, Domnei*, and *The Music from Behind the Moon.*

Of the books of short stories, *Chivalry*, which deals with England and France in the thirteenth and fourteenth centuries (the earliest story, "The Tenson," is dated 1265) comes first and immediately precedes or really coincides with *Jurgen*. Jurgen's story is told in 1277 but it is retrospective over the period of his own lifetime, nearly forty years—Jurgen being then aged "forty-and-something." Then comes the collection of short stories entitled *The Line of Love*, which begins precisely on April 30, 1293, and covers episodes illustrating the lives, *semper idem*, of Manuel's and Jurgen's descendants through until 1919. *The High Place*, set completely in Poictesme, follows and recounts more about

---

[2] Carl Van Doren's short study (revised edition 1932), which Edward Wagenknecht described in 1952 as "the best general study," contains a complete list of the order of Cabell's books "according to the Biography," as does the "Bibliographic Summary" in Volume 16 of the Storisende Edition.

Florian de Puysange, who appears at a younger stage of his life in the first episode of *The Line of Love.* Next comes the short stories under the heading of *Gallantry.* These stories are so closely related that they form a single novel of the factual and fictional times of France and England when George II ruled in England and the Marquise de Pompadour in France, when "the King of Prussia and the Empress Maria Theresa had, between them, set Europe by the ears," and "Mr. Washington was a promising young surveyor in the most loyal colony of Virginia," in other words in the 1750's. In *Gallantry* the blood of Manuel and Jurgen is represented by the line of De Puysange, of which Florian, of *The High Place* and *The Line of Love*, was such a prominent member. The setting moves easily from fact to fiction, for example from Dover to Bellegard-en-Poictesme, or from Paris to Breschau in Noumaria.

Then comes *Something About Eve,* one of the most important, followed by the next group of short stories, entitled *The Certain Hour.* Some of the stories here are earlier in time than those in *Gallantry*—that of "Judith's Creed" features Shakespeare and marks the year 1609 and the season of September for the beginning of the action, and that of Robert Herrick is in the 1670's. Yet these stories carry on through William Wycherley in 1680 down to the unusually modern story of John Charteris in the twentieth century, so the final note is more recent than that of *Gallantry.*

Next come the three early novels of contemporary life already mentioned, *The Cords of Vanity, The Rivet in Grandfather's Neck,* and *The Eagle's Shadow,* as they stand in the Biography and bring Manuel's line down to its descendants in Lichfield in the 1900's.

Finally in the fiction is *The Cream of the Jest.* This features Felix Kennaston (who appeared in *The Eagle's Shadow,* Cabell's first work, in 1904) as the hero who exists in Lichfield but lives in the past. Felix Kennaston, guided by the puppet-shifter Horvendile, and accompanied by the ageless beauty Ettarre, journeys back from the twentieth century across the long ages of history, down to the times of Caesar and beyond and up again to Manuel and Storisende in his search for the meaning of man.

In *The Lineage*, Cabell observes of Kennaston's return to the past:

> . . . through this return, the perpetuated life of Manuel ends its seven hundred years of journeying at the exact point of its outset. The circle is thus made complete, as my last poet annihilates . . . the intervening twenty generations.

As *Beyond Life* forms a fitting prologue to all these works of the Biography, so is *Straws and Prayer Books* (1924) the epilogue. In the prologue, Cabell discusses every aspect of his art; in the epilogue he sums up on the note of *lusisti satis* even as he is taking stock of himself for future works.

This Biography spans seven centuries of human existence. It provides the means to portray all the chief concerns of man on, above, and below the earth, and it well merits the description of "the most ambitiously planned literary work which has ever come out of America." As Edwin Bjorkman observed:

> As far as I know, Mr. Cabell is the only one of our living literary artists in this country who has worked out something like a truly philosophic conception of human existence.[3]

The idea of *The Lineage* (which was not actually written down until 1921) no doubt occurred some time after numerous writings, originally not included, had already taken shape; yet the comparative ease with which the revisions have related all to the superimposed pattern of the Biography is a direct indication of the remarkable unity which connects the latest of Cabell's work with his earliest.

There is a noteworthy similarity between the attitude and ideas of Cabell and those of Carlyle, between their conceptions of a spirit or being animating certain individuals and moving through all history. Teufelsdrockh, fleeing from his shadow, stumbling at random through the corridors of time, anticipates Manuel, Jurgen, and Felix Kennaston. Carlyle, in appending significant reviews to the end of *Sartor Resartus*, again anticipated Cabell's similar

[3] "Concerning James Branch Cabell's Human Comedy," *The Literary Digest International Book Review* (December, 1922).

gesture with the revised version of *The Eagle's Shadow*. The philosophic nature of Cabell's mind coupled with his lifelong yearning for beauty could be expressed only in some such vast sequence of four dimensional worlds. These worlds are complete with their own endless ramifications as one corridor opens up upon another with further echoing implications in this saga of the questing spirit of universal man.

It is now time to examine in detail the precise nature of these, the greatest concerns known and unknown to man, as they are displayed in the twenty generations of The Biography of Manuel the Redeemer, as well as to illustrate something of the profundity and mastery of Cabell's art as a whole.

PART THREE

THE PHILOSOPHY AND ITS CONVERSION TO ART

8: The Prologue

Many a man lives a burden to the earth; but a good book is the precious life-blood of a master-spirit, embalmed and treasured up on purpose to a life beyond life.

John Milton

Beyond Life was written in 1918 immediately before *Jurgen*, with which it was published in 1919. It consists of a series of essays concerning everything which was of most concern to Cabell; in the writing of these essays he was hammering and forging his own master-spirit into the shape required for his best work.

Sir Hugh Walpole had said:

I had not been two weeks in the United States before someone said to me: "Well, at any rate, there is Cabell." That was a new name to me. I was given *Beyond Life* to read. My excitement during the discovery of that perverse and eloquent testament was one of the happiest moments of my American stay.[1]

For a long time the romanticism of Cabell has been regarded as akin either to that in *The Prisoner of Zenda* or to decadent escapism. An analysis of *Beyond Life* may correct both these notions. With the most ruthless honesty, Cabell probes within himself to assess just what it is which makes humanity "tick." The answer he finds is many sided, and very often, as at Elsinore, one side contradicts another. There is always that terrible barrier preventing any clear-cut conclusion such as that which enabled Milton to

[1] "The Art of James Branch Cabell," *Yale Review* (July, 1920), 687.

55

sally forth at once with his ready and easy way to govern without a king. . . . That barrier is an awareness that nothing is good or bad but thinking makes it so. What, in the name of goodness (or badness) is the sensitive artist to do in the face of such a predicament? It was the predicament of Dreiser and of Robert Penn Warren and of E. M. Forster. Cabell, also, refuses to stay on the surface, and in plunging, he reaches rock bottom with this eternal and unanswerable theme forever nagging in the minds of thinking men.

It is worth noting here that it is not forever nagging in the minds of Cabell's women. It seems to come back to the difference between the reactions of Macbeth to a given situation and those of his wife. While Cabell would be the first, in any mixed company, to acknowledge the "intelligence of women," he would also be the first to suggest that it has—unwittingly it may be—as a prime objective the desire to guarantee that the cries of the lover be perpetuated in the wails of an infant. These two important facets of Cabell's work are dealt with in *Beyond Life* under chapters headed "The Demiurge" and "The Witch-Woman."

As offering most hope of satisfaction for his pursuit of an answer, or answers, Cabell turns to an examination of the "penetrative common sense of poets," those "chillingly astute persons," in relation to the matters which so vitally concern the art of living. In this chapter, headed appropriately enough for his day and age, "The Economist," we see Cabell's sympathy with that which Marlowe and François Villon represent in his work.

Vernon Parrington noted[2] of Cabell that "such Homeric absurdities of comment have been flung at him, that he is in a fair way to become our classic example of the fatuousness of contemporary estimates." Of the work in question he says that:

> *Beyond Life* is an essay altogether remarkable for it haunting beauty of phrase, its honest agnosticism, its brooding irony. It is enough to turn one cynic to consider that so noble a book should have called forth from a reputable gentleman . . . the comment that it "contains cheap and shallow pessimistic observations on human

2 "The Incomparable Mr. Cabell," *Pacific Review* (1921).

limitations." . . . An inquisitive mind, deeply concerned with ultimate values, cannot be cheap and shallow.

The central column of Cabell's work is his concern with "ultimate values." The base of this column is rooted in the chapter in *Beyond Life* entitled "The Reactionary," which deals directly with Cabell's conception of Christianity. This extremely significant aspect of his work has been completely overlooked—the worst immediate consequence being the censorship of *Jurgen*. Arising out of the "cause" of Christianity is the "consequence" in fiction of the themes of gallantry and chivalry—from "the petty villains of Wycherley to the eternal verities of religion." In the Author's Note of April, 1927, Cabell states:

> Above all does the book attempt to outline three possible attitudes towards human existence which have been adopted or illustrated, and at times blended, by the many descendants of Manuel. I mean the Chivalric attitude, the Gallant attitude, and what I can only describe as the poetic attitude. The descendants of Manuel have . . . viewed life as a testing; as a toy; and as raw material. They have variously sought during their existence upon earth to become—even by the one true test, of their private thoughts while lying awake at night—admirable; or to enjoy life; or to create something more durable than life.

While the emphasis on each of these aspects may vary, they are all consistently present, the poetic underlying the gallant chivalry.

As Cabell links Christianity to romanticism,[3] so does he link the Church to realism, unfolding these matters in the chapters entitled "The Candle" and "The Mountebank." Restoration comedy is closely examined as the means of illustrating the arguments which involve the role of the church and the role of the artist,

---

[3] T. E. Hulme, discussing "Romanticism and Classicism" in *Speculations* (1924), observed, "Romanticism then, and this is the best definition I can give of it, is spilt religion." Hulme's remarks about the classical attitude explain exactly the element in Cabell's thought which keeps him in touch with reality and gives rise to the banter and mockery; e.g., "In the classical attitude you never seem to swing right along to the infinite nothing. If you say an extravagant thing which does exceed the limits inside which you know man to be fastened, yet there is always . . . an impression of yourself standing outside, and not quite believing it, or consciously putting it forward as a flourish."

not to mention "chief-justices and archbishops and kings and statesmen" and that most valuable of all sedatives, patriotism.

Cabell's search involves considerations of romance and realism as these are reflected in the works of his minor contemporaries and in the classics of English literature. Then, in the final chapter, "Wherein We Await," the finishing touches are made, with full use of the spokesmen to fill in any remaining gaps in the central arguments. This chapter culminates in the urbane but positive credo which constitutes the cornerstone of Cabell's art and which can be used at all times to understand dubious ambiguities. For life is perverse, and to a greater extent than many of the realists, Cabell presents life. As an artist as well as an intellectual realist, Cabell determines to capture as many as possible of the ambiguous complexities of our universe in his universe, and we must follow patiently as he suddenly places his tongue in his cheek, throws in counterarguments like large spanners, becomes frivolous, denies his deepest and most firmly-held convictions and flaunts perversities.[4] For life itself is perverse, and Cabell presents life—not only its stupidity and ugliness but also its music and its beauty, its poetry and its pathos. In Cabell's world, we wash the dishes *and* watch the skylark.

There is early evidence in *Beyond Life* of Cabell's learning. Cabell observes, in the Author's Note of 1927, "Most of this book was stumbled upon in talk with [Guy Holt], during the five years or so that he was quite fruitlessly endeavouring to sell my books." On John Charteris' library shelves he puts "the cream of the unwritten books—the masterpieces that were planned and never carried through." These, he says, are much more difficult to understand, and in some ways more revealing, than those which were actually completed. They include Thackeray's medieval romance of Agincourt together with several novels of Dickens' "later and failing period"; Keats's epic which is "rather disappointing," and Milton's *King Arthur*—"quite his most readable performance"; the last six books of *The Faerie Queen* and the last

---

[4] Cf. Oscar Wilde's remark in *De Profundis:* "what the paradox was to me in the sphere of thought, perversity became to me in the sphere of passion."

Canterbury Tales "are simply beyond human patience"; Sheridan's fine late comedy *Affectation* is his materpiece, while the main treasure is the unbound collection, the intended edition, of *The Unwritten Plays of Christopher Marlowe*. There is also the 1599 version of *Troilus and Cressida*—"the only edition in which the play is anything like comprehensible!"

Having set his scene with his introductory comments on these major romanticists, John Charteris continues "in very much that redundant and finicky and involved and inverted 'style' of his writings." In his preface to the Storisende Edition of *Beyond Life*, Cabell supplies the fullest justification for his mellifluous but accurate style. John Charteris speaks:

> In that hesitating and hair-splitting manner of men seeking the last refinement of truth, full of reservations and qualifications and after thoughts (the footnotes all included in the text, as De Quincey rather suggests they should be), and with every grade of subordination duly recorded in the flexible medium of adverbial modifiers. For the sentence and the complete thought stay always his units: and he strives to make them correspond exactly, at the price of requiring the minds of his hearers to remain continuously alert.

Cabell's prose is thus a classical example of that complex simplicity consisting of the shortest and fewest words possible in the most logical and harmonious order.

John Charteris starts with a rapid but incisive survey of numerous periods of literature. From Hellenic literature and Sophocles' boast that he painted men "as they ought to be," he passes on to medieval and Elizabethan English literature, where the best of Chaucer unites with the best of Marlowe and Shakespeare in selecting, not contemporary events and settings, but ancient and mythological ones and remote Italian backgrounds, and on again to the "impossible" behavior of Restoration so-called realistic comedy where "momentary competence and happiness and all important documents, as well as a sudden turn for heroic verse, were regularly accorded to everybody toward eleven o'clock in the evening." When the novel replaced the drama, the novelist had no need to resort even to partial truth "and this new style of writing at once became emblematic. And so it has been ever since." Proving the exception to the rule he is stating, Cabell, or Charteris, observes:

> The truth about ourselves is the one truth, above all others, which we are adamantine not to face. And this determination springs, not wholly from vanity, but from a profound race-sense that by such denial we have little to lose and a great deal to gain.

This observation is directly linked to the first major conclusions concerning romance, or the demiurge, that Charteris advances, covering it with a qualifying observation from another of Cabell's spokesmen. This conclusion is worth giving in full as it embodies a fundamental cause of Cabell's own urge to create:

> Meanwhile in theory—without of necessity accompanying my friend Felix Kennaston all the way to his conclusion that the sum of corporeal life represents an essay in romantic fiction—I can perceive plainly enough that the shape-giving principle of all sentient beings is artistic. . . . [This principle] shapes too the minds of men, by this universal tendency to imagine—and to think of as in reality existent—all the tenants of earth and all the affairs of earth, not as they are, but "as they ought to be." And so it comes about that romance has invariably been the demiurgic and beneficent force, not merely in letters, but in every matter that concerns mankind.

Romance or the demiurge is quite clearly described here as a *beneficent* force. Where in any previous age, or for the sentimentalist, the matter would rest here, Cabell does not let his theory escape so easily. The odds against romance were now too high: man was to be responsible for more misery and waste in the first fifty years of the twentieth century than in the preceding thousand. On the one hand this amounted to *An American Tragedy*; on the other it was summed up by H. G. Wells's *Tono-Bungay*. The thoughtful were petrified by the extent to which the salesmen and the shopkeepers were persistently polluting the inner sanctums of the national mind with the national excrement—however necessary and ultimately beneficial the process may be.

For anyone so unfortunate as to possess compassion, the spectacle was inevitably sickening—the deadening icecap of despair ever pushing on toward the heart. It was not enough that these things were eternal; their scale and extent made them unprecedented. It is no wonder, then, that there is bitterness here, that a note of pessimism occasionally dominates. This spirit of the age, which marks all modern literature, touches also the work of Cabell and casts the eternal romantic impulse in a modern mould. This makes Cabell's romanticism apparently very different from what he himself describes as the full-blooded, wholly positive romanticism of those with an all powerful zest for living, such as Scott. It is here that we must be very careful indeed. For minor-key romanticism expresses a nostalgic yearning to escape everyday life by a return to childhood, or with residence in Arcadia, or wanderings with Oisin. Major-key romanticism is buoyant and full of rich color and action with the emphasis on life. Minor is lanquid, sombre, and pervaded by the wish for death. Cabell's romanticism is very easily misunderstood not only because it is unique in its time but because it does contain deliberate undertones of the minor kind of romanticism.

These undertones lead Cabell not to decadence but to urbanity; they consistently embody intellect instead of yielding to the emotions whereby romanticism becomes sentimentality. To eat carefully with cutlery instead of ravenously with the bare hands is improvement rather than decline. That the food is occasionally unpalatable and the expression consequently wry is another matter altogether. Cabell presents life imaginatively and so qualifies as a romanticist; his view is cohesive and embodies a philosophy of life and is thus full of thought. As Shakespeare has shown us, anything which deals profoundly with life must acknowledge unpleasantness; it cannot, in other words, be glib and superficial but must, at times, dare to be sad—even, in the face of such evidence, reflect a little despondency. But despondency, or an awareness of unpleasantness, is not decadence unless the artist either does not go beyond it or is diverted by it into avenues of escape which lead away from considerations of life as it is, into fanciful representations of life as it is not. Cabell never evades the consequence of his analysis of life as it is. He entered avenues and these avenues are complete with alcoves, but if they lead to beauty they do not lead to escape for he carries his problems with him. Cabell was not the first to regard beauty as a synonym for truth.

What enables him to retain truth and yet imaginatively to capture beauty is his sense of irony. This, the sane man's defence against an insane world, is an all-important ingredient in both his approach and in his treatment. This sense of irony provides the emotional catharsis necessary for urbanity. At the same time it satisfies the requirements for intellectual integrity. The result is a combination of both beauty and truth of the highest order, expressed with the serenity of wisdom.

Much misconception about Cabell's work has arisen because he has written, in the classical tradition, about general qualities of universal human nature in an age more interested in the complexities of individual predicaments. The consequence has been criticism such as the following:

> Mr. Cabell has carried this novel of escape, pretence and sophisticated grandeur to the point of exhaustion. . . . [His] is a simple philosophy to the effect that life is tedious and disillusioning and scarcely worth the effort, though it may be somewhat relieved by a dream-escape.[5]

And, of his stories:

> Energy and originality they do not have, logic they need not have . . . since environmental reality is dismissed and character cannot exist without it, we are left with nothing to talk of but the pleasurable esthetic qualities of style and composition.[6]

If this were true about "environmental reality" it would seem to curtail considerably any discussion of, for example, *The Tempest*. Because he does not always call a spade a spade, Cabell is not an "escapist." One secret of great art has always been to express one thing in terms of another. It is true that Cabell has always seen

---

[5] Peter Munro Jack, *New Republic* (January 13, 1937).
[6] *Ibid.*

too much into things to commit himself naïvely to a too clear-cut or one-sided statement of beliefs. There is always the possibility that man is of no importance whatsoever to anybody; whereupon there is immediately the co-ordinate possibility that all his theories, religions, sciences, and even arts amount to no more than self-deluding presumptions.

These are the two chief concerns in Cabell's work. One expresses the workings of the spirit of romance or the demiurge and leads to a christian and chivalric attitude which is positive and constructive; the other takes the form of an attitude of "gallantry," like that of the Restoration. The latter is an antidote to any latent sentimentality in the former, and both are complementary. An example of the combination of both is in the episode in *Gallantry* entitled "In The Second April." John Bulmer, Duke of Ormskirk, is the equivalent of a successful businessman, easy-going in his power, who has "bungled this affair of living." Considering "the world a healthy and not intolerable prison, where each man must get through his day's work as best he might, soiling his fingers as much as necessity demanded—but no more . . . ," John Bulmer can state, ". . . for in every man, as I now see quite plainly, there is a god. And the god must judge, and the man himself must be the temple and the instrument of the god. It is very simple, I see now. And whether he goes to church or not is a matter of trivial importance, so long as the man obeys the god who is within him."

Linking these two concerns and an important part of both is a third. Cabell calls this domnei, the worship of woman.

In the chapter in *Beyond Life* headed "The Demiurge," Cabell describes the culmination of these romantic tendencies, primordially inherent in man, the only animal that plays the ape to its dreams. Romance, "the first and loveliest daughter of human vanity," expressed itself in the chivalric attitude toward life. Again, Cabell's is a later version of Spenser's, which stated, in effect, that the manners are the morals. But in Cabell's case there is a far more ruthless analysis of the underlying significance of chivalry. Long past are the days when a work could be written ostensibly to fashion "a noble person in vertuous and gentle discipline." As Cabell himself writes, "The cornerstone of Chivalry I take to be the idea of vicarship: for the chivalrous person is, in his own eyes at least, the child of God, and goes about this world as his Father's representative in an alien country." Chivalry made, and still makes, its appeal to man's pride because it elevates his own importance as an individual with a personal contract with God.

> So man became a chivalrous animal; and about this flattering notion of divine vicarship builded his elaborate medieval code, to which, in essentials, a great number of persons adhere even nowadays, . . . perhaps it was never, quite, a "practical" attitude,—no, *mais quel geste!*

After concluding that on any realistic assessment the human race has shown itself "to be beyond all wording, petty and ineffectual," Cabell sees this chivalric tendency, with its root in vanity, as a prime cause of human advancement toward something better.

> To spin romances is, indeed, man's proper and peculiar function in a world wherein he only of created beings can make no profitable use of the truth about himself . . . so he fares onward chivalrously, led by *ignes fatui* no doubt, yet moving onward.

This, then, is a fundamental concern, this "dynamic Illusion"— "man's big romantic idea of Chivalry, of himself as his Father's representative in an alien country." In spite of all factual or realistic evidence to the contrary, Cabell observes, "And still—behold the miracle! still I believe life to be a personal transaction between myself and Omnipotence; I believe that what I do is somehow of importance."

Three qualities necessary for great art are, first, a sense of compassion; second, comic awareness of man's insignificance; and third, a tragic awareness of man's denial of this insignificance. If the intellectual drive balances or predominates over the emotional, there is almost sure to be a move towards the classical tradition, towards material that reflects an interest in the gods or fate or destiny; also, towards the logical and symmetrical handling of that material, towards harmony and balance—the sort of attitude which eventually produced the Parthenon as opposed to Knossos. Cabell's major concerns of chivalry and of gallantry, as seen most frequently in connection with domnei (the Provençal ideal of courtly love), permit, indeed almost insist upon, the above three qualities. These concerns are the compound; the pestle is the sense of irony and the crucible generally Poictesme. The finished product embodies both the alchemist's elixir of life and the modern economist's views on the best distribution of energy.

In *Beyond Life* it is the chapter headed "The Demiurge" which deals with Cabell's conception of the origin and role of chivalry. He illustrates his views in action in the book of short stories entitled *Chivalry*. The complementary concern of Gallantry is dealt with in, among other places, the chapters headed "The Reactionary" (along with one of Cabell's most straightforward pronouncements—or perhaps admissions—concerning Christianity or religion), "The Candle," and, with a consideration of Sheridan which gives full play to a fine sense of paradox, in the chapter "The Mountebank." It is, paradoxically enough, in his conception of the gallant attitude toward life that Cabell expresses his tragic awareness of man's attempt to overcome his insignificance. It is paradoxical because his gallants come very near to the ethical heart of things just because they attempt an amoral approach to them. And, as with the Porter scene in Macbeth, these gallant activities supply an easing of tension, an off-loading for a moment of the cares of conduct, at the very same time that—as in the Porter scene—they supply further most relevant information at the very gates of Hell itself. Yet, it should be remembered, in Hell, Jurgen does well. One simply does not know—hence the attitude of gallantry; but, one *feels* to the extent that these feelings amount to instinctual knowledge; hence, the gallant attitude, which is a tragically magnificent gesture, is not, in itself, enough. This seems to be Cabell's conclusion, which he illustrates in action in the book of short stories entitled *Gallantry*. These stories are very closely related, often consecutive, and they counterbalance or complement those in *Chivalry*.

The essence of Cabell's gallantry is that of Gawain's behavior when presented, first with the overtures of his host's wife in the Castle and then with the Green Knight himself; also of Arthur's in Book VI of *The Faerie Queene*, when he had to learn to suffer fools, if not gladly, at least with equanimity; and also of Gareth's in Tennyson's *Gareth and Lynette*, when, unseated at last in his conflicts, he replied with laughter and earned the help of the gods in the shape of Lancelot. Thus, Cabell's gallantry is akin to his chivalry. The chivalric aspect relates more obviously to the spiritual and religious in man while the gallant gives freer play to the physical, to action in general, in a more obviously secular environment. Many of these stories, setting forth in action the consequences of the gallant attitude, have the flavor of Restoration drama as in Congreve and the later-flowering Sheridan.

Cabell stands, in his estimate of Restoration drama as "very real literary art," midway between Lamb's idealized representation of it as a utopia of gallantry and Macaulay's view of it as a scandalous and scurrilous array of heartlessness and bad taste. Cabell is nearer Lamb than Macaulay; but where Lamb overlooked those aspects indicated by drunken performances and audiences, Cabell has fewer illusions about the nature and scope of human behavior; on the other hand, Cabell is more sympathetic than Macaulay to the predicament of dramatists who had to write comedies for such people. As Johnson said, the great end of comedy is to make the audience laugh. Although Shakespeare had shown that good box office could be good art, the circumstances were now too difficult, in the main, for the Restoration dramatists. Following the classical tradition of drama initiated by Ben Jonson, aided by Dryden and further augmented by the drama of situation and intrigue in France and Spain, they became "realistic."

As Cabell observes in the chapter "The Reactionary,"

> For Wycherley and his confrères were the first Englishmen to depict mankind as leading an existence with no moral outcome. It was their sorry distinction to be the first of English authors to present a world of unscrupulous persons who entertained no especial

prejudices, one way or the other, as touched ethical matters; to represent such persons as being attractive in their characteristics. . . . There was really never a more disastrous example of literature's stooping to copy life. For of course the Restoration dramatists were misled by facts.

Cabell then illustrates the manner in which great literature must always ignore the "facts," that in reality seemingly unscrupulous persons can be likeable, that the material prizes of life fall mostly to them and that it is only they who apparently possess untroubled consciences. In his own rehandling of such themes as gallantry in his stories, Cabell is not misled by such facts but reverts to a more poetic truthfulness in fuller accord with the dictates of his demiurge. It is the spirit rather than the spiritual which Cabell admires in these dramatists as seen in his estimate of Congreve, who, like Wycherley, "in his first youth wrote in a manner that will always delight the elect, because the desire to write perfectly of beautiful happenings was, with him also, innate." Congreve—and there is a fine and moving estimate of the eternal beauty of his figmentary women as opposed the merely lifelong appeal of their real-life counterparts—gave himself to art until, like Marlowe, he died at the age of twenty-nine, though leaving a physical body which persisted for another thirty years. It is Congreve who most sums up the gallant attitude to life which Cabell describes as follows:

> One must make the best of this world as a residence; keep it as far as possible a cheery and comfortable place; practise urbanity toward the other transient occupants; and not think too despondently or too often of the grim Sheriff, who arrives anon to dispossess you, no less than all the others, nor of any subsequent and unpredictable legal adjustments:—that is what the creed of Gallantry came to (long before Congreve played with verbal jewellery under the later Stuarts) when Horace first exhorted well-loved persons to accept life's inconveniences with a shrug—*amara lento temperet risu.*[7]

Both Johnson and Voltaire would have agreed with this; yet Cabell seems to have accredited much more of his own philosophical

[7] Horace, C. II.16.27.

depth to these dramatists than, in fact, they really possessed. At any rate, in the outcome as represented by his own books, this attitude of gallantry is merely the outward appearance, which acts as a steppingstone to far more profound inward and spiritual conceptions. For in Cabell's work there is always a persistent awareness of values, an awareness which indicates the ability to distinguish, to discriminate, and finally, therefore, to judge—in the pursuit of beauty which is truth. For example, in his brilliant presentation of the paradox that was Sheridan, the bankrupt whom they made secretary to the treasury, Cabell comes eventually to this:

> Thus far the drama has sped so trippingly that one rather boggles over the last act. . . . It would appear that life was fumbling at some lugubrious moral. If not as apologue how else are we to interpret. . . . Yes, it must be that life was fumbling at a moral, of just that explicit sort which every writer worth his salt knows to be unforgivably artificial.

Cabell's conclusions appear to be that here are people who put a brave face on things, who talked and acted boldly and brilliantly —in fact, gallantly instead of apathetically. This is an attitude suitable for the outward expression of Cabell's much more substantial inward thoughts. Yet it has ambiguous elements in it, for it smacked of a heartlessness which was counter to compassion and to Cabell's expressed wish for tenderness—a civilized quality essential to urbanity. Thus he recognizes discrepancies in Sheridan's superficial intellectual brilliance which created a glossy society yet which had no roots. This recognition leads to a contradictory cynicism which Cabell relates to his awareness that possibly man may be really quite an unimportant animal after all. This cynicism, or scepticism, often called Cabell's disillusion, serves to offset any sentimentality latent in the desire for tenderness. Thus we have the equivalent of Dreiser's duality of good and evil as Cabell enters the hearts and minds of his most gallant villains to illustrate the complexities of the demiurge or spirit of romance as it fights to withstand the slow contagion of the world's disease or, in other words, as youth battles with the age that betrays it. So Cabell's spirit of gallantry is a much larger thing than was possessed by the followers of the School of Manners.

I have read that the secret of gallantry is to accept the pleasures of life leisurely, and its inconveniences with a shrug . . . the gallant person will always consider the world with a smile of toleration, and his own doings with a smile of amusement and Heaven with a smile that it not distrustful—being thoroughly persuaded that God is kindlier than the genteel would regard as rational.

So speaks Charteris in *Beyond Life*. For the Restoration dramatists and Sheridan this attitude embodied heartlessness and evasion of any such alien things as personal or social obligations; in Cabell's case the smile of tolerance is for human limitations but also for human aspiration which seems so heavily outweighed in the pursuit of happiness. As Professor Parrington observed, "Those shameless and selfish roués began as artists but they ended as mountebanks; life taught them cynicism and not tenderness. . . . The higher irony lay quite beyond their natures."[8] Cabell, then, takes the Gallantry of the seventeenth and eighteenth centuries and their settings and weds them to his own philosophical observations on man's predicament in a perverse universe. This profound version of *The Way of the World* is much more far reaching, even enlightening, than any *School for Scandal*, even though it assumes a similar outward nonchalence.

These two concerns, of chivalry and gallantry, are seen at work most obviously and most frequently, in life and in the Biography, in man's relations with woman. These relations, in one way or another, take the form of woman-worship or domnei. In *Beyond Life*, Cabell deals with his theories about this in the chapter headed "The Witch-Woman." It is, it seems, all a matter of witchcraft and all are potentially liable to the spell whether the Thane of Cawdor or John Donne or Henry VIII. But it is the poets, the seekers after beauty who are most susceptible. Our clearest examples are, perhaps, Spenser and Milton—not to men-

[8] *Pacific Review* (December, 1921).

tion the causes and consequences of the Sonnets to the Dark Lady nor the impact of the face that launched a thousand ships. It is this domnei which transmutes the weighty intellectual elements in Cabell's work into the star-spangled gossamer of poetry that it is. It is also the vehicle which expresses the weariness consequent upon the many years' climb to romantic heights swathed at all times in the cloying mists of the drudgery of life as it is. Briefly, domnei is the expression, at a much later stage of the civilization, of the medieval neoplatonic attitude to women which saw their beauty as one of God's chief works on earth. The worship of this beauty was part of the worship of God. Against the background of Poictesme it is the reincarnation of the code of courtly love as maintained by the wandering troubadours of Provence from the eleventh to the thirteenth centuries. "For," says Charteris, "there is that in every human being which demands communion with something more fine and potent than itself." Cabell's unfolding of the workings of domnei embody the struggle which this romantic notion must undertake to survive the encroachment of mundane monotony. This attempt of man to make real in marriage this primordial dream becomes *The Cream of the Jest*. It is sufficient at this point merely to observe that it is a jest moving enough to provide the laughter of exalted tragedy as man, that forked animal, postures his defiance of the gods like a not very upright empty bottle awaiting an incoming tide.

Cabell notes, in his afterword to *Domnei:*

> . . . it was the very essence of Domnei that the woman one loves is providentially set between her lover's apprehension and God, as the mobile and vital image and corporeal reminder of Heaven, as a quick symbol of beauty and holiness, of purity and perfection.

As in other activities of man, whether they be the waging of war, politics or education, in domnei also it is possible to subordinate the end to the means.

As Cabell sees this matter, domnei is initially responsible for courtship and marriage, and then "the quick symbol of beauty and holiness" changes into "the mother of his children, that rather likeable, well-meaning creature" who is no longer the person who once set him ablaze with a religious ardour. If the male is fortunate he relapses into a staid and mediocre acquiescence in accord with that of his neighbors, people who, like himself, have bank balances and are accepted as respectable and therefore sensible. If, however, he is one of those unfortunate Minions of the Moon, cursed with an imagination, then he may, like Madoc or Alfgar, King of Ecben, be smitten by a dream. And in this dream is music. With this music comes doubtfulness and discontent as come to those who hear the music of the ageless beauty Ettarre, "the most dear of Dom Manuel's daughters," who leads them out of the set ways of life. When they awake they know their doom is upon them: Madoc and Alfgar, who possess imaginations, become artists and insist on a lifelong pursuit of perfection. "For every art is a confession of faith in that which is not yet." Thus we have once more the conception that Milton embodied in *Samson Agonistes* that in God's service is perfect freedom, a conception that may be coupled to that of Charteris when he observes that art was not a religion. On the contrary, religion is one of the loveliest forms of art. So Cabell's heroes enter the elect company of the happy few who have their moments of splendor one way or another, by hook or by crook, in a perverse world and "surrounded by ugly people doing stupid things." Of domnei, Professor Parrington wrote, "Now of all the dreams which lure men, the one universal and potent dream, Mr. Cabell asserts with Freudian understanding, is the woman dream. Its roots are deep in the ape-animal; it drives men inexorably, for upon it depends the very existence of the race."

These observations concern the theories in *Beyond Life* about the material which, in the volumes of the Biography itself, becomes art. Before examining these volumes there remain the final chapters of *Beyond Life*—chapters which, with careful ambiguity, seem intent to debar us, at all cost, from the author's inherent proclivities, so great is Cabell's fear of pronouncing words which "are such stuff as deans are made on." These chapters are indeed an area where angels may fear to tread. The duality in Cabell's approach seems to derive from the clash between his instinctive desire to preach and his reasoned acknowledgement that this is presumption and therefore folly and therefore to be ridiculed—life is larger than its dictums. Charteris neatly evades any tendency to preach openly, and this aspect is left to another spokesman. Charteris has been expounding about man's "proper attitude toward the universe he temporarily infests and to show you that this must always be a purely romantic attitude." In the chapters "The Reactionary" and "The Candle" the chief product of romance or the demiurge was held to be Christianity with its chief work, the Bible. It is in his treatment of Christianity, the Bible, and the "Christ legend" that Cabell puts forward his most positive theories about God, man, and the Universe. The most that can be said about Cabell's statements is not that he believed them —which he quite possibly did—but that he acknowledged them to be the ones he would most like to be true.

> . . . the Bible is past doubt the boldest and most splendid example of pure romance contrived by human ingenuity. But if it all really happened—if one great Author did in point of fact shape the tale thus . . . it very overwhelmingly proves that our world is swayed by a Romancer of incalculable skill and imagination. And that the truth is this . . . what I have been contending from the start.

Gradually there emerges a conception that resembles the theme of vicarship: God himself is the prime Author who places on earth eternal forces which weave and interweave in contradictory goodness and evil, potential worth and evident waste. These forces continue through the countless generations, each of which act out their repetitive parts. Occasionally, in spite of great odds, come those few who contribute positively to the civilization so that, at long last, a movement forward is seen to have occurred—almost imperceptibly but undeniably. These few are those who listen faithfully and obey the demiurge according to seeds planted within them by the Author himself. Thus in the Biography, which spans twenty generations, we have the poets (Shelley's unacknowledged legislators) inspired and given life by Queen Freydis, who placed within them "Sparkes and smalle Flamings of the Fyer of Audela," and set them down among men. They differ from ordinary mortals because they possess the imagination to be virtuous—purely, or impurely in self interest. Byron, who was in a position to know, observed in a letter that virtue is the only thing that pays in this world. Inevitably these virtuous poets suffer great harm and hurt from the Tumblebugs because they were "unlyke to Beings naturallie conceyved." The attribution of divine origins to poets explains Cabell's statement in *Beyond Life* that "The Christ legend should always be believed in, without relation to the 'realism' of inscription and codexes, because of the legend's beauty and usefulness to art." It explains why Cabell's heroes are "possessed," and why one often reads of great artists who disclaim personal credit for genius on the grounds that they were merely the instruments or mouthpieces (Blake, for example); it illustrates the French phrase "un homme engagé," which is only partially matched by the English "one who is dedicated." And Einstein's belief and Jung's, that they had glimpsed parts of a pattern, hint at a similar idea.

Thus Cabell is dealing with the greatest concerns, with the eternal questions. He does so in the rational spirit of classical Greece with a marked bias toward the sensuous grace of Ionia. His disillusion is not by any means merely the mark of twentieth-century decadence.

> Thing of a day! Such is man; a shadow in a dream
> Yet when god-given splendor visits him
> A bright radiance plays over him, and how sweet is life!

The sombre note that time was that of Pindar.

> For you and I are going a queer way, in search of justice, over the grave of a dream and through the malice of time. So you had best put on this shirt.

And so, wearing the shirt of Nessus, the shining garment which ensures that a bright radiance plays over him, Jurgen—thing of a day, shadow in a dream—begins the universal quest. Both poets deal with the more solid reality of the intangible spirit.

73

The final chapters are "The Arbiters" and "Wherein We Await." As impartial a selection as possible produces the following views as the core or heart of all Cabell's artistic activity— remembering that he has made it a special rule to break all rules in his attempt to be as perverse as life. In "The Arbiters" he writes: "Through a merciful dispensation we are one and all of us created very vain and very dull: and by utilizing these invaluable qualities the demiurgic spirit will yet contrive a world 'as it ought to be,' " Our vanity enables us to aspire; our dullness prevents us from accepting defeat. It is on this basis that Cabell ironically erects his artist's creed as he states the consequences of his attitude. On the impulse of vanity and protected by the stubborn obtuseness of our dullness,

> . . . our caravan accepts romance for guide; and strains and flounders toward goals which stay remote, and yet are fairly discernible. For that to which romance conducts (concluded John Charteris), is plain enough—distinction and clarity, and beauty and symmetry, and tenderness and truth and urbanity.

John Charteris is the chief mouthpiece in *Beyond Life*, but another spokesman argues with him, and this secondary spokesman speaks in the first person.[9] It is necessary for the reader to put two and two together to attempt to draw a conclusion. For Charteris consistently evades any artistic responsibility for preaching or propaganda. It is this attitude which raises Cabell's work above the levels of minor "art with a message." Yet Hamlet is the hero, not his uncle; Othello, not Iago; and the developments within Macbeth do, after all, constitute a tragedy. Thus, even when an artist is big enough to recognize the fact that life is larger than its dictums, that it cannot be seen simply in moral terms of black and white, it does not necessarily follow that that artist may not have something to say about life which may be quite enlightening— in fact, all the more enlightening because it refuses to claim omniscience or even the aim of enlightenment.

[9] See *As I Remember It* (186), where Cabell describes his indebtedness to Guy Holt for this culminating duologue. While Cabell was rather close to the trees, he immediately acknowledged Guy Holt's ability to see both the trees and the wood.

It is now safe, perhaps, to quote the secondary spokesman who, in *Beyond Life,* is so sorely buffeted by the tormentor Charteris.

For art is truly "a branch of pedagogy," because the artist is affiliated to priesthood. To only a few of us is it given, or desirable, to see within. . . . Yet since it is our nature to learn by parables, we turn to the artist who is also a seer, in search of entertainment, and more or less consciously hoping to acquire understanding . . . something like an answer to the great question which I can only word as "what is it all up to?"

To this, Charteris does agree that "art and religion are kindred," though the latter is merely a branch of the former. It is tempting to treat Charteris, especially as he is at times in these final pages, as did Hugh Walpole. Charteris observes, "Romance is an expression of an attitude which views life with profound distrust, as a business of exceeding dulness, and of very little worth." Such nihilism does make for critical difficulties, and Hugh Walpole countered simply with, "That was never Mr. Cabell's judgment, and we cannot but feel that at the last it is the author rather than Charteris that we would prefer to hear." Walpole had just previously stated, ". . . towards the last the crabbed and irritable personality of the little jaundiced author separates itself quite deliberately from its creator."[10] These opinions have the following evidence to support them.

In his time a man plays many parts, and Cabell distributes these parts to his various spokesmen, a neat and very convenient method for the writer. It is worth noting now the final story in *The Certain Hour,* a collection of stories wherein a number of figures contained the "Sparkes and smalle Flamings of the Fyer of Audela" do, at a certain hour, have to make the decision which will govern the nature of the rest of their lives—"there is a tide in the affairs of men . . . ." These stories were published in 1916, and on the whole, still show stronger regard for sounds than for meanings and may represent a stage of artistic development similar to that of *Love's Labour's Lost.* They were not revised after the notoriety

---

10 "The Art of James Branch Cabell," *Yale Review* (July, 1920).

of 1919–20. In his author's note to the Storisende Edition (which, incidentally, is one of the funniest of his many witty sallies at life), Cabell explains his inability to revise by reference to the economy of "zinc plates which were made from a copy of this first and only printing." The final story in this collection seems to be the only one set in modern times. It has the title "The Lady of All our Dreams" and is about John Charteris. The prologue to the story may have bearing on this matter of the inner integrity of an evasive artist:

> In John Charteris appeared a man with an inborn sense of the supreme interest and the overwhelming emotional and spiritual relevancy of human life as it is actually and obscurely lived; a man with unmistakable creative impulses and potentialities; a man who, had he lived in a more mature and less self-deluding community— a community that did not so rigorously confine its interest in facts to business and to the supplying of illusions—might humbly and patiently have schooled his gifts to the service of his vision. . . . As it was, he accepted defeat and compromised half-heartedly with commercialism.

This does suggest that, in *Beyond Life*, we are justified in listening also to the secondary spokesman, who speaks in the first person, as well as to Charteris, who was, after all, speaking in "those dark hours just before the dawn."

It is now possible to complete this analysis of *Beyond Life* with a necessarily full statement of "the vision" which, in actual fact, Cabell himself has served so faithfully.

> To what does the whole business tend?—why, how in heaven's name should I know? We can but be content to note that all goes forward, toward something. . . . I prefer to take it that we are components of an unfinished world, and that we are but as seething atoms which ferment towards its making, if merely because man as he now exists can hardly be the finished product of any Creator whom one could very heartily revere. We are being made into something quite unpredictable, I imagine: and we are sustained through the purging and the smelting, by an instinctive knowledge that we are being made into something better. For this we know, quite in-

communicably, and yet as surely as we know that we will to have it thus.

And it is this will that stirs in us to have the creatures of earth and the affairs of earth, not as they are, but "as they ought to be," which we call romance. But when we note how visibly it sways all life we perceive that we are talking about God.

This, then, would seem to be the heart of the matter, and it adds up to a positive and indeed Christian belief which, with understandable provision that it might be presumption, moulds the material throughout the Biography even unto *The Way of Ecben*, "the last of all the many stories about the many inheritors of Dom Manuel's life."

9: *Figures of Earth*

The door of death I open found,
And the worm weaving in the ground:
Thou'rt my mother from the womb,
Wife, Sister, Daughter, to the tomb:
Weaving to dreams the sexual strife,
And weeping over the web of life.

—BLAKE

What is one to say of *Figures of Earth* other than to regret, perhaps, that one must use the fettered sounds of words instead of the free sounds of music? For this work is, indeed, a tone poem, a balanced, even, measured dance best illustrated in spirit and movement by, for example, Fauré's "Pavane." Begun in the summer of 1919, finished in that of 1920, and published in February, 1921, *Figures of Earth*[1] is the product of Cabell's supremacy as

---

[1] There is a most useful work entitled *Notes on Figures of Earth* by John Philips Cranwell and James P. Cover, New York, Robert McBride & Co., 1929, which describes the meanings of Cabell's legendary names, the origin and nature of Poictesme and the general significance of Manuel relative to other redeemers, particularly Christ (Appendix A). It is pointed out here that Cabell derived the names of Leshy, Koshchei, Norka, Beda, Kruchina and Zhar Ptitza and characteristics and incidents from W. R. S. Ralston's *Russian Folk Tales*; this work also supplied the origin of some episodes in *Jurgen* and *The Line of Love* and provided some influence, via translation, on Cabell's phraseology.

both an artist and a thinker. It is fully equal to *Jurgen* in literary status. Structurally, *Figures of Earth* is the more symmetrical. It is more even in development and in the flow of ideas: the ideas receive their significance, add to it, and hand it on to the following portions for further accretion. *Jurgen* is more episodic. Jurgen undergoes numerous experiences which represent all aspects of life for a sensitive, curious, and thoughtful individual, but in *Jurgen* these aspects are not so interdependent; they are all connected in so far as they all illustrate different facets of man's life, but they are almost separate entities within themselves as Jurgen moves his spiritual spotlight here and there over life. The history of Manuel develops along a continuous line through consecutive happenings that form a chronological whole. The end returns to the beginning so that the line becomes the unbroken circle of antiquity, the oriental circle of eternity, a symbol buried deep in the primordial subconscious the world over.

In the Biography, *Figures of Earth* is the beginning. Manuel is the Founding Father of the race who repeats with variations his own life's themes in Poictesme, Europe, and America. In this work we learn of the conquest and origin of Poictesme, of the rise of Manuel from swineherd to noble count, possessor of

> . . . a noble country, good to live in, rich with grain and metal, embowered with tall forests, and watered by pleasant streams. Walled cities it had, and castles crowned its eminences.

The foreword to *Figures of Earth* is dedicated to Sinclair Lewis, while the five portions into which the book is divided are dedicated to Wilson Follett, Louis Untermeyer, H. L. Mencken, Hugh Walpole, and Joseph Hergesheimer, all "six most gallant champions." There are a number of features like this about *Figures of Earth* which demonstrate the close relation of art to life, the inner transmutation by the artist of those outer experiences which supply the initial raw material. There is a much more serious note to this music, much less of the gaiety and apparent flippancy of *Jurgen. Jurgen* is an astute balancing of imponderables and unknowns against enigmas and ambiguities; against a universal back-

78

ground is the pursuit of a laughter which is, perhaps, the supreme and only wisdom. *Figures of Earth* presents a narrower view of life. This particular "life" embodies a pursuit of wisdom involving the practical spirit of romance as moulded by the hard facts of existence, the desire for beauty exposed to experience.

Figures of Earth concerns a young person called Manuel who has low beginnings but high ambitions. Manuel is at first a swineherd. He falls in love with one Niafer. He believes her to be beautiful when, in fact, she is quite plain; he believes her to have remarkable intelligence whereas she has really quite ordinary mental ability which is abnormally exalted for a brief spell when she first meets Manuel (the spell was cast by Miramon Lluagor). To fulfill what he regards as his destiny, which is to cut a fine figure in the world, Manuel is prepared to sacrifice even Niafer, and during another spell, she is as dead to him while he follows his own thinking and his own desires. At last Manuel finds himself in a forest acting as a servant to a small head of white clay called Misery. Manuel grows old in its company and as its servant, but for the loss of his youth, he regains Niafer. Reunited with Niafer, Manuel abandons his youthful intentions of traveling to the corners of the earth to form judgments and, at the request of his wife, takes possession of his fief of Poictesme and sets up a household and a family. Niafer appears content. This portion of the book (Chapters XVIII through XXI of Part III) is the spiritual and dramatic or structural center. Manuel acquires children and is tempted to repudiate Niafer again to pursue the joys and beauties of phrase-making. But he refuses this temptation and, as judged by the standards of his neighbors, becomes increasingly renowned and prosperous. The whole, it should be remembered, is a comedy of appearances.

Another aspect of the theme should be underlined, perhaps, as being of much importance in understanding and appreciating Cabell's art and artistry. While his work contains the stuff of his own experience, it is by no means simply autobiographical. The themes of *Figures of Earth* and of *Jurgen* provide the clearest evidence of this. Jurgen is a retired poet, one who relinquishes the

79

chase after beauty to follow his business and to enjoy his wife's cooking if not, at all times, her company. Manuel turns away Sesphra and his phrase-making magic and abides by his obligations to wife and family—even bricking up a magic window which opens onto other ways. But whereas Jurgen accepts his inadequacy and seems to acknowledge, as an important part of his findings, man's worthlessness, Manuel insists to the last on his personal worth and even on his worldly accomplishments. Of course, Manuel faces the world and Jurgen considers the universe, as we learn in the foreword; even so, the insistence on worth and accomplishments means more than the statement of a bigger man climbing a smaller mountain. Manuel's is the comedy of appearances, and he keeps up appearances even unto the preposterous end. And yet just because of this, the culmination of *Figures of Earth* is much more genuinely heroic, in the best sense of that much-battered word (in the sense that Fielding's life, for example, was as heroic as his histrionic epics), than even Jurgen, who is himself heroic enough in his ultimate denial of heroics. For behind the masks of Dom Manuel, as Death only too willingly points out, there speaks a "sick and satiated and disappointed being."

Whereas Jurgen stresses the laughableness of man's insignificance, Dom Manuel stresses the magnificent tragedy of his attempts to overcome it. Manuel, count of Poictesme, having been called on by Grandfather Death, looks back and sees:

> . . . only the strivings of an ape reft of his tail, and grown rusty at climbing, who has reeled blunderingly from mystery to mystery, with pathetic makeshifts, not understanding anything, greedy in all desires, and always honeycombed with poltroonery. So in a secret place his youth was put away in exchange for a prize that was hardly worth the having; and the fine geas which his mother laid upon him was exchanged for the common geas of what seems expected.

Thus, again, is the philosophy of *Beyond Life* transmuted into art. Misery went about the world "in the appearance of a light formless cloud." To the above observations Grandfather Death replied:

> Such notions . . . are entertained by many of you humans in the

lightheaded time of youth. Then commonsense arises like a light formless cloud about your goings, and you half forget these notions. Then I bring darkness.

In his immediately following behavior, Manuel reveals a sense of worthiness that exists in the best of humanity, a worthiness that speaks for itself and that is quite distinctly opposed to any theoretical nihilism in Manuel's speech or thought. For he is great unto the end. Grandfather Death starts toward the door that leads to darkness:

> "Now, pardon me," says Manuel, "but in Poictesme the Count of Poictesme goes first in any company. It may seem to you an affair of no importance, but nowadays I concede the strength as well as the foolishness of my accustomed habits, and all my life long I have gone first. So do you ride a little way behind me, friend, and carry this shroud and napkin, till I have need of them."

Dom Manuel, the Achilles of Poictesme, is a man of action, and in his actions, as opposed to his innermost thinking, lies his greatness. "Our thoughts are ours, our deeds none of our own"—this enigma is part of the puzzle of these figures of earth whose actions so frequently belie their intentions as they empty themselves to fill their coffers. Cabell's realism is confirmed by a remark of a real-life Manuel—Francis Bacon, Lord Verulam, Viscount St. Albans—who observed at the time of his downfall that he had misspent his talents "in things for which I was least fit, so as I may truly say, my soul hath been a stranger in the course of my pilgrimage." And, similarly, note the exact parallel of the theme of *Figures of Earth* in the more realistic renderings of contemporary American fiction:

> We see this theme in Warren, in Wolfe, and we have found it in Mark Twain. Not the repudiation of success and practicality, but the achievement of it. . . . Yet along with it there is the sense of something impractical and spiritual lost in the doing.[2]

Figures of Earth is as rounded and satisfyingly complete as *Some-*

[2] Louis D. Rubin, Jr., "Tom Sawyer and the Use of Novels," *American Quarterly*, Vol. IX, No. 2, Pt. 2 (Summer, 1957).

thing About Eve. In it there is much more of a philosophical approach to the predicament called life, a much more harmonious melody in this version of the universal cycle of living, as if the author has a serener confidence in his personally achieved convictions. In *Jurgen* there is a series of implicit questions at the heart of the banter and mockery as Jurgen measures up to this and that human remedy for all ills, whether spiritual (philosophic or religious), physical (natural or perverted), or artistic. In *Figures of Earth* there is no interrogation: the theme is not so much the object of man's quest as the quest itself.

> Such and such things were said and done by our great Manuel. . . .
> Such and such were the appearances, and do you make what you
> can of them.

The author adds one of his most straightforward comments linking his art to his personal attitude to life:

> . . . in real life also, such is the fashion in which we are compelled
> to deal with all happenings and with all our fellows, whether they
> wear or lack the gaudy name of heroism.

As in the majority of Cabell's writings, the inspiring principles underlying, indeed governing, the nature of the action are religious. That is, the plot consists of considerations embodying not advocated themes of Christianity or modes of conduct but the Christianity and modes of conduct themselves as they actually do appear in world-wide human behavior. But this is the starting point, not the culmination as it tends to be in Meredith and Hardy or, more realistically, in Shaw. Meredith's insistent chapters opening *Diana of the Crossways*, for example, would seem sacrilege, artistically, to Cabell. For Cabell designs his plot so that it illustrates the interaction between such an attitude as that of romantic or chivalrous Christianity and the world and life as they really are. Thus Manuel's motto becomes not *Mundus decipit* but *Mundus vult decipi*.[3]

---

[3] "The world wishes to be deceived," originally ascribed to Petronius but possibly acquired from Burton's *Anatomy of Melancholy*, where it appears as "Si mundus vult decipi, decipiatur." See *Notes on Figures of Earth*, 32.

In following his natural desires and instinctive thinking, Manuel makes figures of wisdom and righteousness in the shapes of Kings Helmas and Ferdinand. Both these kings redeem men through powers that are presented as possible illusions but which nevertheless constitute feathers in their caps, or crowns in this case. For in the certainty of their wisdom and saintliness, mountains become molehills; indigestion derived from worry and uncertainty disappears as the consequence of faith. But Manuel, who made these figures and knows how they acquired their expressions, cannot be satisfied but must journey on looking always for a better appearance. In the process he comes to reside with the small head of clay, and, in the most irrational part of the forest, does service to Misery. He strikes the Hamlet time barrier that lies athwart all life and his wings are strained to breaking point. And now he yields increasingly to the demands of what is expected as he builds a home and raises a family for his wife and in accordance with the notions of his neighbors.

One escape is offered in the person of another of Manuel's images—Sesphra of the Dreams. Manuel, whose living, since his residence with Misery, consists of "days made up of small frettings and little pleasures and only half-earnest desires," in the presence of Sesphra, is again possessed by passion, "the passion which informs all those who make images." Manuel asks Sesphra what it is that Sesphra demands of him.

> "It is my will that you and I go hence on a long journey, into the far lands where I am worshipped as a God."
>
> "I cannot go on any journey, just now, for I have my lands and castles to regain, and my wife and my newborn child to protect . . ."
>
> ". . . What are these things to me, or you, or to anyone that makes images? We follow after our own thinking and our own desires."
>
> "I lived thus once upon a time," said Manuel, sighing, "but nowadays there is a bond upon me to provide for my wife, and for my child too, and I have not much leisure left for anything else."

Sesphra is pagan; Manuel is, at this particular time, resident of an abode governed only by Christian terrors and Sesphra is ousted.

Yet the significance and the power of Sesphra are unceasing. The dual demands of art and obligations have been standard features in the lives of many, from Langland, where Sesphra was a grimly possessive plowman, to Shakespeare, who left Anne and married the Globe; to Milton whose young Royalist wife refused after a matter only of months to compete with his muse, and whose daughters were offered up as burnt offerings to the music of sounds they recited but knew not; to Wordsworth, who sacrificed Annette Vallon; to Shelley, who attempted to put into practice Milton's views on divorce all at the beck and call of Sesphra; and to Meredith, whose transient first marriage was at least in part wrecked by Sesphraic ideals and whose marital difficulties were rendered into the phrases of *Modern Love*. And so it goes on as these pursuers of beauty attempt to mould figures of earth in the shape of their desires or to impress the pattern of their desires upon figures that are all too often only of earth.

And yet Manuel's love for Niafer, as Jurgen's for Lisa and Kennaston's for Kathleen in *The Cream of the Jest* (not to mention recurrent confirmation in the short stories), is an enduring thing and not to be denied. Even appearances sometimes tell the truth, as when, at the last, Manuel says to his daughter Melicent:

> "Go to your mother, dear, and tell her . . . ." He paused here and his lips worked.
> Says Melicent, "But what am I to tell her, father?"
> "Oh, a very queer thing . . . you are to tell Mother that Father has always loved her over and above all else, and that she is always to remember that . . ."

But this is sentiment and as such must not go unqualified. So Grandfather Death hastens to label this as a posture, a gesture, and to assert that it is an attitude due to vanity rather than to devotion. Nevertheless, it seems clear that this time Manuel almost means what he says and that his assiduously pursued appearance of blissful marriage indicates at least something of the truth. In spite of incidentals, as far as the general action of the theme is concerned, Manuel is making a moving farewell to his wife at a point of climax and culmination. This is very often the case in Cabell's writings and, being so, would seem to speak for itself.

Manuel's life draws to its close. The pipings of his youth were stilled only to be reborn, Phoenix-like, as the full orchestra of valiant old age, but even as Tamburlaine, he must at last leave the stage.

> Then the Count armed and departed from Storisende, riding on the black horse, in gold armour, and carrying before him his shield whereon was blazoned the rampant and bridled stallion of Poictesme and the motto Mundus vult decipi. Behind him was Grandfather Death, on the white horse, carrying the Count's grave-clothes in a neat bundle. They rode toward the sunset, and against the yellow sunset each figure showed jet black.

And thus they enter the swirling waters of the dark stream of Lethe, where strange things happen.

In *Figures of Earth* a most amazing thing is seen—the fact that, in one of his chief works, Cabell is guilty of having told a story with a moral. And that moral—staring us in the face in the final chapter—is, "If you have been yourself you cannot reasonably be punished, but if you have been somebody else . . . ." As Wilde wrote in *De Profundis*, "A man whose desire is to be something separate from himself . . . invariably succeeds in being what he wants to be. That is his punishment. Those who want a mask have to wear it"; similarly Sir Thomas Browne, "Do thou be singly what thou art."

It is here that Cabell reveals something of the extent and nature of his thinking. For the structural circle which brings Manuel back to the Pool of Haranton, to begin again, owes much to the kind of comprehension embodied in that gospel of Hinduism, the Song of God or the *Bhagavad-Gita*. In this we are told how man must distinguish between his inner spiritual self and his outer material and physical self. Unless he lives by and for the inner, he cannot come to the prime creator or to himself, but must enact his spurious role again until purified of desire and greed for things transient:

> Great souls who find me have found the highest perfection. They are no longer reborn into the condition of transience and pain. All the worlds, and even the heavenly realm of Brahma [God as Creator] are subject to the laws of rebirth. But, for the man who comes to me, there is no returning.

The beauty with which this conception rounds out the total significance is such as almost to convince one of its truth. Whereas Manuel was misled by appearances and was reborn, Gerald Musgrave, in *Something About Eve*, was more discriminating; even so, he did not get beyond Maya, even as Manuel returned to the love that was Niafer. It was for precisely this undue exaltation of woman that Milton's Adam was chastised in *Paradise Lost*. Even if the apple (the temptation of the senses) was the cause and the serpent the instrument, the immediate responsibility was in the act of Eve, the guilt for which Adam elected to share in their joint fall. This aspect is more fully treated in *Something About Eve*, but it helps to indicate here the intricacy of Cabell's range and craftsmanship.

Cabell creates symbols, and it has been said that it is very difficult to feel affection for symbols. Yet his greatest are filled with the spirit of living individuals. Horvendile the puppet shifter is one; Jurgen is another. In his foreword to *Figures of Earth*, Cabell wrote:

> . . . with Jurgen all of the physical and mental man is rendered as a matter of course; whereas in dealing with Manuel there is, always . . . aloofness. . . . He is "done" from the outside, always at arm's length.

This has the consequence, the foreword continues, of creating a national hero who can be admired but not really loved. Manuel does acquire a stature of mythlike proportions; yet, perhaps of all Cabell's symbolic figures, he is most likeable for himself. For of Manuel may it be said (as his dance moves to the end which

is a beginning), as of that other confused Achilles for whom
Cassius was something of a Sesphra,

> His life was gentle, and the elements
> So mixed in him that Nature might stand up
> And say to all the world, "This was a man!"

Historically, *Figures of Earth* is naturally followed by *The Silver
Stallion*. This deals with the deeds of the immediate followers of
Manuel, the fellowship of those who lived in Poictesme with him
and who governed areas of it under him. But, to assess Cabell's
artistry and philosophy it must be noted that *The Silver Stallion*
was not published until 1926: that is, it was written not only after
Figures of Earth and *Jurgen* but after *Straws and Prayer Books*.
The spiritually conflicting elements that make *Straws and Prayer
Books* such a dangerous venture for any artist intent on the pursuit
of anything, let alone beauty, are present also in *The Silver Stallion*; they make of it, not a "tainted" work, but one fraught with
the implications of darkness and despair to a greater extent than
any of Cabell's previous fictions. Whereas, in *Straws and Prayer
Books*, these implications are developed to their logical conclusions and tend to dominate the final effects of that work, in *The
Silver Stallion* they are controlled and rendered artistically subordinate to the whole; the whole becomes as positive, spiritually,
as the works published earlier.

In *Figures of Earth* is revealed Manuel's greatness in all its
ambiguity—how, while always in doubt himself, while never hesi-
tating to use foul means as well as fair, his ultimate achievements
are real and tangible; indeed they come undeniably to represent
greatness as even the most material achievement must derive from,
and be in proportion to, feelings of some kind. On his death, and
thanks initially to the ramblings of the child Jurgen, his life becomes that legend that men have fashioned since time primordial.
He comes to signify not only the greatness that gets things done,
but the goodness that gets the right things done. Inevitably, in
accordance with the religious desires of humanity, he becomes
that mythical redeemer who will return and set the world to rights

one day, and without too much effort on the part of humanity itself. This conception is well expressed in three dedicatory verses to Carl van Doren, the last of which is:

> Out of the bright—and, no, not vacant!—heavens
> Redeemers will be coming by and by,
> En route to make our sixes and our sevens
> Neat as a trivet or an apple-pie.

The Silver Stallion records the growth of Manuel, the bold but spiritually dubious warrior, into a great legend capable of influencing human development and behavior, and also human happiness, as even Jurgen is finally obliged to acknowledge. Yet the followers of Manuel, the Fellowship of the Silver Stallion, the willy-nilly perpetrators of the legend, at the beginning of the book all know what Manuel was really like and how he made his money. But it makes no difference; all are gathered up into the consequences of the legend itself, even bluff Coth, who went

> . . . blundering westward to fetch back Dom Manuel into his Poictesme, which, as Coth asserted, skinny women and holy persons and lying poets were making quite uninhabitable.

At the beginning, the Fellowship is gathered together, along with Manuel's wife Niafer and Holy Holmendis, who has recently arrived from Philistia to offer religious guidance to Niafer on the administration of Poictesme. Here also is Horvendile. Cabell is always inspired to his very best when he deals with certain specific themes through certain specific people—themes like Christianity and true marriage (formal or informal), and people like Jurgen or anyone else who most immediately is the vehicle for one of these themes, including Horvendile. And Horvendile sustains the high level of his performances in many of Cabell's works. What is he and who is he? As Bradley said of Hamlet, he has upon him that "inexplicable touch of infinity." Ever young, he is quiet in his strength, implacable in his foresight and yet, withall, most likeable in his fey but eternal mystery. He ordains, even as the emissary of his creator, who may be the emissary of his Creator.

88

As a consequence of what he ordains, the members of the Fellowship depart to fulfill their destinies and perpetuate the legend of a redeemer in accordance, not always with their own desires, but with those of Horvendile, as even Coth himself almost conceded "long afterward."

The significance of each book is an epitome of all the most fundamental elements of Cabell's art. In most of his novels of Poictesme, Cabell deals in more detail with one particular aspect. Thus in *Figures of Earth* we have the development of the inarticulate but curious man of action; in *Jurgen* we have the experiences of the all-too-complicated man of poetic thought; in *Chivalry* we see more obviously the clash between life and the chivalrous and christian ideals of man; in *Gallantry* the emphasis is upon man's impudent gestures on behalf of his personal freedom, gestures which, of gallant, are seen to be just as fettered, spiritually, as the ideals of chivalry with which they are interwoven. In *Domnei* we have, unadulterated for once, the pure pleasure and fulfillment of romantic love between a man and a woman; in *The High Place*, Florian places his romantic youth upon the altar of experience and we see what is left of his offering to life, the burnt offering of the younger idealist as he discovers his elders; in *The Cream of the Jest* the significant fact is that the hero is married, the intended significance being connoted by the title. And thus we see how the artist deals, one by one, in volume after volume of essentially the same story of Manuel and his descendants, with each aspect of a romantic's concern with life, with the clash between the pursuit of beauty and the facts of living. In *The Silver Stallion* the representation of various aspects is distributed among the chief followers of Manuel; in their stories are epitomes of most of Cabell's chief interests as the foundational legend is launched into the perpetuity of the Biography, to be repeated with greater individual emphasis and variety through a multitude of descendants over many centuries. At times the members of the Fellowship are strangely reminiscent of certain features of the "six most gallant champions" to whom *Figures of Earth* was dedicated; it is quite likely that Cabell has drawn

89

features from the web of real life as he knew it for the web of his creative life as he has spun it in *The Silver Stallion*, written during those years when Cabell was most actively concerned with the most outstanding crusades and crusaders of the "twenties."

Book One sets the general scene immediately after Manuel's departure; the Fellowship convenes, receives instructions or comments from Horvendile, and then each member leaves upon his particular mission. The first of the Fellowship to die is Gonfal.[4] He goes South, where the people adhere strictly to traditional and orthodox tenets under Morvyth their Queen. Gonfal is a realist and hence concentrates on the things of most importance, that is, on peace and quiet and the contemplation of the beauty which is Morvyth, instead of dissipating his energies in ostentatious deeds and the pursuit of worldly wealth as do his rivals for the throne, honor, and renown. Unlike Ford, Rockefeller, Carnegie, or Woolworth, the artist stays quietly at home and writes perfectly of beautiful happenings. Vergil's Empire outlived Caesar's, and Gonfal—who had nevertheless suffered some pain to achieve his position—moved among the fundamentalists with an amused detachment which much intrigued the Queen, who would have given him for his love the supreme prize over and above all the more active contestants. But Gonfal is a realist and so knows that Ettarre must elude all men in the end. Refusing to lose his head one way, he loses it another. The beheading of Gonfal by the Queen fits in with the legend of a redeemer, being reminiscent of the beheading of John at the request, through her dancing daughter, of Herodias—a beheading related to the legend of another redeemer. In this way, Cabell consistently approaches and frequently deals directly with man's innermost and eternal thoughts and desires.

Miramon represents, among many other things, that tendency to seclusion, privacy and the evasion of vulgarity embodied in the movement of art for art's sake. In his ivory tower he makes

---

[4] See *As I Remember It* (185), where Cabell states that Guy Holt "invented the entire story of Gonfal, somewhat as Thomas Beer presented me with the gem of Guivric."

dreams to occupy sleeping minds. His activities are hindered by his marriage, yet his wife is indispensable and when she almost brings an end to his universe and deprives him of his creative powers, Miramon still wants her. His wife almost succeeds in destroying his universe and in ending the "divine contentment of all gods in any place." As it was, she merely causes them to appear temporarily "as flimsy and incredible inventions" and in the end Miramon re-establishes his worlds intact and the supremacy of the more familiar gods of Koschei. The artist in his imaginative isolation resists the demands made through his wife, of ordinary workaday humanity, of conventional if not sterile and static religion, attitudes, respectability and orthodoxy. Miramon's victory is apparently a fortunate one, for, as he said:

> It would be a sad happening if I were never again to sway the sleeping of men, and grant them yet more dreams of distinction and clarity, of beauty and symmetry, of tenderness and truth and urbanity. For whether they like it or not, I know what is good for them, and it affords to their starved living that which they lack and ought to have.

Cabell has used some of these words before, of course—in the statement of John Charteris (who, like Miramon, seems to represent a fundamental element in Cabell's make-up but not the whole of Cabell) in *Beyond Life*. So Miramon expresses the author but, also, a facet of mankind; for have not whole societies, indeed civilizations, embodied one kind or another of hedonism as the ultimate reality? It should not be overlooked that Charteris' romance and Miramon's dreams are initiated by the certainty of pleasure but continue to the equal certainty of the qualities of "tenderness and truth and urbanity," which amount not just to a form of hedonism but to a way of life that places equal emphasis upon conduct. Cabell's art was developed in visually pleasant and comfortable security and, perhaps, in its emphasis on pleasure-giving forms, it has some affinity with art for art's sake as practiced in an ivory tower; yet it is indeed much more profound; it contains much more essential verisimilitude than any art created simply to please the aesthetic sensibilities. So, while Miramon can enjoy his magic, he also knows "what is good for them" and "that which they . . . ought to have." It seems clear enough now that his observations refer not simply to the entertainment of dreams (which, in this sense, include legends), but also to the quality in his art, which elevates man's conduct, however slightly. For, after all, Manuel is the creation of one of Miramon's finest dreams; and Manuel was a redeemer whose eventual significance taught men what was good for men—not only through the static religion of Holy Holmendis or the orthodox church, but also through the dynamic religion that Jurgen saw was also the begetter of much charity, forbearance, bravery, and self-denial, and of its devotees' so strange, so troublingly incomprehensible, contentment. So Miramon's mission, too, was more than to enjoy himself in an ivory tower; and his chapters here show that his art, the practice of which so pleased him, also contributed to the extension of an essentially Christian legend even as Horvendile required it should. If Horvendile controls all within the book, he still speaks for Cabell, who controls him.

Books Four and Five concern the bluff and grumpy Coth, who goes farther than anyone in his attempt to recapture the real Manuel. So it is not surprising that he finds himself deep in the pollution, corruption, stench, and putrefaction of *Straws and Prayer Books*. At his worst he finds that he is smaller than he had been and even than he was to be again. Coth reaches the Place of the Dead and talks with Manuel, only to be commanded to forget the true Manuel and join in perpetuating the legendary one. Coth asks, "Should this truth be disregarded for a vainglorious dream!" And Manuel answers, "The dream is better. For man alone of animals plays the ape to his dreams."

So Coth, too, must acquiesce in reality even if he himself refuses to compromise. He returns and, while making the most of his material advantages—like the General of Jean Anouilh—he nevertheless ages even as he acknowledges with appropriate publicity the motto of Poictesme, *Mundus vult decipi*. And in Coth's ageing, Cabell, without prevarication, expresses another of his fundamental themes. For, as time passed, Coth became puzzled, "For all, everywhere, appeared to have failed and deserted him." Coth realizes the worst fears and actualities of *Straws and Prayer Books.*

> In the end you were . . . a withered hulk, with no more of pride nor any hope of pleasure nor any real desire alive in you.

Deprived, as at the command of Nemesis, of the presence and affection of Jurgen—"his Jurgen in dozens upon dozens of stages of growth"—Coth loses his wife, finds himself alone, and awaits his last enemy. Coth, "who could make no wheedling compromise with the fictions by which fools live and preserve alike their foolish hopes and their smirking amenities," expresses again that conception which Cabell summed up in his views on Joseph Hergesheimer and Marlowe in *Straws and Prayer Books,* when he noted "men labouring toward the unattainable, and a high questing foiled." But the aspect emphasized in Coth is the more human one, as we are shown the tragic heart of human suffering itself in the shape of this gruff Falstaff.

Thus is unfolded in *The Silver Stallion* a grand summary of the numerous themes and strands of human living as they supply the foundation for the edifice of the Biography as a whole. Guivric became only the phantom of his former self while his false self becomes pious, charitable, and wholly respectable for his last years; in his support of the legend of Manuel, Guivric's false self is a "fervent adherent and expounder"; he becomes "a marked favorite" with the established church, with static religion, and he helped to convert the ageing Kerin also to the legend until Guivric "died in the assurance of a blessed resurrection, which he no doubt attained." The subtlety and complexity of myth and symbol, phrase and deed, are at their most abundant as Guivric sees himself in all the members of his ancestors, meets his appointed youthful enemy in the perversion of his saga, and talks with Horvendile, who tells him that successful persons cannot afford to live, for life needs passion and passion lacks the caution needed for worldly success. And so Guivric gradually becomes but the shadow of himself as his living wears thin on an adequate income in his pleasant suburban home filled with efficacious gadgets and with two cars in the garage.

Kerin, on the other hand, is a scholar. With the rather too prompt help of his wife, who is ominously named Saraide and is possibly a witch, Kerin goes underground and acquires all knowledge in the pursuit of truth. Pleasantly enough, Kerin reads book after book, interrupted only by a gander creating romances about "beauty and mystery and holiness and heroism and immortality and . . . other unscientific matters." But Kerin, like a good social scientist and positivist, wants the facts, and to get them he accumulates endless data concerning externals and refuses to be diverted by the gander's version of the inner realities. When, many years later, he returns to his wife, who wanted to know the truth when she was young, he corrects her notion that the "bird down yonder" has the true wisdom; instead in a "fine historical and scientific library" such as is to be found in almost any civilized country, Kerin has found the truth, the one thing which is wholly true, and this he has copied upon a piece of paper, which Saraide uses to light the lamp. And, yet, in so doing, she revealed another truth—that:

> It was the summit of actual wisdom to treat the one thing which was wholly true as if it were not true at all. For the truth was discomposing, and without remedy, and was too chillingly strange ever to be really faced: meanwhile, in the familiar and the superficial, and in temperate bodily pleasures, one found a certain cheerfulness.

Kerin and Saraide "make the best of this world as a residence; keep it as far as possible a cheery and comfortable place" with the gallantry defined in *Beyond Life*. They have found by the aid of Kerin's unimaginative objectivity, "that the main course of daily living is part boredom, part active discomfort and fret," in the words of *Straws and Prayer Books*. We see Cabell consistently rendering his theories artistically as he builds, brick by brick or chapter by chapter, his mythological representations of the eternal subjects of the greatest art—life and death. For while Kerin had been searching for truth among the facts, his wife had discovered truth much more directly; her version is valuable too, for while Kerin used merely reason—which, used alone, was the cause of all the poison in *Straws and Prayer Books*—his wife had expected him to listen to the wisdom of the singing gander. So it is Saraide who produces the antidote when she observes:

> But life is a fine ardent spectacle; and I have loved the actors in it: . . . their youth and their high-heartedness, and their ungrounded faiths, and their queer dreams, my Kerin, about their own importance and about the greatness of the destiny that awaited them.

The author, spinning his web most intricately, with dazzling ingenuity capturing a thousand subtle shades of suggestion and innuendo constituting the profoundest wisdom, balances the positive against the negative. Without becoming sentimental, Cabell's thought is permeated with the strongest feeling so that he does full justice to human desires and sorrows without pathos: yet objectively he exaults these desires and sorrows into something akin to a religious affirmation acceptable to, because produced by, the most exacting logic.

These chapters in Book Seven represent the lowest point of the spiritual developments in *The Silver Stallion*. With Kerin and Saraide comes the cold truth of *Straws and Prayer Books*, worded here, "Life is a pageant that passes very quickly, going hastily from one darkness to another . . . and there is no sense in it," as Saraide says, or as Kerin affirmed, ". . . no man, I find, has ever known for what purpose life was given him, nor what ends he may either help or hinder." And it was the truth, also, that these truths had to be ignored, while "in the familiar and the superficial, and in temperate bodily pleasures, one found a certain cheerfulness."

All Cabell's writing is permeated with humor. His catharsis is largely a comic one though it embodies pity and terror. But such is the profundity of his objectivity that frequently he produces entertaining philosophy as much as philosophic entertainment— as seen most clearly in his essays and autobiographical nonfiction. In other words, Cabell's humor, like that of Shakespeare's clowns, is a very serious thing. It underlies everything, but it can be grim and foreboding if not forbidding. At its most effective it manages to express reality but without being dispiriting. This is a very real achievement, because the result is depth without darkness and weight that is not a burden. The laughter brings a release that is profound because compassionate, yet light because exalted. In particular the treatment of Florian in *The High Place*, of John Bulmer, Duke of Ormskirk, and of Gerald Musgrave in *Something About Eve* displays that bantering drollery which Cabell adds to a long tradition of the very greatest art from Aristophanes, through Rabelais, some of Swift, Sterne, Peacock, George Meredith when the sun was shining, and Carlyle after a good meal to himself, a Virginian with his front to the fire and his back to the flag. In *The Silver Stallion* this purest humor emerges once again in Book Eight, "The Candid Footprint," which deals with "Poor-spirited, over-easy-going Ninzian."

Cabell's secret in the concoction of this magic brew is that, life being what it is, we weep for joy even at the possibility of getting what we want. So Cabell increases, just occasionally, the admixture of "what we want." For example, in that most easing of openings in *The High Place*, the central character, for once, is wholly innocent and pleasing in name and appearance; he begins his quest in fair but rare weather and scenery. Similarly does the Duke of Ormskirk consistently but convincingly transcend human limitations in the achievement of his desire, and consequently we share his joy even as it is humorously communicated. This does not involve a relaxation of artistic discipline on Cabell's part; it is a readjustment of emphasis to produce a happier humor but not a more shallow one. It must be done sparingly because it is too easily cheapened; it too easily becomes facile or glib. As it is, these episodes constitute the high-water mark of Cabell's entertainment. They make the most of what we most want to be true. In "The Candid Footprint," Cabell gets off to a good start with a legitimate and happy marriage. It is evening and Ninzian and his wife are walking in the garden:

They were a handsome couple, and the high-hearted love that had been between them in their youth was a tale which many poets had embroidered. It was an affection, too, which had survived its consummation.

After all, there *are* successful marriages. Cabell makes of this relationship a thing wholly of mirth and gentleness, of understanding and, it is tempting and perhaps not inappropriate to say, of experience. For Cabell wrote of his first wife in *As I Remember It*,

> . . . I know that from the midsummer of 1912 onward, this brown-haired, soft-voiced but emphatic woman entered into virtually everything I wrote: she contributed to never so many of the feminine characters in my never so many books.

All the characters and relationships in *The Silver Stallion* are individualized, a fact which constitutes not the least of the novel's achievements. In this episode of Ninzian the love between Ninzian and his wife is never really in doubt, whereas, to put it at its mildest, that between Kerin and Saraide, for example, is never consistently stressed; even when this love is acknowledged, it still expresses itself ambiguously, as in Kerin's departure down the Well of Ogde—a modern equivalent of which would be a wife's not only pushing her husband under a bus but arranging for the driver to reverse to make sure.

All elements combine to provide this sunnier laughter. The situation involves the return of Lucifer, who seems to inspire Cabell even as he did Milton. The significance involves a reversal of values, as Ninzian, the agent of Lucifer, relapses into goodness. Many are the subtle touches building up a host of shades from cloistered and ancient cathedral towns to Episcopal Richmond, from vestry small talk to cautious teas on sedate lawns. In other words, with what is here a gentle irony, Cabell pokes fun at aspects long traditional in English-speaking communities. But this is not Dickens and "there are always corners and bedrooms and other secluded places where one strikes a balance." But even here, when Cabell and his readers may so obviously enjoy themselves,

97

the profundity is not less apparent—the paradoxes are pungent both for and against Lucifer; they take us to the essence of man's situation as his deeds confound his desires and intentions.

> Man rises from the dust: he struts and postures: he falls back into the dust. That is all. How can this midge work good or evil? His virtue passes as a thin scolding: the utmost reach of his iniquity is . . . superorogation. . . . Meanwhile his sympathies incline—I know —by a hair-breath or so, toward Heaven. Yes, but what does it matter? is it even a compliment to Heaven? Ah, prince, had I the say, I would leave men to perish in their unimportant starveling virtues, without raising all this pother over trifles.

The breadth of outlook—counterbalancing this against that even unto the last confines of man's sadism as it is inherent in his conception of celestial reward and punishment—is all embracing in its philosophic observations. This breadth is matched by the fluidity and seeming spontaneity, the unsoured nature, of the cream of these Cabellian jests in *The Silver Stallion.*

Book Nine concerns Donander of Evre, the youngest of the Fellowship and "the only one of the lords of the Silver Stallion who accepted with joy and with unbounded faith the legend of Manuel, and who in all his living bore testimony to it." In this book, Cabell expresses that aspect of his philosophy which in *Beyond Life* states most clearly his positive hopes for mankind. This aspect appears in the evolutionary principle inherent in the credo at the end of *Beyond Life*; it appears again in *The Cream of the Jest*, for example, in Felix Kennaston's conception of an artist-god working, in one corner of his studio, on the planet earth. Here, in the experiences of Donander, are expressed the fuller version of this "playing with worlds," a play which at once widens human vision even as it dwarfs man and his world to the size and significance of the least worthy of repellent insects. Whereas in *Beyond Life* and *The Cream of the Jest* this conception implies some sort of guiding hand in the outer universe, in Donander's playing there is really just an artist's interest in his own craftsmanship: the worlds he makes are destroyed at his will as soon as he graduates to better things. Earth is not important beyond the experience it provides the artist as he improves his skill. And Donander himself is under the command of a greater god. The philosophical implications are carefully worked out while not stating anything finally or conclusively. Thus Cabell avoids the pitfall of precise limitation in his versions of man and his universe. Consequently, his ultimate significance echoes like a voice in a series of underground caves; yet throughout all the subtly continued ramifications of suggestion there appears a symmetrical and harmonious imitation of life, not in its externals but in its spiritual verities, in those internal experiences which always seem to amount to the same things in the best minds of every civilization. The greatest minds really do seem to think alike, and, as he deals with destiny, Cabell also achieves this wisdom. Ruthlessly he reveals man's smallness as compared with his universes spinning in eternity. Yet there is much compassion for the ineffectual hopes and loves of humans as they call upon, ultimately, gods who are either indifferent or powerless. Yet, if in this version of Donander and his toys appears the despondency of *Straws and Prayer Books*, there appears also at the end the triumphs of Donander's faith. As Jurgen recovered from being shown all in the forest, so Donander persists in his faith even after he has seen truth through the window. Donander regards what he saw as contrived illusions to undermine him, and he persists in his original faith.

The Silver Stallion concludes, symmetrically of course, by gathering once more around the tomb of Manuel all those who were personally most concerned with him when he was alive, together with Jurgen, whose early eloquence had first launched the legend.

In the book as a whole Cabell endeavors to show the emergence of this legend, which, by its nature, is reminiscent of those legends that man has always made ostensibly fundamental to his civilizations—those of a redeemer. Even in spite of the hypocrisy, pretence, and self-interest inevitably inherent in the spread of such legends, Cabell sees a certain hard core of real achievement—aptly enough through Jurgen, who sums it up in the last chapter in his survey of the exploits of the Fellowship of the Silver Stallion. The tomb of Manuel is, indeed, a paradox:

These trivial fripperies were, to the eyes of a considerate person, worthy of a reverence undemanded by mere diamonds, because of the deeds which they had prompted: and this emptiness was sacred because of the faith which people had put in it. And that this glittering vacuity could, as a matter of fact, work miracles was now fully attested: for it had reduced Jurgen to silence.

No, you could never, shruggingly, dismiss this tomb . . . .

The pattern of Cabell's philosophy unfolds itself with many paradoxes but no real contradictions. He does justice to all aspects of human folly and iniquity through the motives and deeds of the followers of Manuel. In this way, the scepticism of John Charteris and the "realism" of Richard Fentnor Harrowby are acknowledged, indeed with a now more skillful and fictionally more truthful art; but still it is Kennaston, the Edward of *Chivalry*, and even Nicolas de Caen who have the final word about the silver stallion, along with that most cautious sinner Jurgen, who, in being frightened before the paradoxical tomb, becomes what is for him the soul of indiscretion:

> Meanwhile, you knew the shining thing to have been, also, the begetter of so much charity, and of forbearance, and of bravery, and of self-denial,—and of its devotees' so strange, so incomprehensible, contentment,—that it somewhat frightened Jurgen.

Technically, the craftsmanship of *The Silver Stallion* seems well-nigh perfect. The wizardry of the interweaving of symbol and myth with plot and action is more complicated than that in *Figures of Earth* and fully on a par with that in *Jurgen* and *Something About Eve*. But the bitter tang of *Straws and Prayer Books* is here, particularly in the sections dealing with the deeds of Coth, Guivric, and Kerin, (Books Four, through Seven). In fact this work begins on a note of easy good humor and light playfulness, with the amused detachment of Gonfal at the Court of Morvyth, and then takes us steadily through the mire of the worst doubts of *Straws and Prayer Books*. But whereas we are left, in *Straws and Prayer Books*, wondering about the future sanity of its author (much as we might wonder about the future well-being of the creator of Lear), in *The Silver Stallion* we are led upwards again, with Kerin (in Book Seven, Chapter XXVIII), to something like an almost acceptable world. For, against that knowledge (after which, as T. S. Eliot asked, what forgiveness?) is placed domestic, if not "bliss," then that acquiescence which Jurgen finally placed above all else. In *Straws and Prayer Books,* Cabell most fully yields to that destructive, negative, sceptical side of his most objective intellect. Yet even in that mass of festering sores illustrating disenchantment at its honest worst is given the cure for the disease even as is given its medical report. And, as Jurgen illustrates beside Manuel's empty and falsely bedecked tomb itself:

> Performances like these [of Manuel and his followers] were well worthy to be commemorated in history: and Jurgen regarded them with a warm, gratifying thrill of purely aesthetic appreciation.

Thus, consistently and over many years of endeavor as well as pleasure, Cabell continues to supply artistic verifications of the philosophical hypotheses expressed in his analytical essays in *Beyond Life* and *Straws and Prayer Books.* Very few modern writers have displayed such tenacious or convincing unity of thought and achievement.

10: *Domnei, the Music from Behind the Moon,* and *Chivalry*

> *Man hath never failed in duty*
> *Who hath drunk the wines of Beauty*
> WILSON MACDONALD

According to the author's note to the Storisende Edition of *Domnei,* it was begun in 1910 and completed in 1912. During that time its writing was interrupted by a visit to England. The work was published in 1913 as *The Soul of Melicent; Domnei* is the revised version of 1920. According to this same author's note, *The Soul of Melicent* sold 493 copies as compared with, for example, 163,000 copies of *Laddie, a True Blue Story,* by Mrs. Gene Stratton Porter, "very close to the heart of nature, in flower and bird, and to the heart of man in the purest and best emotions of life, with four illustrations in color." Yet, such is the diaboli-cal ambivalence of language that *Domnei* also comes "very close to the heart of nature . . . and to the heart of man."

It is the clearest expression in the Biography of that which is called "love" between a man and a woman. Perion and Melicent are supreme specimens of the race and they maintain their re-lationship from the first unto the last—they are strong enough in their love to maintain it intact against all the onslaughts of life through separation, suspicion, material and physical temptation, and even through rape that appears as acquiescence. The marriage is wholly successful and the ideal triumphs. Why is it that this triumph should be so moving, so right, so satisfying and, indeed, so beautiful?

In his espistle dedicatory to *The Lineage of Lichfield*, Cabell, in effect, explains the chemistry of his creative method. It seems to verify completely the scientific hypothesis of the creation of myth as a "founding," a preliminary based on introspection of one's life, followed by the creative flowering of representative symbols into myth. Cabell writes:

> The first act is the imagining of the place where contentment exists and may be come to; and the second act reveals the striving toward, and the third act the falling short of that shining goal.

Cabell observes that this is the comedy which Manuel has enacted over and over again on every stage between Poictesme and Lichfield. Thus Cabell undertakes the examination of what his spirit yearns for—or needs for its growth—and represents the conflict between the growing spirit and the opposing forces sur-rounding it. The third act is the natural dramatic culmination which, in the structural circle, must be followed by the fresh be-ginning as the comedy is repeated with the next generation.

Domnei represents one particular aspect of this process. This aspect concerns that particular phase of the spirit's growth con-tained in man's struggle to achieve fulfillment by uniting with his counterpart in the opposite sex. What is a bare frigid rationaliza-tion in criticism becomes warm, fluid, profoundly moving poetry in art.

The action of *Domnei* begins at Bellegarde but moves quickly elsewhere. In fact, the general background and atmosphere of *Domnei* is akin to that of Moorish Spain and, in particular, of the halls and gardens of the Alhambra. Here broods the dark, barbaric passion of Demetrios, who acquires Melicent and opposes Perion. According to the bibliography at the end of *The Lineage of Lichfield,* the action of *Domnei* falls between August, 1256, and July, 1274, while that of *The Silver Stallion* occurs between November 23, 1239, and May 23, 1277. The historical table at the end of *The Silver Stallion* states in effect that Perion and Melicent leave Poictesme in 1257 and do not return until 1275—one year after their reunion at the end of *Domnei.* Thus, while *Domnei* represents a fundamental attribute of romanticism it is not portrayed directly against the background of Poictesme.

Domnei tells of how a young mercenary, Perion de la Foret, falls in love with Melicent. But this relationship is profound and vast in its significance. We are concerned not merely with the carnal aspects between Melicent and any of her lovers, Perion, Demetrios, or Ahasuerus, but with the significance of the emotions, beliefs, actions, and their consequences, engendered by the spiritual effects of the relationship. Perion is the ideal hero, Demetrios the villain, and Ahasuerus a Jew like Shylock; in a way we are shown the effects of this love upon three widely differing but fundamental and universal temperaments—the idealist, the conqueror, and the merchant, or a younger Hamlet, an even more sensual Mark Antony, and an elevated Shylock. Yet all are enmeshed in the same spiritual web at the center of which is Melicent and all she symbolizes. In the afterword to *Domnei,* Cabell discusses Melicent as a symbol:

> In her the lover views—embodied, apparent to human sense, and even accessible to human enterprise,—all qualities of God which can be comprehended by our restricted human faculties.

Cabell states that, although rather differently to each, Melicent is this symbol to both Perion and Ahasuerus. With Demetrios we see that tendency fulfilled for which Adam was rebuked in Milton's *Paradise Lost*—the "darker and rebellious side of Domnei, of a religion pathetically dragged dustward by the luxuriance and efflorescence of overpassionate service."

But whereas in Chaucer's *Troilus and Criseyde* Diomedes is a sensual Greek who corrupts the beloved of Troilus, and whereas in Shakespeare's version Cressida is a slut who drives Troilus well-nigh insane, here the lover Perion and his beloved Melicent withstand all inroads upon their fundamental integrity.

The book begins with festivities at Bellegarde during which Perion, masquerading under the title of the Vicomte de Puysange, whom he is supposed to have murdered and robbed, reveals his identity to Dame Melicent, the purple of whose eyes "made the thought of heaven comprehensible." Perion and Melicent seem natural, inevitable lovers—she for obvious reasons, he through her wise discernment of his innate idealism. At first Perion recalls much of the François Villon of "In Necessity's Mortar" (written before 1905, revised 1921) in *The Line of Love*. But he soon crystalizes into his own individual mold as a young knight, impeccable in his strength, strong in his innocence. Innocence is not the only quality from which strength derives, of course, and in Demetrios, too, is the counterbalancing force which produces dynamic tension. But in acquiring Melicent—by means which fully reveal Cabell's ability for dramatic irony in the Elizabethan manner—Demetrios is not simply the villain. While "the mainspring of his least action was an inordinate pride" he does dimly perceive that there is that in Melicent's love for Perion which renders her, even to him, spiritually inviolable. He expresses something of his predicament when he converses with Perion on board ship "in the manner of a Tenson, as these two rhapsodized about Dame Melicent until the stars had grown lustreless before the sun." For Demetrios sees, intellectually, the lack of rational justification for chivalry and its associated faith and behavior. "You and I are different, messire, in that I imagine every looking-glass to afford me nourishing food for mirth and wonder and derision." And yet, even at this point, Demetrios realizes that his anger is due largely to the fact that he is left outside of a relationship the emotional strength or faith of which stands between him and Melicent like an unscaleable wall. And on the other side, or the in side, of that wall—which turns out to be a garden wall—Melicent and Perion are not one whit interested in him or in the world he represents. And Perion's reply to Demetrios is a religious one:

> . . . you pass blindly by the revelation of Heaven's splendor in Heaven's masterwork; you ignore the miracle; and so do you find only the stings of the flesh where I find joy in rendering love and service to Dame Melicent.

Demetrios counters with what, in this incident, is the last word when he informs Perion that "Heaven is inaccessible and doubtful" and that every woman has her price. Yet in the outcome of the book itself Melicent proves Demetrios wrong; Perion is right, if only on a pragmatic basis.

This conception of domnei pervades the Biography at all times, in one form or another, as it displays Perion's or Demetrios' side of the argument or tenson. But, as *Chivalry* gives perhaps the clearest revelation of the Christianity within Cabell's thought, so does *Domnei* gives the clearest expression of a primordial tendency in western man's attitude toward woman. In *Domnei* the exaltation of this chivalric and Christian conception is infinitely more whole in its artistic integrity than it is in, for example, Chaucer's *Troilus and Criseyde,* where the traditional view had become weakened and confused to the point of being ready for burlesque as Chaucer's realism undercuts traditional sentimentality. Just for once Cabell lets his statement stand finally unsmudged by the ambiguities of reason. The culmination of *Domnei* is a very fine achievement in the communication of ultimate intangibles, accomplishing the near-impossible in the reunion between Perion and Melicent by revealing factually something quite beyond the reach of fact. And this is done partly through the use of nature—of the sunrise, "the serenity and awe and sweetness of this daily miracle" as the myth maker establishes his cosmic synthesis, his spiritual unity. The relationship of two lovers is seen against the much larger canvas of cosmic forces as Perion experiences, first disappointment as he loses the superficial love of his youth, then "joy and terror" as he acquires the profounder love of his maturity.

The place of Ahasuerus in *Domnei* is structural as well as spiritual. From the beginning of the book, the Jew has his special role as servitor, first to Perion, then to Demetrios, and then to himself, as, in effect, he acquires full power upon the death of Demetrios. Ahasuerus uses his power—which, in the circumstances, is overwhelming—to imprison Melicent. Cabell handles this situation to make the utmost use of horror and revulsion at the contamination of Beauty by the Beast, with Perion, at long last, within bowshot. The fact that Beauty triumphs does not betoken a fanciful fairy tale. For out of this gross threat (which is dramatically most effectively handled) emerges the final proof—that Melicent is willing to sacrifice all to retain that faith which is the foundation of the happiness of herself and Perion. She knows what is really in her own interest and pursues it with a ruthless singleness of purpose that brings even Ahasuerus to heel as he observes:

> We may deny, deride, deplore, or even hate, the sanctity of any noble lady . . . but there is for us no possible escape from worshipping it.

Ahasuerus, like Demetrios, finally reveals something akin to likeableness even in his repulsiveness; in the large heart of Melicent is the understanding that breeds forgiveness. The significance of the Jew is so revealed as to become shadowy, mysterious, and legendary. In his author's note to *Gallantry*, Cabell, writing of the persistent and seemingly uncontrollable evolution of Horvendile, wonders:

> Was he also Ahasuerus, that ever-living being with no superhuman trait save that of deathlessness, whose existence is everywhere reported, and is but very inadequately explained by unsatisfying legends about the Flying Dutchman and El Khoudr and the Wandering Jew?

There is something diabolical in him, but, as in so much of the

Biography and life, the diabolical can produce, and thus contain, goodness. As he reveals for one brief emotional moment, Ahasuerus is human; yet he is also inhuman as he transcends the limits within which Perion, Demetrios, and Melicent are constricted, and at the last, he vanishes. The suggestive range of the work is greatly extended as Cabell creates his own unknowable even as he penetrates and represents the original unknowable.

With these three aspects of masculine temperament, Cabell reveals all men's conscious and unconscious attitudes, feelings, and thoughts toward woman, in that process which perpetuates the species.

Domnei is a clarification of this relationship which, in the other books, meets with such varying fortunes. Here we have the process of woman-worship carried to fulfillment and consummation because both parties were sufficiently worthy. The illustration of it is one of the finest of Cabell's earlier prose poems.

Yet *Domnei* is not the most profound of Cabell's works, because it deals so purely with only one aspect of the web of life. This aspect may be, indeed, central to the web, but the web itself must be represented also if the significance is to be all embracing. Ultimately it is the all-embracing quality of Cabell's art which gives it a stature far greater than that of novels which represent "a slice of life."

In the Storisende Edition, Cabell combined *Domnei* with a short novel called *The Music from Behind the Moon.* It was written in 1926 and does not belong intrinsically to the Biography; it does not concern Poictesme except that it features Ettarre. It is worth considering at this point because of its relevance to an understanding of Cabell's irony. *The Music from Behind the Moon* creates in Ettarre that symbol which hovers over all Cabell's symbols along with the hierarchy of his highest gods, the creators of the creators of the creators, from beyond Koschei, through God and Horvendile, through the human author and his compatriots, down to the created puppets, who, like Prometheus and Manuel, yearn to create. Matters are so arranged that humanity derives its greatest pleasure from creative activity, by night or by day. Ettarre is the symbol of the eternal beauty which these creators pursue in their creating. Cabell's most explicit view of Ettarre is contained within *The Sigil of Scoteia*, but *The Music from Behind the Moon* is one of his most substantial offerings made directly to her. Like Horvendile, who is her natural escort and equal (whom, too, she evades at the last), she appears here and there throughout the Biography like a wraith of consistent shapeliness but variable substance.

In the Storisende Edition, Cabell juxtaposes *The Music from Behind the Moon* with *Domnei*. In his author's note he explains that his reason for the juxtaposition concerns his curiosity about what happened to Perion and Melicent after their reunion.

> When in 1919 I wrote "The Wedding Jest" I surmised the answer at least from Melicent's point of view. But it was not until I wrote, in 1926, "The Music From Behind The Moon" that I knew quite well what . . . had happened . . . and that I perceived these two brief tales are in reality one story.

"The Wedding Jest" is a fine short story written in 1919 to be added to the collection in *The Line of Love*, when that volume (first published in 1905) was reissued in November, 1921, in the Kalki Edition. The general subject is that of young love and its effects on the young themselves, on the one hand, and upon their elders on the other. We meet Perion and Melicent again but much later in life. What it amounts to is that Cabell now enshrines young love in a mist of wistful remembrance and knowledgeable condescension: Melicent has become a homely and sensible, practical old woman. To young Florian, who has told her that love is immortal, she replies concerning Perion and his and her love:

> . . . Perion and I grew old together, friendly enough; and our senses and our desires began to serve us more drowsily, so that we did not greatly mind the falling away of youth . . . and we were content enough. But of the high passion that had wedded us there was no trace.

And Melicent falls to recounting domestic failings. Is this the outcome of the triumphant advance of Perion upon the castle to recapture his shining bride? Cabell is an intellectual realist as well as an emotional romanticist, and in this outcome we see the applied irony that results from this combination. But while the contrast given us is an indication of the full range of his treatment of life, it does not diminish in any way the significance or beauty or artistic integrity or stature of domnei, the attitude, or of *Domnei,* the triumphant everlasting song of chivalric love fulfilled. Also, it may be significant that dramatically, physically, and spiritually, the characters of *Domnei* tower above those of "The Wedding Jest" as the pageant of a royal court above pursuant and motley jesters or the leading noteables in an army on campaign above their camp followers.

In *The Music from Behind the Moon,* however, the poetic level is raised to the heights again. In Madoc there is, indeed, another side to Perion's coin; while it counterbalances his youth—even as in "The Wedding Jest" the youth of Melicent is counterbalanced by later developments—it does so with the same poetic substance so that, like *Domnei, The Music from Behind the Moon* becomes a perfect poem. But because it deals with much more of the web, with the full length of life, it is far more profound. Of course, fourteen years of Cabell's own living had elapsed between the finishing of *Domnei* in 1912 and the publication of *The Music from Behind the Moon* in 1926. Madoc seems to express the same poetic attitude of *Domnei* but at a later stage of its development; it is as if Perion as Madoc has, simply, much more material now to remake. The Melicent of "The Wedding Jest" expresses the attitude of *Domnei* in a different mood, a mood which does comic justice to the mundane aspects of later life. The Melicent of "The Wedding Jest" may mock her earlier self but she does not contradict or deny her. In fact, as Madoc represents Perion, so Melicent is represented by Ettarre, who represents all women who, however contemptuously, partner their husbands.

The Music from Behind the Moon consists of what amounts to thirty prose stanzas, none of which is more than one page long. These stanzas form four parts which constitute a circle or cycle of living as perceived in its inner essentials. Cabell constructs a continuum of interpretation from unity of observed facts in the known to unity of spiritual awareness in the unknown. He extends the web until it embodies not only the tangible but also the intangible. At the center is Ettarre, Horvendile, Cabell, Koschei, Donander, Miramon Lluagor, and the Norns—all, in fact, who participate in the hierarchy of creators. In the web struggle the characters of the Biography, humanity, in endless perturbation even if and as they themselves struggle toward the center and attempt to create, and even as, occasionally, the spider at the center visits, inspects, or associates with victims. In these myths the spirit which permeates all may be personified by animals or nature, for example, death by a grey wolf, inspiration or recollection by a greyhound, or the sunset communicating the love of the prime creator in *Domnei*. In this way man again seems a coordinate part of the forces in his whole universe—he can once again achieve unity with the total spirit. Indeed the men of action of the Biography, like Manuel, Edward, Perion, and Demetrios, pace their cages like tigers "burning bright / In the forests of the night," and are at least powerful in their bewilderment; those who, like Jurgen, think too precisely on the events, swing like so many chattering monkeys or gaily plumed parrots from one environmental trapeze to another.

To begin with, Madoc is the least promising of poets, and like Cabell with *The Eagle's Shadow*, he himself does not like his composition. Madoc meets Ettarre, the "woman like a mist," who makes music upon heartstrings until there is forever after upon Madoc "a loneliness and a hungering for what he could not name." Madoc tunes in, however inadequately, through his cursed gift of an imagination, to the source of all creation, symbolized by a woman and by art. Madoc goes through one form of creation, his art, to another, his woman, so that he is entirely dedicated to the service of creation—primarily to perpetuate the race and secondarily to elevate it. Remember that in *Beyond Life*, Cabell, is "grounding himself," observed, "all goes forward, toward something. . . . We are being made . . . into something better." As he sees it, romance, which is synonymous with God, is the means of this advancement. The first act of a myth-maker must be to establish wherein lies man's contentment. Of course, it is in creation through the medium of woman and art—and art presumably includes everything constructed for the purpose of integration: bridges, statesmanship, religion, laws of relativity, sciences of the sub-conscious, and cooking utensils, everything in fact, that is *made* and produces unity, order, symmetry, or harmony. Thus this maker of genuine myths is at the center of the universe, participating in the universal forces and revealing for us the entire nature of their ambiguous duality, which produces the tension necessary for the action by which "all goes forward." The measurements are not so much good and evil or even strength and weakness, but beauty and ugliness as signified respectively by unity and chaos; real art is synthesis consequent upon analysis, not just the analysis. Romanticism succeeds and completes because it achieves also the spiritual synthesis of content and not just of form.

Madoc represents all art and artists, particularly in their poetic aspects. He at first fashions music to beguile and possibly to elevate people who are patriotically and democratically inclined. Even while doing this and just when he is at his best, Madoc hears the music of Ettarre, which is beyond, and more profound and moving than, anything of his own and quite unperceived by his public. While he entertains, fortifies, and even perhaps edifies his public, Madoc himself becomes increasingly discontented; eventually he is compelled to abandon his activities and set off again over the desert toward his mirage. Precisely as Gerald Musgrave comes to Maya in *Something About Eve,* so does Madoc. In fact, in his note to *Something About Eve,* Cabell writes:

> . . . in this tenth volume, the Biography reverts to the clan of old Madoc, who was neither chivalrous nor gallant, but merely a poet—a never-idle "maker"; and to whom all life afforded, in the ultimate, only the raw materials which his half-tranced imaginings might remake into something more comely, more symmetrical, and

more diverting. Gerald Musgrave alone of the sober minded Musgraves was of the clan. Gerald Musgrave turned inevitably, neglecting all else, toward this or that rather beautiful ideal to play with.

Gerald Musgrave stayed with Maya, even as Perion did with Melicent and as many husbands do with their wives; but Madoc left Maya and continued, with that strange compulsion toward beauty within the hearts of poets, in pursuit of Ettarre, leaving this world where he had increased love of country, philanthropy, peace, and all constructive activities, for the "pale mists and the naked desert space behind the moon," where "Ettarre was at her accursed music." Ettarre is fascinating, of course, and in accordance with the design of nature satisfies Madoc naturally; the desert becomes "a sylvan paradise" of which Ettarre remarks, biblically, "Love has wrought this lovely miracle."

Madoc finds that Ettarre must bewitch men for an allotted time until, even as Prospero released Ariel, Sargatanet is to release Ettarre—after 725 years of music-making, as is written in the giant Book of Norns. But Madoc inserts, with his mighty pen, a decimal point after the number 7; Ettarre, thus released, is taken by Madoc back to the olden days. Of this, Sargatanet observes: "A poet is bold. There is no god in any current mythology who would have made bold to cheat the Norns."

On returning to earth, Madoc and Ettarre take up residence among the Northmen, and Madoc makes songs for them of the "splendid and luxurious future which was in store for their noble Nordic race," the essentially practical people whose favorite recreations were "drunkeness and song-making and piracy." Ettarre becomes domesticated, and there is now no music from behind the moon. While Madoc flourishes materially and has everything his body needs, even as did Manuel, he misses that music. Thus Madoc and Ettarre come to represent, on this profounder level, not only the Melicent of "The Wedding Jest" but the ageing Perion and Melicent of *Domnei*, until Ettarre dies. Only myth can express what is so clearly a form of revelation. Ettarre "died sedately, with the best medical and churchly aid," and for Madoc,

"His loneliness closed over him like a cold flood," as his living is robbed of purpose and of every joy." But suddenly,

> Old Madoc heard another music, unheard through all the years in which he had held Ettarre away from her lunar witcheries . . . and the bereaved widower shocked everybody by laughing aloud, now that he heard once more the skirling music from behind the moon.

Many are the wondrous subtleties of Cabell's vast weaving which have here been omitted. Only his works themselves can fully reveal them. But perhaps these few salient pointers may indicate something of their intricacy, of his skill, and of the significance of his creation.

There are ten stories in *Chivalry.* They were written between 1904 and 1907, collected and published in 1909, and then revised for the Kalki Edition and reissued in 1921. They are somewhat uneven in their artistry, but they nevertheless contain clear evidence of the means by which Cabell was persistently to present the ideas embodied in *Beyond Life.* Here, "after the simple cunning that God hath sent to me," he deals with the noble acts of chivalry, "to the intent that noble men may see and learn." Indeed, *Chivalry* represents one of the occasions when Cabell most permits himself, not to be didactic, but to deal more straightforwardly with the ways of God on earth.

Burton Rascoe wrote, in his introduction to the revised version, that there is "a superb craftsmanship in recreating a vanished age, an atmosphere in keeping with the themes, a fluid, graceful, personal style, a poetic ecstasy, a fine sense of drama, and a unity and symmetry which are the hall-marks of literary genius."

This atmosphere is established partly by the elaborate paraphernalia of "precautional" and prologue, assisted by numerous quotations constituting asides before the main business. Cabell always approaches the main business delicately, building up precise shades of atmosphere and setting his stage in detail, thereby ensuring something of the leisurely approach of the medieval readers or listeners, who had all the time in the world, it seems, to enjoy what may even have been to them the most important things. In his own time, Cabell was in competition with magazine stories that were prefixed by a statement of the time required to read them.

It is with *Chivalry* that Cabell substantially launches his notorious figure Nicolas de Caen, who is supposed to have written these accounts in French, in 1470, while a dependant of the Duke of Burgundy. Nicolas is rather biased in favor of York and Burgundy and a little slow to praise Lancaster and Valois. Historical figures intermingle with those even from Poictesme, as Manuel—who knows all noblewomen of note—knows Alianora of Provence; their supposed descendants illustrate the workings of the Biography.

In the precautional, Cabell discusses the themes of these stories. He recalls that the chivalric code was world-wide, unquestioned, and unquestionable. Its root was the belief in a benevolent Father to whom all were traveling. This "not foolishly indulgent Father" kept an eye on the least doings—he was a divine eavesdropper. Heaven was as actual a place as Alaska or the cinema today.

> This Chivalry was a pragmatic hypothesis: it "worked," and served society for a long while. Like all the other codes of conduct yet attempted it created a tragi-comic mêlée wherein contended "courtesy and humanity, friendliness, hardihood, love and friendship, and murder, hate, and virtue, and sin."

These stories set out to illustrate numerous aspects of this tragi-comic melee and, at all times, the hero is found to display the assumption "that a gentleman will always serve his God, his honour and his lady without any reservation."

Cabell is dealing with the ideals of chivalry, which are primary principles of human motivation; yet they are the most difficult to make convincing and interesting. Ariosto was faced with much the same problem, as was Cervantes, and Cabell solves his problem in much the same way as they did—with irony.

The chivalric person regards life as a test or a trial; each of these stories sets out to illustrate how, in matters involving women, the men are put to the test. Those who maintain their ideals—which circumstances and all practical considerations, including those about the women, suggest are ridiculous—pass spiritually even if they fail materially. The women are frequently one thing while the men, looking at them through the ideals of the code, see them as something else. Yet it is just this dullness, this ingenuousness, in the men (the heroes not the villains), permitting them to live by ideals, that constitutes the fire that attracts the women.

To illustrate the substance of this material, and the possibility that this dullness, obtuseness, or ingenuousness may be the supreme wisdom, here are extracts from the work entitled *Mysticism and Logic* by Bertrand Russell, one who is not overprone to superficial thinking. His essay "A Free Man's Worship" is a handbook to Cabell's works. In this, Bertrand Russell writes,

> In all the multiform facts of the world—in the visual shapes of trees and mountains and clouds, in the events of the life of Man, even in the very omnipotence of Death—the insight of creative idealism can find the reflection of a beauty, which its own thoughts first made.

And again, in what reflects considerably Cabell and the Greeks,

> Brief and powerless is Man's life. . . . Blind to Good and Evil, reckless of destruction, omnipotent matter rolls on its relentless way; for Man . . . it remains only to cherish . . . the lofty thoughts that ennoble his little day . . . to worship at the shrine his own hands have built . . . to preserve a mind free from the wanton tyranny that rules his outward life . . . to sustain alone, a weary but unyielding Atlas, the world that his own ideals have fashioned despite the trampling march of unconscious power.

Also, Cabell had stated, he "desiderated" tenderness; if he could find little of it in life, it runs like a vein of amber through these stories of *Chivalry.*

The first story is that of "The Sestina." A sestina is an ancient French verse form, originating in Provence and northern Italy; it consists of six stanzas of six unrhymed lines plus a final triplet. The story takes place around a sestina in salutation of spring.

While Cabell's poem keeps precisely enough to the traditional form, he follows later variations which introduced rhymes, with an *ababab* rhyme scheme.

Osmund Heleigh is a scholar, an observer, and rather ineffectual in action. Thirty years prior to this story he had been a troubadour at the court of Raymond-Berenger in Provence, where he had hymned as unattainable the second daughter Alianora. The story begins with a request to Osmund by Alianora for help.

The plot in "The Sestina" is straightforward and well knit. It depends on the substance of the situation rather than on any twist of circumstances in a surprise ending. There is the atmosphere of a foregone conclusion which is satisfying because it fulfills "what should be." The aged troubadour is one of the many of Cabell's "retired poets." He follows once again the youthful creed of his sestina, which had won the laurels at the betrothal of this ageing woman, then a young sorceress about to become Henry III's wife. He agrees, reluctantly because it means discomfort, to lead the Queen through the enemy to rejoin her forces at Bristol. The Queen wonders if he can be trusted as she is worth much money and Osmund is not wealthy.

> "You may trust me, mon bel esper"—his eyes were those of a beaten child,—"because my memory is better than yours . . ."
> When he had gone, Dame Alianora laughed contentedly. "Mon bel esper! My fairest hope! The man called me that in his verses—thirty years ago! Yes, I may trust you, my poor Osmund."

Cabell is handling very difficult material, liable, in its high flying, at any moment to sideslip into maudlin sentimentality. He succeeds, as he almost always does, by carefully counterbalancing pathos by a display of ruthless violence which plays continually around the "omnipotence of death." These realistic notes are rendered all the more effective because they are deliberately and consistently underplayed. The main shock of the sentence is bottled up in a subordinate compartment as if casually introduced and of merely incidental significance. Life does it that way and Cabell achieves a lifelike impact with the cruel and unexpected.

116

This is a standard feature of Cabell's technique, but it is allied with, indeed inextricably part of, his ironic approach. Where Thomas Hardy countered his hostile gods with a somber determinism, Cabell uses humor. The gods are cruel and they delight in jerking the strings so that man jigs ignominiously, ridiculously, and helplessly. In retaliation, the artist creates his own characters and is then free to manipulate strings in imitation and even, at times, to produce movements that are gracious and noble, as in Greek tragedy or *Samson Agonistes,* or, in their own way, these movements of Osmund Heleigh, the pathetic book-muddled pedant turned knight-errant. For a moment, the artist enjoys a bright radiance which may bring a moment's contentment. But when the artist is continually pestered with probing introspection, he is inevitably aware, even in the act of creation, of the peculiarity, incongruity, and possible folly of his behavior. Hence the protective shield of banter and irony toward all of life, even the most tragic, and thus conscience makes irony an alternative to cowardice, as is found in Sterne, Rabelais, and Hemingway. It is one way that man can strike back at the gods—by playing, for a moment, their own game and by manipulating the strings with the same pungent cruelty to which the artist is himself subjected in outer life. And, as Aristotle pointed out, in this creation the turbulence is purged from the emotions, leaving them temporarily at rest and composed in the process of catharsis. It is this irony and its humorous expression in action and comment that is the intellectual core, the hand of iron in the velvet glove, in Cabell's work.

It is effective only because it is deeply felt. As Fielding said, "he who will make me weep must first weep himself." It is exactly this depth of feeling, rigidly controlled by the mind, which Gibbon, Fielding's admirer, expresses ironically in *The Decline and Fall* (especially in his comments about Christianity, which are a parallel to Cabell's). And Gibbon's views about the fall of Rome coinciding with the invasion of the barbarians and Christians have been repeated in the twentieth century by Bertrand Russell, who also uses the ironic approach and whose views, as indicated, are the theories which Cabell has put into practice in the Biography. Thus we should be very wary of such criticism as the following:

Closely allied to his humour is his never-absent irony. Cabell, fundamentally a genial sceptic, can comment on nothing without sardonically bantering it. There is no passion, no spirit of agony, in Cabell's pessimism:[1]

It is suggested that, on the contrary, Cabell's irony is the direct and natural outcome of considerable passion and an intense spirit of agony.

In this example, "The Sestina," the journey to Bristol has one pleasant consequence. As the disguised Queen trudges through charred ruins and rancid flesh, she comes into direct contact with the consequences of orders given in the airy abstractedness of the palace or council-chamber. But it is Osmund Heleigh's story and he replies to a grief-stricken, grey-faced Queen:

I detect only one coward in the affair. Your men and Leicester's men also ride about the world, and draw sword and slay and die for the right as they see it. And you and Leicester contend for the right as ye see it. But I, Madame! I! I who sat snug at home spilling ink and trimming rose-bushes! God's world, Madame, and I in it afraid to speak a word for him . . . .

Cabell seldom, if ever, again expresses such clear and positive statements. And even here is that duality of meaning essential to an art which aims at re-creating the ambivalence of life.

Osmund and the Queen are detected. It is at this point that the action acquires its characteristic blend of pathos and humor as Osmund must now put his chivalric pretensions to the test and defend the queen against young Camoys who has trapped her into speaking court French and recognized her. Osmund has no hope at all in this combat, but he is resigned and knows, as Camoys observes, ". . . people will speak harshly of us if we lose this opportunity of gaining honour."

Like Don Quixote, Osmund goes forward to battle. He is im-

---

[1] "James Branch Cabell: An Introduction by John J. Gunther," *The Bookman*, (November, 1920).

mediately severely wounded in the thigh and begins to bleed heavily. Osmund, in near-hysterical desperation, throws away his sword and turns the duel into a brawl. Camoys' helmet rolls to the ground.

> Osmund caught up this helmet and with it battered Camoys in the face, dealing severe blows.
> "God!" Camoys cried, his face all blood.
> "Do you acknowledge my quarrel just?" said Osmund between horrid sobs.
> "What choice have I?" said Camoys, very sensibly.
> So Osmund rose, blind with tears and shivering. The Queen bound up their wounds as best she might, but Camoys was much dissatisfied.

Camoys demands a return bout, to be to the death, "in consideration of the fact it was my own helmet," then rides away, and sings as he goes.

Cabell is to do much better than this but it is already a clear example of what is to become a superb mastery of the unexpected. And already there are numerous complex issues which become standard ingredients. For example, here is that situation whereby age betrays youth and, by breaking the rules, successfully retains something akin to respectability which, whatever else it will overlook, insists upon outward success.

Macbeth is a tyrant and a murderer but he retains the audience's sympathy. Similarly, Cabell so establishes the complexities which surround his own "heroes" that they can, as it were, do no wrong. By all the natural odds Camoys should win, but Osmund remains the hero—by villainous means. He does this because we know he is the victim, not the master, of circumstances. And, like so many of Cabell's heroes, he has been debarred from the placidity of action and condemned to the turmoil of contemplation. This does make a difference. Hamlet, in actual fact, was responsible for more deaths than anyone else in the play. By the time the author has established the various complexities there is really no question of direct blame. The writing, a veritable mess of meanings, becomes "a representation of life."

Nevertheless, Osmund is killed in the return bout and this, too, seems right. He had passed his test and fulfilled the ideals of his youthful sestina by acting out, during a sestina of six days of manly common living, "a folly that is divine."

And all the time the author appears to sit aloof, undermining with mocking banter the highest flying pronouncements of devotion, neatly balancing each attempt at a magnificent gesture with some ridiculous incongruity. The dramatic effect would be murdered completely by further dissection but, as Camoys observed when he returned the body of Heleigh to the Queen, "this man was frank and courteous." This, also, has meaning.

Some of the stories in *Chivalry* are loosely linked by Nicolas. For example, there are two about Edward I, "The Tenson" and "The Rat-Trap," these being the second and third stories of the ten.

In "The Tenson" it is the young Prince Edward with whom we deal, a Prince who has just won the battle of Evesham, thus ending the Barons' War; such behavior is "reminiscent of Count Manuel of Poictesme, whose portraits certainly the Prince resembled to an embarrassing extent." "The Tenson" tells how, free for a moment from public matters, Edward goes to France to claim the wife to whom he has been betrothed ten years previously. Having decorously rid himself of his mistress, he rides alone into Lower Picardy coming eventually to Entrechat, where his wife lives. Edward is, in everything but the one thing, the opposite of Osmund Heleigh. Edward, descendant of Manuel, is a man of action, of big build and of less subtle but more decisive intellect. Yet—and Cabell often keeps remarkably close to historical facts—Edward is a man with a mission. But, again unlike Osmund, he lives this mission throughout his life, not merely for six dramatic days. Edward, "a gigantic and florid person . . . of handsome exterior, high featured and blonde, having a narrow, small head and vivid light blue eyes, and the chest of a stallion," a brusque man of deeds, not words, has a clear conception of his own destiny or vicarship. He illustrates Cabell's ability to draw vividly and effectively men of action. In "The Tenson" is the modern equivalent of the country in Spenser's *The Faerie Queene* as Edward moves through these woods of southern France toward Castile. In fact, making allowances for the difference between Spenser's medium of poetry and Cabell's of poetic prose, there is a remarkable affinity between each artist's representation of ruthless action conveying similar mixtures of masculine brutality and feminine sensuous grace and beauty against similarly sunlit woodlands.

For example, in Book VI, Canto I, stanza 23, of *The Faerie Queene,* Spenser describes Calidore's action against Maleffort who fled within the castle:

> But *Calidore* did follow him so fast,
> That even in the Porch he him did win,
> And cleft his head asunder to his chin.
> The carkasse tumbling down within the door,
> Did choke the entrance with a lump of sin,
> That it could not be shut, whilst *Calidore*
> Did enter in, and slew the Porter on the flore.

Cabell's work has the same virility and strength which derive from rapidity of masculine action. This technique Cabell later raises to a high level, as seen particularly in *The First American Gentleman,* where dramatic interest is retained and heightened by consistently springing twists in rapid action on the basis of dramatic as well as intellectual irony. Perhaps the classic example is the episode in this novel of a slaughter in Florida of the French by the Spaniards, while "just around the corner" the unwitting French commander discusses with the Spaniard their shared youth. The beginnings of this method are obvious in *Chivalry.* In "The Tenson" and even more so in "The Rat-Trap," these dramatic twists and an air of detached and cold-blooded impartiality are in full evidence. At times, these touches do not succeed—the language falls into the artificial or too casual—but these slips are rare and were later to disappear entirely as mastery was achieved.

In "The Tenson," Prince Edward falls into conversation with a group of Spaniards drinking about a stone table in a wood near the home of his wife, whom he is still to meet. Edward accepts hospitality and is soon in "amicable" discourse.

One fellow asked his name and business in those parts, and the Prince gave each without hesitancy as he reached for the bottle, and afterwards dropped it just in time to catch, cannily, with his naked left hand, the knife-blade with which the rascal had dug at the unguarded ribs. The Prince was astounded, but he was never a subtle man: Here were four knaves who . . . desired his death: manifestly there was here an actionable difference of opinion; so he had his sword out and killed the four of them.

However, in ten years of neglect, Edward's "wife" has her own experiences. She falls in love with De Gâtinais, who, with the aid of the Pope, cancels the youthful contract, marries this sister of Alphonso, and then completes negotiations to extend his possessions to include Sicily and Apulia. Alphonso in return receives De Gâtinais' vote toward making him King of Germany. This marriage would be in nearly everyone's interest, a fact not to be taken lightly. However, it is not in Edward's interest, and on the basis of his divine right, he takes action. Cabell uses a favorite Elizabethan device whereby a page who accompanies Edward is in fact his wife. This situation is revealed early to the reader but not to Edward.

A tenson is a verse competition between two troubadours before a tribunal of love. The tenson which forms the fulcrum of this story consists of the two opposing points of view. These are sung to a lute accompaniment by the page and the Prince in an inn yard near Burgos in Old Castile on the southern slopes of the Pyrenees. "About them was an immeasurable twilight, moonless, but tempered by many stars, and everywhere they could hear an agreeable whispering of leaves."

The page presents the woman's case, which is to step aside from the trodden path, to pause and seize joy for itself for that moment, for in the trodden path—which leads only to oblivion—one becomes ever more dusty and weary. The Prince takes the opposite view and, like Bunyan's Pilgrim, is for forging ahead, unafraid, to and through the gateway of a citadel.

At the end the page observes, "You paint a dreary world, my Prince." The Prince replies in what is another key statement on behalf of chivalry.

> My little Miguel, I paint the world as the Eternal Father made it. The laws of the place are written large, so that all may read them; and we know that every road . . . yet leads in the end to God. We have our choice,—or to come to Him as a laborer comes at evening for the day's wages fairly earned, or to come as a roisterer haled before the magistrate. . . . we have sung, we two, the Eternal Tenson of God's will and of man's desires.

As they proceed south to Burgos, the page's dilemma becomes an increasing burden. For she is enamoured of De Gâtinais to the full extent of her passionate being, yet she is also increasingly respectful of this "very dull and very glorious Prince" who is her lawful husband.

Cabell's sense of character and situation is unerring and as realistically perceptive as Shaw's. De Gâtinais and the Prince meet. De Gâtinais is also handsome in the world's eyes.

> And at sight of him awoke in the woman's heart all the old tenderness; handsome and brave and witty she knew him to be . . . and the innate weakness of de Gâtinais, which she alone suspected, made him now seem doubly dear. Fiercely she wanted to shield him . . . from that self-degradation which she cloudily apprehended to be at hand; the test was come, and Etienne would fail. This much she knew with a sick, illimitable surety, and she loved de Gâtinais with a passion which dwarfed comprehension.

The action moves forward now almost entirely by dialogue, revealing that Cabell has no difficulty in conveying a consistent character through dialogue as well as through physical action. The Frenchman twists and turns from one emotional but sutble argument to another on a personal basis of straight hate; the Englishman, standing righteously on a firm moral foundation, is unshakable but very fair and magnanimous in what he regards as a simple logical sequence of reasoning—"always it is granted us to behold that sin is sin."

The two fight; Edward stumbles, strikes his head and victory would have been to De Gâtinais but for the intervention of the "page." Nursing the unconscious Edward, this "big and simple man," she is recognized by De Gâtinais, who states:

"I was afraid. Never in my life have I been afraid before today. But I was afraid of this terrible and fair and righteous man. I saw all hope of you vanish, all home of Sicily—in effect, I lied as a cornered beast spits out his venom."

"I know," she answered. ". . . you and I are not strong . . . we can enjoy only the pleasant things of life. But this man can enjoy —enjoy, mark you—the commission of any act, however distasteful, if he think it to be his duty. There is the difference. I cannot fathom him. But it is now necessary that I become all which he loves— and that I be in thought and deed whatever his toplofty notions require. For I have heard the Tenson through."

By her decision, Edward's wife not only achieves an incurious content but life seemed "though scarcely the merry and colourful business which she had esteemed it, yet immeasurably the more worthwhile."

"The Rat-Trap" is a story which illustrates a dramatic technique that becomes a standard element in Cabell's writing. It is about Edward again, but he is now an ageing man near sixty. The date is 1298 and Edward's first wife has died in 1290. Again, this story concerns a question of marriage which will extend the royal domains in France. A standard device of Cabell's is used here: he presents a naïve, innocent idealist being led into a trap by men and women who exploit his ideals and then shed their pretence and become lifelike as they move in to the kill. But at this point they discover that their gullible victim is fully aware of things as they are and has prepared himself accordingly. Thus in "The Rat Trap," Edward is surrounded by his enemies only to inform them that they in turn are matched two to one by his own men. This is paralleled in a series of personal incidents of essential concern to the central characters.

The outward circumstances thus color and comment upon the inward events as the genuine emotions of love and self-sacrifice become confused and made ambiguous by the treachery and subtle dishonesty of the general action. To be right, Right must have Might. Part of Edward's might consists of his ability to learn from experience without shedding the ideals by which he thrives and grows stronger. In the end, he is invincible, and his invincibility shows itself in his ability to match his enemies' cunning. In a sprint, cunning can outpace wisdom but not in the long run. Cunning is presented as the Devil's wisdom and, as such, is not to be used except when survival demands. It was a lesson that Tom Jones had to learn.

In life, cunning often triumphs perhaps, but in *Chivalry* Cabell deals with the godlike exception whose wisdom is ultimately impregnable. The mesh or web is woven and we may watch the lifelike struggle of cunning and wisdom as they strive, like a snake and a mongoose, for mastery.

Mention must be made of one other story in this collection by Nicolas de Caen called "The Choices." A portion of the dialogue in this story which seems to represent the vital problem that lies at the heart of the thought and action of most of Cabell's characters is used as the prologue for "Which Deals with the Demiurge," the key chapter in *Beyond Life. The Choices* is thus the fictionalized version of a philosophical career most close to Cabell himself.

What is man, that his welfare be considered?—an ape who chatters to himself of kinship with the archangels while filthily he digs for groundnuts. . . .

Yet more clearly do I perceive that this same man is a maimed god. . . . He is under penalty condemned to compute eternity with false weights and to estimate infinity with a yardstick; and he very often does it. . . .

There lies the choice which every man must make—or rationally to accept his own limitations? or stupendously to play the fool and swear that he is at will omnipotent? DIZAIN DES REINES.

"The Choices" takes place in 1327 during the reign of "the unworthy son" Edward II and the choices are whether to follow Ariel or Caliban.

The central character this time is a woman, Ysabeau of France, who is endeavouring to acquire England from Edward. She is something between Lady Macbeth and the mother of Hamlet, "a handsome woman, stoutening now from gluttony and from too much wine." Like Elizabeth, she moved at the center of intrigue and treachery with her own person a bargaining counter. She is much interested in one of her prisoners, with whom she has had more than a long acquaintance. He, Sir Gregory Darrell, is enamored of Ysabeau but in love with one Rosamund. Ysabeau offers Darrell either death, or herself with all the power and riches that go with her.

On this simple and eternal triangle, Cabell builds his imposing edifice complete with numerous ramifications. The Queen Ysabeau is a complicated woman handicapped by the fact that her desire for Darrell includes, or is even based upon, admiration for what he represents. Consequently, when Darrell—who is a mortal man—hesitates before choosing death and love instead of power and glory, she is stricken with a terrible fear.

"The Choices" is a masterpiece-in-miniature for the manner in which the author makes solidly convincing the ephemeral matter of the interplay between the weak flesh and the willing spirit, with the outcome never happiness but always its pursuit. The story involves the tragic opposition between genuine friendship and the need to survive; survival is most often not of the fittest but of the cruelest and most vicious—and the Devil takes the foremost. It is on this note that the story ends with its final unexpected twist which reveals just how difficult the choices are.

As Ysabeau departs alone, "a handsome woman, stoutening now from gluttony and too much wine," she sings:

> As with her dupes dealt Circé
> Life deals with hers, for she
> Reshapes them without mercy,
> And shapes them swinishly,
> To wallow swinishly,
> And for eternity;

Though, harder than the witch was,
Life, changing not the whole,
Transmutes the body, which was
Proud garment of the soul,
Whose ruin is her goal;

And means by this thereafter
A subtler mirth to get,
And mock with bitterer laughter
Her helpless dupes' regret,
Their swinish dull regret
For what they half forget.

Thus, in these stories, Cabell presents the tangled consequences of these "chivalric" impulses as they occur over several generations involving the Plantaganets and the Barons. The spirit impelling the heroes and claimed by the villains is essentially Christian; at times the key statement actually embodies Christian dogma as, for example, in "The Satraps":

"Heaven help us, nor you nor I nor any one may transform through any personal force this bitter world. . . . Charity and Truth are excommunicate, and a king is only an adorned and fearful person who leads wolves toward their quarry, lest, lacking it, they turn and devour him . . . and lechery and greed and hatred sway these glittering inconsiderate fools. . . ."

The Queen answered sadly: "Once and only once did God tread this tangible world, for a very little while; and, look you, to what trivial matters He devoted that brief space! Only to chat with fishermen, and to talk with light women, and to consort with rascals, and at last to die between two cutpurses, ignominiously! If Christ Himself achieved nothing which seemed great and admirable, how should we two hope to do any more?"

Frequently an outcome involves the renunciation of place and power for anonymity and a measure of ambitionless stoicism amounting to content. The style is downright, but the well-chosen words give a final impression of polished strength. The substance of the stories is the most important thing in *Chivalry*, but the artist renders this enlightening substance entertaining by full use of situation and intrigue. Character portrayal is highly developed, and these descendants of Manuel are usually portrayed through their actions. The ingredients character-in-action, spiritual significance, intrigue and situation form the staple of Cabell's fiction. The society is aristocratic in the sense that it is royal and revolves around the crown and nobility; the heroes and heroines are, in their intellectual probity, on a par with the mythology of Henry James.

As far as development is concerned, these stories are in themselves artistic achievements of a very high order. As a craftsman, Cabell is well on his way to the art which conceals art. The spiritual content and the poetic treatment reach yet higher levels later. The intricacies of situation and intrigue become still more intricate and more pungently presented in, for example, the more secular *Gallantry* (written a shade earlier but revised for republication in 1922) and *The Certain Hour*.

But these stories of Nicolas de Caen have their very special place and significance in Cabell's work. Never again, perhaps, was he to embody in his fiction so clearly, positively, and consistently the spirit of genuine Christianity as a fundamental source of lasting life. Many complexities were to enter more obviously into Cabell's work later, ranging from the pungency of extreme bitterness to perverse scepticism; but this relatively serene atmosphere underlying *Chivalry* is best summed up by the description of the fictitious author Nicolas de Caen as given in *Domnei* in a "Notice sur la vie de Nicolas de Caen," written under the name of Paul Verville:

> Nicolas de Caen est un représentant agréable, naif, et expressif de cet âge que nous aimons a nous représenter de loin comme l'âge d'or du bon vieux temps. . . . Nicolas croyait à son Roi et à sa Dame, il croyait surtout à son Dieu. Nicolas sentait que le monde était semé à chaque pas d'obscurités et d'embûches, et que l'inconnu était partout; partout aussi était le protecteur invisible et le soutien; à chaque souffle qui frémissait, Nicolas croyait le sentir comme derrière le rideau. Le ciel par-dessus ce Nicolas de Caen était ouvert,

peuple en chaque point de figures vivantes, de patrons attentifs et manifestes, d'une invocation directe. Le plus intrépide guerrier alors marchait dans un mélange habituel de crainte et de confiance, comme tout petit enfant. A cette vue, les esprits les plus émancipés d'aujourd'hui ne sauraient s'empêcher de crier, en tempérant leur sourire par le respect: *Sancta simplicitas!*

If Charteris is a major spokesman for one feature of Cabell's work, Nicolas de Caen speaks for another and much more important feature. For, as Fielding maintained, a man is what a man does, and the Biography is itself a deed which, taken as a whole, speaks more loudly than its individual parts.

Nicolas personifies the spiritual impulse that represents a fundamental impulse behind all Cabell's best work. The aspects represented at odd despondent moments by Charteris extend the artist's range to include questioning scepticism and protective banter; these lead to the intellectual integrity that pursues life's ambiguities and remakes them in a tragicomic blend that is finally polished to finely wrought beauty. This spiritual basis should be remembered at all times when considering what appears to be Cabell's greatest work. For *Jurgen* was censored.

11: *Jurgen*

> *So this, your* Jurgen, *travels*
> *Content to compromise*
> *Ordainments none unravels*
> *Explicitly . . . and sighs.*

Artistically, the most important years in Cabell's life may well be those from 1917 to 1927. These years saw *The Cream of the Jest, Beyond Life, Jurgen, Figures of Earth, Straws and Prayer Books, The Silver Stallion,* and *Something About Eve.* Seemingly in substance, and most probably in treatment, these are the summit of his endeavors. Much good work, even great work, was still to come; but although Cabell's work still had its spells among the best-sellers (*Something About Eve*, in 1927, is "the last of my books to have any general circulation"), after 1921 the music was becoming familiar. For a reading public which was to be bombarded with thousands of realistic novelties a year, this familiarity bred generally a certain contempt.

Cabell's artistic development never ceased. His style became ever closer knit with the consequence of ever-increasing forcefulness and vigor. This may be noteworthy in view of his remarks about the weary way ahead, but this sustained vigor and evident enjoyment are tangible facts, as seen in his later work.

The attitude underlying this later work is important, for it is above all critical, a fact which denotes a continuing intellectual attitude. The prose is less poetic, but construction, unity, and balance of parts remain first rate. These points suggest that, unlike Shakespeare for example, Cabell's later years show more, not less, reliance upon thought. With Shakespeare, after the tragedies there was a weakening of mental striving and a relaxation of control over such technical matters as plot, although for his farewell in *The Tempest* he unpacked all the tools of his trade just once more and even kept an eye on the three unities in case Ben Jonson was right. But the final romances of Shakespeare are noteworthy for their relative emotional serenity, even self-indulgence in the insistence on happy endings, and for their predominant spirit of reconciliation. In its continued cognitive activity, Cabell's final development seems to be, in certain respects, just about the opposite of Shakespeare's.

Cabell's later prose is less poetic. Consequently its appeal is increasingly to the mind and less to or through the emotions. Poetry is the highest form of artistic endeavor in the medium of words, if not in all mediums. One of the reasons for this is that only poetry appeals through a blend of both feeling and thought —that blend which brings to life the greatest part of a being. The vocabulary of poetry is more limited than that of its greatest rival, music; but poetry approaches music and, in this way, makes its emotional appeal. For words to make music they must inhabit a context which turns images to symbols so that feeling, rhythm, sound, and picture blend to amplify each other's significance to form a total that is new and not contained in the individual parts.

It is for this reason, perhaps, that myth and allegory are the great-est methods of representation. For they are most akin to music and least earth-bound of literary forms. They were standard in medieval Europe from the renaissance of the twelfth century to that of the fifteenth and sixteenth centuries. In this earth-bound age of stratospheric flight, genuine myths are almost unknown.

Considerations such as these seem to indicate the years 1917–27 as Cabell's best years, for these are the years of his profoundest poetic prose. In 1919 Cabell was forty. Chronologically, he had behind him works dealing, separately and together, with his in-dividual concerns of chivalry and gallantry. In the prose essays in *Beyond Life* he had hammered out his own views on these things, views ranging from deepest-held desires at least bordering on convictions, to flippant denials of the sun and moon. These denials also contained their grains of truth, for he had seen beyond good and evil to the good that is evil and the evil that is good. Thus, with the superior thirties behind and the fattening forties ahead, Cabell was at the one point where the chivalric and gallant, the positive and negative, the serious and the flippant could blend to most purpose and effect. Cabell was very obviously on the crest of the wave of his ability. Like the Fielding of *Tom Jones*, which Fielding wrote at the age of forty-two after purging himself of the venom in *Jonathan Wilde*, Cabell could look down from his eminence of urbanity and laugh at what he saw. As suggested by *Straws and Prayer Books*, this laughter was to become strained, more barbed with a bitterness which was to lace the mirth with an unpleasant tang of more than the macabre before it was to settle to its final even pungency.

Beyond Life was begun in 1917 and received final touches at Virginia Beach in August, 1918. *Jurgen* was begun in March, 1918, and completed in October, 1918, but was retained to allow for the publication of *Beyond Life* in January, 1919, with the consequence that *Jurgen* received "a liberal amount of retouching" in the early part of 1919. Thus *Jurgen*, the synthesis, flowered directly out of the analysis in *Beyond Life*. Cabell's opinion is that it developed more logically from its first draft than did *Figures of Earth*; in fact, *Jurgen* seems to have emerged almost as reasonably as *Something About Eve*, the profoundest synthesis, perhaps, produced by the analysis in *Straws and Prayer Books*. For the Biography, *Jurgen* is almost the beginning. The setting or starting point is Poictesme, where Jurgen is a pawnbroker who makes his way home past the Cistercian Abbey. He is forty-something but he dons the shirt of Nessus and regains his physical youth. With this, he goes again in search of happiness. He samples, in a variety of worlds, most of man's prescribed sources of happiness, mostly through one form or another of domnei. For the women represent a wide range of philosophies and ways of life and Jurgen is ever willing to learn.

But Jurgen meets also many notable males such as Gogyrvan Gowr, who observes:

> Youth can afford ideals, being vigorous enough to stand the hard knocks they earn their possessor. But I am an old fellow cursed with a tender heart and tolerably keen eyes. That combination . . . is one which very often forces me to jeer out of season, simply because I know myself to be upon the verge of far more untimely tears.

It is tempting, now, to diverge into intuitive criticism and say that this attitude of Gogyrvan Gowr represents exactly the attitude of the author in writing *Jurgen*. This would account for so much. It would account for the flippancy that paradoxically reawakens the genuine spirit of what is traditionally sacrosanct to the point of being moribund; and it would account for the constant organ music of the deeply-stirred emotions. If youth is a song, age is a symphony. For all the sadness and despondency of its individual parts, the symphony is an infinitely greater achievement, as shown in *Jurgen*, than the song, however joyous and spontaneous. Thus this unique combination of jeers and tears would be explained. But, for the following reasons, *Jurgen* is not the kind of book safely approached solely through intuitive criticism. *Jurgen* is a comedy of justice. It is a Greek theme. Jurgen, armed with the conception of what justice should be, accepts eventually the definition of what it is. His definition is very much akin to that of the Sophists, for example of Thrasymachus, who declared that "Justice is simply the interest of the stronger." With an even more economical use of words, Jurgen decides that justice is expediency. This is the agelong and reiterative universal quest and Jurgen is the symbol of man as he undertakes this quest. It was the quest of Hamlet, the concern of Lear, the bane of Othello, and the poetic justice of Macbeth and Antony, not to mention the Greeks, including Socrates, and the last words of *Plato's Apology*. There could hardly be a greater theme.

The book itself is approached through the usual maze of introductory quotations and comments, some of which must be noted in full. The first is,

> Of JURGEN eke they maken mencioun,
> That of an olde wyf gat his youth, agoon,
> And gat himselfe a shirte as bright as fyre
> Wherein to jape, yet gat not his desire
> In any countrie ne condicioun.

As a preliminary, which needs to be much qualified, it may be of use to compare this with another quotation which has been suggested[1] as the starting impulse for *Pilgrim's Progress:*

> They were strangers and pilgrims on the earth. For they that say such things, declare plainly that they seek a country . . . they desire a better country, that is, an heavenly: wherefore God is not ashamed to be called their God: for He hath prepared for them a city.[2]

To this city journeyed Cabell's re-creation of the first Edward in *Chivalry:*[3] and there is still much of this compulsion in Jurgen, who sought and desired a better country. But Jurgen had fed from the poisonous tree of knowledge and his shining city was only Pseudopolis, inhabited by Greeks not from Periclean Athens but from *Troilus and Cressida*; and Pseudopolis is at war with the

---

[1] Sir Charles Frith, article on Bunyan's pamphlet *The Strait Gate, English Association Leaflet*, No. 19 (1911).

[2] Hebrews XI: 13–36.

[3] The description of Edward is used again, almost word for word, to describe Dom Manuel in Figures of Earth. Edward, the reincarnated "savior," did return again to Poictesme, but not very benevolently.

Philistines, who always win, and Jurgen did not stay there very long.

Like the final chapter of *Rasselas,* Cabell's foreword is one which asserts nothing; it is preceded by the observation, "Nescio quid certe est: et Hylax in limine latrat," from the eighth *Eclogue* of Vergil. This foreword openly throws down the gauntlet of subtlety as Cabell weaves his mesh of false authorities and their interpretation of his symbols.

> . . . Dr. Codman says, without any hesitancy, of Mother Sereda: "This Mother middle is the world generally (an obvious anagram *of Erda Es*), and this Sereda rules not merely the middle of the working-days but the midst of everything. She is the factor of *middleness,* of mediocrity . . . of the eternal compromise begotten by use and wont."
>
> And, of Prote,:—"Sereda typifies a surrender to life as it is, a giving-up of man's rebellious self-centeredness and selfishness: the anagram being *se dare.*"

After thus indicating the possibilities of his art Cabell continues:

> Yet possibly each one of these unriddlings, with no doubt a host of others, is conceivable: so that wisdom will dwell upon none of them very seriously . . . this volume is presented simply as a story to be read for pastime.

Concluding a life's work, Shakespeare remarked in Prospero's Epilogue:

> Gentle breath of yours my sails
> Must fill, or else my project fails,
> Which was to please . . . .

The artist, especially if associated with a box office, must always emphasize his intention to please: the spectacle of ageing Lear makes for tumultuous entertainment. Thus *Jurgen* is presented simply as a story to be read for pastime.

There are three critical "notices" prefixed to the contents. The third, in its relative straightforwardness, is useful:

> Too urbane to advocate delusion, too hale for the bitterness of irony, this fable of *Jurgen* is, as the world itself, a book wherein each

man will find what his nature enables him to see; which gives us back each his own image; and which teaches us each the lesson that each of us desires to learn.[4]

Jurgen is, indeed, as large as life. But in dealing with life it contains, under the guise of symbols, observations about life which are profound, therefore wise, therefore enlightening and therefore, even, pedagogic. Art can be enlightening as well as enjoyable. That *Jurgen* does not set out to teach guarantees its scope and depth. Whether or not Cabell set out to entertain any other than himself, it is entertaining because it is a thing of beauty; this beauty, presented in the best words in the best order, comprises satire, irony, perverse ambiguities, and pungent wit which add up to the human comedy as well as the pathos which underlies it all and converts it to tragedy. In reading *Jurgen* it is not long before one is struck with the author's wonderful freedom, both of mind and of treatment. The entire universe is at his mercy; even time is adapted in whatever way he wishes to suit his particular aims. This freedom, in conjunction with the nature of the material, results in a very special world of its own. It is a world of fantasy which, while apparently a chaotic jumble, nevertheless comprises the stuff of great literature, those things which concern everyone vitally.

More specifically, Cabell uses everything that the imagination of previous ages has created, from ancient classical mythologies to the chivalric romances of the France of Chrétien de Troyes and the England of *Gawain and the Green Knight*; Arthurian legend and the universe of Milton meet with the fairy land of Spenser and the voluptuous nights of the Orient. These are all viewed with a meditative urbanity and an ironic penetration which reveal great depth of humor and pathos and provide echoing implications of searching thought and sympathetic feeling—*Jurgen* is by no means merely a joke.

It is difficult to discuss ordinary rules of construction here—just as with Sterne. The world or worlds created by the author are part of a carefully constructed framework upon which, for all its

[4] John Frederick Lewistam.

135

apparent fantasy, is built a complete representation of life. This, in turn, conveys completely the author's attitude and philosophy. We appreciate this attitude and philosophy by following the experiences unfolded to Jurgen and thus the author may be said to be omniscient. Jurgen, however haphazardly he appears to be whisked here and there without apparent meaning, is, in fact, passing through (partly by review) a universal cycle of human experience. He passes from young love through disillusion, through "sensationalism" (as of Walter Pater, Oscar Wilde and the aesthetes), through religion, and so on ad infinitum. And always the search for values is portrayed with Cabellian breadth of humor, mockery and sensitive sympathy.

Jurgen himself is a universal symbol and does not have a character of his own in the ordinary sense. Nevertheless, we soon come to know him as an individual with a mature knowledge of all things even as he reveals, by action and dialogue, that, like Socrates, he knows nothing. All is placed in focus by an unfailing urbanity and humor. Whatever devastating spiritual or physical experience encompasses Jurgen, a lovely woman is always just around the corner, and inevitably, in her hands, he acquires further enlightenment in accordance with the fundamental psychology of subconscious human motivation.

The physical background is very important, not only because it gives Cabell mediums suited to his theme but also because it helps to encourage a frame of mind amenable to the author's particular brand of realistic idealism. When all is said and done, the author is a poet recording the history of sensitive idealism, and in an age which seems to insist that idealism is no longer called for in prose. The humorous Rabelaisian attitude of the hero is ideal as a guard against sentimentality which does not however prevent the author from using to the full the poetic depths of romantic feeling which have been the prerogative of art for centuries. In other words, the setting, quite apart from the action it contains, is in itself a unique achievement.

The style accords with both aspects (poetry and humor): it can be richly and colorfully poetic and suggestively and ironically humorous. It is lucid even if it does rely on innuendo. The nearest comparison is, perhaps, Meredith's *The Shaving of Shagpat* which has a similar richness of fantasy and allegory but not quite the urbanity of Cabell's work—life was more immediate for Meredith.

Although, in his foreword, the author mock-seriously denies the seriousness of his mythology, *Jurgen* does contain meanings obviously capable of interpretations varying in their degrees of inaccuracy—after all, it *was* censored. Thus, to dissect the significance may be vivisection rather than murder. The two concerns of *Chivalry* and *Gallantry* unite in *Jurgen*. The spectacular role is played by gallantry. Jurgen's behavior is nothing if not gallant, yet he also is on a journey and his visiting places have by their very nature their special meanings. His conclusions do, in spite of their inconclusiveness, add up to a positive total. Yet often any direct affirmation of a positive philosophy is countered by its negative. For example, the nineteenth and twentieth chapters balance each other as follows.

Chapter XIX is entitled "The Brown Man with Queer Feet," and in it Jurgen is escorted into the Druid forest and shown all. In *Beyond Life* Cabell had observed that man was the only animal unable to make profitable use of the truth about himself; *Jurgen*, which is the fictionalized version of *Beyond Life*, illustrates this observation as Jurgen refuses to believe what is shown him in the forest.

> ". . . I will not believe in the insignificance of Jurgen." Chillingly came the whisper of the brown man: "Poor fool! Oh shuddering, stiff-necked fool! and have you not just seen that which you may not ever quite forget?"
>
> "None the less, I think there is something in me which will endure. I am fettered by cowardice, I am enfeebled by disastrous memories, and I am maimed by old follies. Still, I seem to detect in myself something which is permanent and rather fine . . ."
>
> "Now, but before a fool's opinion of himself," the brown man cried, "the Gods are powerless. Of, yes, and envious, too!"

This is a restatement of the chapter in *Beyond Life* entitled *The*

Demiurge. In *Beyond Life* Cabell describes the chief expression of the demiurge as being Christianity.

Chapter XX of *Jurgen* is entitled "Efficacy of Prayer." After the shock of seeing into the innermost heart of things, Jurgen hastened to the Cathedral of the Sacred Thorn in Cameliard and prayer in terror for his dead, "that they should not have been blotted out in nothingness, for the dead among his kindred whom he had loved in boyhood, and for these only." In the morning,

> He paused before a crucifix, and he knelt and looked up wistfully. "If one could only know," says Jurgen, "what really happened in Judea! How immensely would matters be simplified, if anyone but knew the truth about You, Man upon the Cross!"

Whereupon Jurgen questions the Bishop of Merion, who replies:

> ". . . was He Melchisedek, or Shem, or Adam? or was He verily the Logos? and in that event, what sort of a something was the Logos? Granted He was a god, were the Arians or the Sabellians in the right? had He existed always, co-substantial with the Father, and the Holy Spirit, or was He a creation of the Father, a kind of Israelitic Zagreus? Was He the husband of Acharamoth, that degraded Sophia, as the Valentinians aver? or the son of Pantherus, as say the Jews? or Kalakav, as contends Basilidês? or was it, as the Docetês taught, only a tinted cloud in the shape of a man that went from Jordan to Golgotha? Or were the Merinthians right . . . ."
> Thus speaking, the gallant prelate bowed, then raised two fingers in benediction.

Here are Cabell's own chivalric instincts counterbalanced by actual behavior as seen in the world at large. But it may be inadvisable too quickly to label all this nihilism.

Any extensive examination of *Jurgen* must include considerations of the author, but the prime object is to attempt to evaluate the work of art not the man. We have seen something of the composite forces at work within the man and, as always, these forces represent considerations of the ambiguities and contradictions of good and evil. This is not a crime. The core of Shakespeare's tragedies is contained within his sixty-sixth sonnet, which epitomizes the essential attitude behind it all. Some people see farther into things than others, and while their visions prevent them from painting in black and white, they frequently claim to have glimpsed a pattern. On this basis Cabell has taken all the instinctive desires within himself—all those desires which he would most like to be true—concerning man and the universe, and he has, in *Jurgen*, presented them as he has seen them at work in the world. Beauty combats ugliness; truth, falsity. And there is always the shadow, apparently unnoticed by others but ever looming larger. But—and this is perhaps a crowning glory of this work's realism—Jurgen himself is not just. And so he eventually becomes the lackey of use and wont and the fine fire within burns lower and lower. In *Straws and Prayer Books*, writing of the works of Joseph Hergesheimer, Cabell states:

> Here always I find portrayed, with an insistency and a reiteration to which I seem to detect a queer analogue in the writings of Christopher Marlowe, men laboring toward the unattainable, and a high questing foiled.

This is the heart of the tragedy in Cabell's writings; all his desired "truths" are erections heaped up like a barrier against this final truth. Dreiser had said that people talked and talked but he saw no morals anywhere. Cabell is not a moralist in that he offers no clear-cut theory on behalf of good to the detriment of evil: he is not a propagandist. Yet his sympathies lie clearly with some things and his hostilities with others. His representations can be broken down into a host of component parts which do not state but which do imply. Art is great in proportion as it captures beauty, for beauty is truth, and truth is more than a question of haphazard taste.

Cabell is just as realistic as Dreiser, for the greatness of *Jurgen* derives from the clash that arises not only from the fact that we have so many ethics and so few morals, but that we think ourselves so well-intentioned. For instance, when Jurgen is on trial before the Judges of Philistia, he observes to them, ". . . I am a poet, and I make literature."

"But in Philistia to make literature and to make trouble for yourself are synonyms," the tumble-bug explained.

He then describes what was done to Edgar, Walt, and Mark before adding:

> "What is art to me and my way of living?" replied the tumble-bug, wearily. ". . . No, no, my lad; once whatever I may do means nothing to you, and once you are really rotten, you will find the tumble-bug friendly enough. Meanwhile I am paid to protest that living persons are offensive and lewd and lascivious and indecent, and one must live . . . .
>
> Jurgen now looked more attentively at this queer creature: and he saw that the tumble-bug was malodorous, certainly, but at bottom honest and well-meaning; and this seemed to Jurgen the saddest thing he had found among the Philistines.

The gods of Philistia are Vel-Tyno (Novelty) and Sesphra (Phrases) and Ageus (Usage), and the Tumblebug, smiling benevolently, depart saying, "Morals, not art." It would seem to be *these* "morals," the misleading oversimplification by the Tumblebug, to which Cabell objects, preferring the spirit of the genuine artist as it enquires, and lives its enquiries, after truth.

Yet, if they know not what they do, where lies the sin? And so Jurgen continues his seeking, Jurgen who is tempted with easy living in Philistia if he will do what is expected. In refusing, Jurgen is exalting right against wrong, and in doing this, he reveals the sympathies of his creator; but his creator does not leave the matter there—it must be art not morals. As Jurgen is deliberating about his verdict, which condemns him to the Hell of his fathers (the one verdict most in keeping with the Judges of Philistia), he is offered three parchments and a letter. These include his pardon, his elevation to Poet Laureate, and his appointment as Mathematician Royal—the Queen has much admired his ability to put one and one together and produce three. The letter from the Queen states, "Do you consider now what fun it would be to hoodwink everybody by pretending to conform to our laws! For we could be so happy!" But a person is what a person does, and there

was the matter of a certain oak tree embodying a treachery tanta-
mount to the sublime. And then, in front of all, Jurgen makes the
gesture magnificent:

> And Jurgen gave a fine laugh, and with a fine deliberateness he
> tore up the Queen's letter into little strips. Then statelily he took
> the parchments, and found they were so tough he could not tear
> them. This was uncommonly awkward, for Jurgen's ill-advised at-
> tempt to tear the parchments impaired the dignity of his magnan-
> imous self-sacrifice: he even suspected one of the guards of smiling.
> So there was nothing for it but presently to give up that futile tug-
> ging and jerking, and to compromise by crumpling these parchments.
> "This is my answer," said Jurgen, heroically, and with some ad-
> miration of himself, but still a little dashed by the uncalled-for tough-
> ness of the parchments.

So Jurgen passes to Hell, where people have consciences, the
religion is patriotism, and the government an enlightened democracy. Hell is in accord with the imagination of Jurgen's father, and
the subtle introduction into the action and dialogue of Victorian
prudishness is brilliantly managed and clear evidence that Cabell
can create character as well as symbols.

There are fifty chapters in Jurgen, and the finest are possibly
the ones dealing with Heaven (Chapters XL and XLI), "The
Ascension of Pope Jurgen" and "Of Compromises in Heaven."
Jurgen clambers from Hell,

> ... upon a ladder of unalloyed, time-tested gold; and as he climbed
> the shirt of Nessus glittered handsomely in the light which shone
> from heaven; and by this great light above him, as Jurgen mounted
> higher and yet higher, the shadow of Jurgen was lengthened beyond
> belief along the sheer white wall of Heaven, as though the shadow
> were reluctant and adhered tenaciously to Hell. Yet presently Jur-
> gen leaped the ramparts: and then the shadow leaped too; and so
> his shadow came with Jurgen into Heaven, and huddled dispiritedly
> at Jurgen's feet.

Some boldness here may be appropriate as the remarks even of
Prote be noted concerning this shadow, when he observed in the

"Origin of Fable" that, "the shadow symbolizes conscience." Jurgen is let into Heaven by the boy he had once been—at least in his Grandmother's eyes. It may be significant that the humor in these chapters is much more gentle and sympathetic, indeed remarkably tender, and that the author of *Chivalry*, the creator of Nicolas de Caen, and the artist who regards Christianity as the greatest product of the demiurge should treat almost with respect and reverence, however yearning, this dramatic culmination to his greatest work. Jurgen has always proved, with his excellent logic, that Heaven is no more than an old wives' tale, and sure enough, the heaven he now temporarily occupies is built precisely according to the notions of his Grandmother, who would not believe in things as they are. It has been built by Koshchei, who makes things as they are, and God himself is a product designed according to the instructions of the Revelations of St. John the Divine found in a Bible brought specially to Koshchei, who was unacquainted with these matters but who was intrigued by what he saw in the eyes of "the decent little bent grey woman" whenever she talked of her children.

In these pages Cabell appears to be drawing in full upon the deepest reserves of his own stored memories[5]; he retains control of these emotions by treating them imaginatively and with a fine and gentle humor. The very nature itself of these memories and emotions becomes tangible evidence amounting almost to the factual in this quest of Jurgen. The illustration of this appears to bring us to the heart of Cabell's own dilemma—the dilemma which gives rise to that duality within his thinking that governs the cause and effect of all his work.

> And everywhere fluttered and glittered the multicoloured wings of seraphs and cherubs . . . .
> Now the eyes of this God met the eyes of Jurgen: and Jurgen waited thus for a long while, and far longer indeed, than Jurgen suspected.

[5] Evidence supporting this opinion seems to be contained in Cabell's autobiographical statement in *Beyond Life* ("The Mountebank," 65–66) concerning his own family.

"I fear You," Jurgen said, at last: "and, yes, I love You: and yet I cannot believe. Why could You not let me believe, where so many believed? Or else, why could You not let me deride, as the remainder derided so noisily? O God, why could You not let me have faith? for You gave me no faith in anything, not even in nothingness. It was not fair."

And in the highest court of Heaven, and in plain view of all the angels, Jurgen began to weep.

This is, in every respect, a magnificent performance and all the more so because, for once, Jurgen himself overlooked this aspect of it. It is almost paralleled in spirit by the final scenes of Marlowe's *Faustus*; the inherent mental situation seems to be almost identical with Marlowe's as seen in *Faustus*. Thus Jurgen's predicament has a long history which will be longer yet. It is the predicament of all the thinkers. It is this fact which helps to make the Biography great art, for it guarantees profundity while retaining compassion. Eventually, Jurgen, trembling at his own audacity, climbs into the vacated throne of God itself:

"And what will you do now?" says Jurgen, aloud. "Oh, fretful little Jurgen, you that have complained because you have not your desire . . . ." And, sitting thus terribly enthroned, the heart of Jurgen was as lead within him, and he felt old and very tired. "For I do not know. Oh, nothing can help me, for I do not know what thing it is that I desire! . . . and nothing can ever avail me: for I am Jurgen who seeks he knows not what."

In heaven Jurgen finds, not justice, which would have debarred his entry, but that the god of his grandmother was love—and he remembers that he is looking, at least ostensibly, "for that Lisa who used to be my wife." Cabell's conception of marriage is best studied, perhaps, in *The Cream of the Jest*. It is one of the elements within his work most prone to misinterpretation. Jurgen, on the way out of Heaven toward more congenial illusions, asks four archangels if they know the whereabouts of Lisa. "He described her; and they regarded him with compassion." In the end, it is his wife to whom he returns—he who had been offered Helen.

In returning to Lisa, Jurgen returns quietly and meekly to reality. And yet he does so with some thankfulness. This return to mundane reality—the greatest tragedy of all perhaps—is the master touch which completes a masterpiece. As Koshchei informed him, in Jurgen's final interview, "he was not giving him justice but something infinitely more acceptable." " 'But, to be sure!' says Jurgen. 'I fancy that nobody anywhere cares much for justice.' " And yet Jurgen observes, in what are his last words:

> So I retain my wife . . . . I retain my home. I retain my shop and a fair line of business. Yes, Koshchei—if it was really Koshchei—has dealt with me very justly. And probably his methods are everything they should be . . . but still, at the same time—!

Jurgen is most important for the ideas on life which are implicit in it. Indeed, it is impossible to escape these ideas for very long in dealing with any aspect of this work, because they dominate the whole. Here is an author who knows life thoroughly, who has aspired, thought, and suffered over it until now he has achieved the position of an urbane but sympathetic observer capable of recording the ways of his fellow men without bias or prejudice. And yet Cabell is not a detached observer, for a precise and definite attitude emerges. It is that of a partisan, for it is that of the poetic idealist, battered but not entirely bowed and with flags still flying, even if at half-mast. He perceives what amounts to the ultimate failure of all aspiration yet still he elevates once more the place of romance, "For that to which romance conducts . . . is plain enough—distinction and clarity, and beauty and symmetry, and tenderness and truth and urbanity." As Manuel is the Achilles of Poictesme, so Jurgen is its Ulysses, says Codman for Cabell in the foreword to *Figures of Earth*. The final lines of "old-fashioned" and "simple" Tennyson's *Ulysses* best capture, perhaps, the subtle and evasive spirit of Jurgen.

> Tho' much is taken, much abides; and tho'
> We are not now that strength which in old days
> Moved earth and heaven; that which we are, we are;
> One equal temper of heroic hearts,

Made weak by time and fate, but strong in will
To strive, to seek, to find, and not to yield.

In view of the preceding evidence of the seriousness of Cabell's artistic and intellectual endeavors, anyone who should ever again feel censorious about any carnal elements in *Jurgen* or Cabell's works as a whole, might do well to recall the words of Jesus to Nicodemus: "Think not carnally or thou art carnal, but think symbolically, then art thou spirit."

12: *The Line of Love* and *The High Place*

The Line of Love is a collection of short stories most of which constitute Cabell's earliest fiction. The earliest, "The Love-Letters of Falstaff," written in 1901, appeared in *Harper's* in March, 1902; the others, except for "The Wedding Jest" and "Porcelain Cups" (both added in 1919), were written by 1905, when the collection was published as a Christmas book entitled *The Line of Love.* Then, in 1921, Cabell revised them for the Kalki Edition and absorbed them into Poictesme and the Biography of Manuel, prefixing each with a prologue acting as a link.

The Kalki Edition has a foreword by Cabell's great champion, H. L. Mencken. H. L. Mencken must have been a very fine man. Shaw's remark about William Morris would seem to be equally applicable to Mencken; "You can lose a man like that by your own death but not by his." With much of D. H. Lawrence's fearless independence of spirit, Mencken could similarly overstate on behalf of greater truth. Like Ezra Pound, with whom also he has a marked spiritual and stylistic affinity, Mencken's writings are outstanding for their punch which seems to render the apparently intuitive insight irrefutable. Mencken had always an ax to grind, for it was constantly in use. Among his greatest achievements were his swings on behalf of Dreiser and Cabell. This introduction to *The Line of Love* was written in Baltimore in 1921 and valuable work it must have done on behalf of "the author of *Jurgen.*"

In view, then, of Mencken's work in general and of his crusading spirit on behalf of Cabell, it is most surprising that, when dealing with the essence of Cabell's art, Mencken should seem completely to misjudge the most important point. When he deals with Cabell's "essence" he states:

> He is an artist whose work shows constant progress toward the goals he aims at—principally the goal of a perfect style. Content, with him, is always secondary. He has ideas, and they are often of much charm and plausibility, but his main concern is with the manner of stating them. It is surely not ideas that make *Jurgen* stand out so saliently from the dreadful prairie of modern American literature; it is the magnificent writing that is visible on every page of it—writing apparently simple and spontaneous, and yet extraordinarily cunning and painstaking.

This is a most unfortunate misplacement of emphasis. It is like praising a soliloquy of Shakespeare only for its euphony. It is like the behavior of the Earl of Chesterfield when he received Johnson's tragic letter only to display it in his anteroom as a good example of English letter-writing. Matthew Arnold gave some good advice about, not only the object of criticism (which should be "a disinterested endeavor to learn and propagate the best that is known and thought in the world") but also about the achievement of style. His advice about style said in effect, "think, the words will look after themselves." By all means tinker and fiddle, chisel and polish, but the prime requisite is thought. The greater the thought the nearer is the approach to the essentials and the simpler the style. Adjustments follow for perfection and the achievement of the flavor and atmosphere of irony, suggestion, banter, or bite. Thus the style is merely a consequence, never a cause—except in initial stages of individual or national development comparable with the prose of Lyly's *Euphues* or Sydney's *Arcadia*. No writing can be great which reverses this order and concerns itself with its appearance instead of its content. Cabell has made clear his ability to concentrate on psychic reality in his own life;[1] similarly, he has concentrated primarily on the content in his writings even if he has insisted on clothing this content more conscientiously and fittingly than was usual in a rather

[1] See his autobiography and his statements in *Beyond Life*.

shabby age. Many of Cabell's heroes are retired poets, but he himself never relinquished his interest in style. And the style is the man. It is fully time to re-examine this tendency to damn Cabell with the faint praise that is the praise of style. His value is predominantly that of what he says. That he says it pleasantly is so much the better. At his finest he says it poetically, as is best. But to praise him primarily for his style is to praise the builder not for the finished building but for his methods. Cabell's methods are of great importance and ensure a structure that will endure— but they can never be as important as the building itself. And, again, as the methods depend on the nature of the building, so Cabell's unruffled ironic style is but the natural, perhaps only, medium for the tears and jeers of his feeling and thought.

In Cabell's own foreword to *The Line of Love* entitled "The Epistle Dedicatory" to Mrs. Grundy, unintentionally he answers Mencken's charge that he is primarily a stylist. These are, although of a rather special kind, love stories, and Cabell indicates the nature of his material; that is, he confirms its essential realism and thus implies the solidity of the thought that is father to the style:

> Love, then, is no trifle. And literature, mimicking life at a respectful distance, may very reasonably be permitted an occasional reference to the cornerstone of all that exists.

Thus the creator of Poictesme and author of *Beyond Life* claims to mimic life. And this is one true statement unclouded by the shifty tricks of humor and intentional caprice. For of course he mimics life even as did the author of *A Midsummer Night's Dream* and *The Winter's Tale*. That he usually transcribes what he mimics is immaterial provided the transcription remains true, in its inner significance, to a pattern we can recognize and measure by our own experience as lifelike.

The Line of Love contains ten stories again (Cabell likes round numbers, which imply a rational finality, order, control, and harmony), described as "episodes." These trace the line of love, that is, of experiences handed on from parents to children for the most part, from "The Wedding Jest" (an experiment in the graveyard macabre), set in 1293, to the national-prize-winning "Porcelain Cups," set in 1593, which recreates, with Cabellian dialogue, the final hours of Christopher Marlowe. Frequently the spiritual center of the stories is not love and its consequences but the terribleness of time's alchemy upon youth and aspiration. Yet often this "expense of spirit in a waste of shame" is shown as Destiny molding an instrument for a particular task so that, even in utmost degradation, the once shining hero is still not by any means wholly responsible or blameworthy but merely a helpless pawn. This can be seen in the episode "The Love-Letters of Falstaff" and, in the supreme example, "In Necessity's Mortar," which concerns François Villon, here called François de Montcorbier. Both these stories illustrate clearly Cabell's compassion and understanding. If unfortified by intellect these qualities run quickly to sentimentality; the thought-filled alternative can appear as ruthless, even heartless and flippant, irreverence. The feelings tend to be suppressed and find outlet in pungently expressed perspicacity, as in the style, the biting lucidity of which makes *The Decline and Fall* read like a fast-moving novel of horror. This same style is equally capable of a drum roll and trumpets introducing magnificence or to a Rabelaisian anticlimax embarrassing the hero outside the wrong door.

In "In Necessity's Mortar" the action falls between June 5, 1455, and August 4, 1462. At the beginning of this period Villon is a young and untested poet on the threshold of a life of luxury and bliss. At the end he is a vice-ridden derelict: he is also a proven artist of the first rank. How is this mixture of decline and rise explained? Partly through the nature of man and partly through the loaded dice of Fate. To begin with, François de Montcorbier is engaged, in the face of self-interested and therefore merciless competition, to Catherine de Vaucelles. He is very much in love, can play the lute to his own verses, and sees his beloved as an angel. Thus the situation has some precedent, a fact of which Cabell makes much use. A merciless competitor involves young De Montcorbier in a brawl during which a man, or rather a drunken priest, is slain.

This episode illustrates a regular feature of Cabell's technique, a feature he had perfected over the years until in the revised version of 1921 it is a fine example of the traditional means of raising dramatic tension through a straightforward action. Yet the action is presented in such a way that there is an additional meaning refracted from the artist's mirror which captures the brutality of life. And when all is said and done, the impact from this particular method of presentation is an emotional one; it takes the form frequently of the chill that comes with shock and it is as subtle and calculated an effect as anything in the mass of sensitive vibrations in the work of Henry James. Cabell describes, in cold blood, hot-blooded events. The events are cast before the reader coldly and impassively, but they convey an overall impression of speed because they are compressed and told with the fewest possible words as the action in *Macbeth*. From the action, the author captures the unexpected; from his method he captures the underlying spirit of malignant cruelty that is conveyed not only by the expression "man's inhumanity to man," but also by the age-old concept of hostile gods. It is really useless to attempt to capture the spirit of this method by quoting bits and pieces, for each story is a mosaic; all the pieces are interdependent, and the climax—the culmination—is carefully played for as by an expert angler so that an isolated quotation tends to be little more than an exclamation mark without the preceding exclamation.

The priest dies:

> Death exalted the man to some nobility . . . he exonerated Montcorbier, under oath, and asked that no steps be taken against him. "I forgive him my death," said Sermaise, manly enough at the last, "by reason of certain causes moving him thereunto."

Thus we cannot say, oversimply, that the priest is black and young Villon or Montcorbier is white. Cabell is mimicking life so that there is always this infernal or heavenly, certainly annoying, mixture, this inextricable blend of protean shades from the whole spectrum.

Young de Montcorbier was, till this time, innocent enough.

Yet, though eventually pardoned by law, he is condemned by the neighbors, and then by his stepfather, also a priest, and, finally, by his former betrothed. However, Catherine, before instructing her new and wealthy escort to thrash him, for a moment reveals her genuine but inexpedient love for François. At this turn of events François de Montcorbier decides for the devil, whose existence is obvious, instead of for any God who seems to be noteworthy only by his absence. De Montcorbier becomes François Villon, vagabond and outcast, resident of muck heaps, peddling his genius through the gutters, and "Fate grins and goes on with her weaving." This reference to fate is used as a refrain in the story, repeated periodically and accumulating more and more meaning, a device frequent in Cabell's writing.

Seven years later Villon returns to Catherine de Vaucelles on the eve of her wedding to successful Noel d'Arnaye. He is now wine-sodden, rotten, weak and honeycombed with vice, no longer able to live cleanly—a hog with a voice. Yet Catherine still wants him. He is much tempted, for he badly needs, for his few remaining years, a more comfortable sty. Like Samson he manages one final act of strength—to turn this woman's love to loathing so that she should be safe. He tells her:

"Listen," François said, "Yonder is Paris,—laughing, tragic Paris,

> who once had need of a singer to proclaim her splendour and all her misery. Fate made the man; in necessity's mortar she pounded his soul into the shape Fate needed . . . that he might make the Song of Paris. He could not have made it here in the smug Rue St. Jacques . . . and, in this fashioning, Villon the man was damned in body and soul. And by God! the song was worth it!"

In this brilliant blend of stage management and music Villon gains his end and converts love to loathing; this bald thief, disease wracked, in glory and in shame, titters over his secret between himself and God. Then, once again in the garden of his youth, voluntarily exiled from his offered sanctuary and en route once more for the muck-heap, he prays:

"O Mother of God," the thief prayed, "grant that Noel may be kind to her! Mother of God, grant that she may be happy! Mother of God, grant that I may not live long!"

And straightway he perceived that triple invocation could be, rather neatly, worked out in ballade form. . . . Yes, with a separate prayer to each verse. So, dismissing for the while his misery, he fell to considering, with undried cheeks, what rhymes he needed.

This writing has a power molded primarily from suffering. Suffering has been rewrought with fine craftsmanship to a finished article that contains intricate filigree work on a solid gold basis of experience. Only the unfeeling, inexperienced, or thoughtless could associate this writing merely with "dream escapes." It is, indeed, the stuff of life in the hands of a master weaver.

The High Place is one of Cabell's most pleasant novels. It is set entirely in and around Poictesme and is pervaded by a Spenserian sunbathed atmosphere of easy graciousness and affability. It was published in 1923 and, thus, is a mature work, the next novel after the heights of *Jurgen* and *Figures of Earth*. But between *Figures of Earth* and *The High Place* are studies, memoirs, and a one act play which possibly account for the atmosphere of release and pleasure in *The High Place*, an atmosphere as of one moving thankfully again in his own home. *The High Place* was begun in July, 1922, on a first visit to Mountain Lake, Virginia. The surrounding woods, together with features recalled from Rockbridge Alum Springs, all combined to contribute to the geography of that Poictesme conveniently and aptly located in the south of France.

The hero of *The High Place* is Florian de Puysange, Prince de Lisuarte. He is a "jaunty little person of the very highest fashion, a dapper imp in eternal bottle green and silver," and he too embarks upon a quest. This is a comedy of disenchantment; where Jurgen went through the malice of time Florian merely approaches the grave of a dream. So, once again, Cabell takes one particular aspect of the problem of life as a romanticist sees it and adds another strand to his biographical tapestry. This tapestry has now advanced, with *The High Place*, to the end of the reign of Louis XIV, to 1698; this is not the period of the mistresses but of religion—*the* mistress. The time is well chosen, for *The High Place* involves religious concerns which become remarkably real under this irreligious handling. So young Florian, under his father's now pious guidance, spends his time at the Duke's two chateaux at Storisende and Bellegarde during a few snatched years of peace between Louis and England.

The keynote of this book is that of enjoyment, and it is expressed by the opening lines:

> Probably Florian would never have gone into the Forest of Acaire had he not been told, over and over again, to keep out of it.

The setting is apt:

> Today, with October's temperate sunlight everywhere, the sleek country of Poictesme was inexpressably asleep, wrapped in a mellowing haze. The thronged trees of Acaire, as Florian now saw them just beyond that low red wall, seemed to have golden powder scattered over them, a powder which they stayed too motionless to shake off.

Florian is only ten and Cabell recaptures with a fine whimsical touch the childlike innocence of Florian's attitude as he is smitten by that dream which contains music and becomes a follower of Ettarre or, in this case, of the Princess Melior; thus he is doomed to the life of a romantic as befits a Puysange. In his later life he goes again in search of Melior. As a consequence of certain arrangements with one Janicot, a brown man like the one who revealed all in *Jurgen*, Florian is permitted to return to the high place in the forest and to possess as his wife the Princess Melior. Florian wins his heart's desire, this haunting beauty that was normally the unattainable; in fact, he wins Helen. With the unattainable, Florian returns from the high place to Poictesme and puts his ideal to the test of married life.

The special arrangement with Janicot enables Cabell to exploit to the full his gift for intrigue and situation. Numerous incidents throughout Cabell's writings culminate at points of climax placed within the action like large beads interspersed fittingly among smaller ones, in conversations between two people who know each other for exactly what they are. Exactly what they are is one of the most difficult things to convey convincingly, for they are sophisticated reprobates, wary as foxes yet with an elegance that betokens thought and much fastidiousness as well as ruthlessness of action. The outer velvet conceals the hand of iron which in turn clutches and protects an exquisite rose that is the innermost self's desired way of life. In the mature and revised writings these conversations are for the most part brilliantly managed; rarely do they cloy, though the earlier stories do have moments where the paint wears thin and the diamonds appear paste. *Chivalry*, *Gallantry*, and *The High Place* all have these Cabellian encounters; in these, and in *The Line of Love*, as they stand finally, these encounters forward action and display character magnificently even if they are generally uniform, as they draw from the same minority of Restoration or neo-Restoration nobility. In *The High Place* an example of this intellectual and sophisticated fencing appears in the thirteenth chapter, aptly entitled "Debonnaire." In this, Florian meets with his childhood friend Philippe of Orleans, now the most powerful man in France. The mental swordplay takes place against the opulent background of eighteenth-century Versailles or Fontainebleau. The Virginian captures authentically the spirit of aristocratic Europe—quite as authentically as the New Englander who spent his life there and fashioned *The Ambassadors* and *The Wings of The Dove*. The interview ends in death, minutely calculated death with most peculiar incidental aspects, but all is completed in the most refined manner possible. The only person really to be inconvenienced is the unfortunate Madame de Phalaris, charming, tiny and "as yet amusingly shame-faced about her adulteries," upon whose lap Orleans dies.

A whole host of complex and subtle shades of meaning are captured in such incidents illustrating various aspects of the problem of life. For example, at the mental center of his action in dealing with the newly dead Philippe d'Orleans, Florian reflects on the casual and chancelike elimination of reigning figures which is a longstanding feature of history, so hazy and haphazard seems providence:

> . . . after his usual fashion of fond lingering upon what life afforded of the quaint. . . . He had, with no especial effort or discomfort, with no real straining of his powers, changed the history of all Europe when he transferred this famous kingdom of France and the future of France from the keeping of Philippe to guardians more staid. Probably Monsieur de Bourbon would be the next minister.

Similarly, in his relationship with his wife, Melior the attained unattainable, Florian is further intrigued by these "incidentals." He has learned by experience that "your wives very often astound you by striking the target of your inmost thinking, fair and full with just such seemingly irrational shots of surmise." Such clairvoyance, delivered with "an air of commingled self-satisfaction and shrewdness," leads to moments for Florian "when his wife appears to be looking over his secret thoughts somewhat as one glances over the pages of a not particularly interesting book." He awaits the return of his wife's normal gullibility and charm, remembering her flawless beauty. These extensive details range from the humorously perceptive to the wisely profound, giving substance to the tapestry's main strands.

T. S. Eliot, in "A Note on Culture and Politics" from his *Definition of Culture*, states his three permanent reasons for reading. These are "the acquisition of wisdom, the enjoyment of art, and the pleasure of entertainment." These central dialogues and these incidental touches which are so important, together with the action, guarantee the elements of entertainment, for Cabell is a true teller of tales who knows that he must entertain. He is so much the artist that he has been praised for his art only. Yet there is in Cabell's work that substance essential to all great art, the substance that permits of the acquisition of wisdom. His work is not pedagogic for it is too all-embracing. But by his selection of some ambiguities and his omission of others a recognizable attitude emerges. In *The High Place,* as in all his books, the very theme itself is a statement of his view of life. This quest is more than an elevation of beauty simply for its own sake or, as Pater recommended, for the impressions from beauty which constitute all we ever know of happiness and which, nursed and indulged, may lead to the creation in the mind of the house beautiful.

Pater's recommendations influenced not only the Pre-Raphaelites of the *fin de siècle,* but much novel-writing and art of the twentieth century. Pater's views would appear to be the views which govern the writing of Virginia Woolf and Elizabeth Bowen. And excellent filigree work their writing is. But it lacks the full-blooded sweeping virility of great art. Its preciosity is a valiant, indeed brilliant, attempt to pursue refinement to its essence— but life is not refined and this preciosity produces eventually a limited reality. Pater's approach leads to escape, as W. B. Yeats realized; in exchanging the inner house beautiful for the market place, Yeats achieved his greatest work and came nearest to self-fulfillment. Cabell's work has been closely identified with that of the Pre-Raphaelites and Pater, but there is much more than this to the creator of the Tumblebug. For Cabell's beauty is composed by no means entirely of impressions resulting from the contemplation of trees and clouds and flowers and streams as shadows strive with the sun. These impressions are a part of his work, for he is as much in tune with nature as was Spenser or Shelley; but his conception of beauty does not stop there. And because it does not stop there he cannot be constricted within the limits of the art of the Pateresque tradition. For Cabell's beauty embodies the manifold workings, the eternal machinations, not only of good and evil, but of good-and-evil or beauty-and-ugliness. This was the beauty of *Jurgen.*[2] Pursuit of this beauty

[2] The intellect of Coleridge, who considered that he himself smacked something of Hamlet, has much in common with Cabell's. In his "Table Talk" of December 27, 1831, Coleridge said.

"The old definition of beauty in the Roman school of painting was, *il piu nell' uno*—multitude in unity. . . . such is the principle of beauty . . . observe the instinctive habit which all superior minds have of endeavouring to bring . . . into unity the scattered facts."

which is truth is the intellectual drive behind all Cabell's work. In *The High Place* this all-embracing pursuit of beauty appears, for example, in Florian's duel with his brother, wherein is captured the tragedy that time works upon love and friendship as youth becomes age and the small beloved brother with the ever-dirty face becomes a garrulous stranger who is yet weirdly and movingly familiar. Likewise, the concerns of Jurgen reappear in the thoughts of Florian as he listens to Philippe, Duc d'Orléans, the most powerful man in France. After an autobiographical survey of wine, woman, and song, Philippe concludes:—

> No, my friend . . . there is nothing in life which possession does not discover to be inadequate; we are cursed with a tyrannous need for what life does not afford: and we strive for various prizes, saying "Happiness is there," when in point of fact it is nowhere . . . the man who attains his will cohabits with an assassin, for, having it, he perceives that he does not want it; and desire is dead in him, and the man too is dead.

Avoid greatness, says the Duke, as he considers reaching for the crown.

> So Philippe d'Orleans also, thought Florian, had got what he wanted, only to find it a damnable nuisance. Probably all life was like that.

Cabell's gift for innuendo is very apparent in *The High Place*. It is with this gift that he welds together and transforms his raw material into the complexity of a maze at the center of which are many things, including a rose, a thorn, a bubble, and a pin. The innuendo is an ever-present ingredient, but it becomes predominant in the chapter "Dubieties of the Master." Deep in the forest, Florian talks with Janicot, who is a blend of Pan, Merlin, the Devil, and a leader of the opposition. Suddenly Florian finds that seated beside him is a tumblebug, and his conversation takes a rapid and remarkable change of direction.

> No, Monsieur Janicot, I can consent to hear no more of these sophomoric blasphemies . . . it is better taste to recognise some drastic regeneration may be necessary without doing anything about it, and certainly without aligning ourselves with the foul anarchistic

mocker of everything in our social chaos which is making for beauty and righteousness . . . you combine a vulgar atheism and an iconoclastic desire to befoul the sacred ideas of the average man or woman.

Thus Florian, with the aid of Sesphra of Philistia, speaks on this occasion certainly for the author himself.

And so Florian wends his way through compromise to acquiescence but never actually to surrender; for he is a Puysange and knows—again in a paraphrase of *Beyond Life*—"incommunicably but very surely, that this unapprehended desire ought to be gratified." For the Puysanges have within them the contemplative trait from old Jurgen and the active blood of tall Manuel, not to mention Horvendile's notions about an Author who clothes his intentions with Puysanges as with masks and temporary garments. So Florian persists in his inherent romantic idealism but outwardly he accepts the law of living. This he defines as "Thou shalt not offend against the notions of thy neighbour." It is the old story of the taboos and the taboo breakers.

All moves toward the deliberations between Michael, representative of God and the reigning religion, and Janicot, Prince of this World who has seen so many religions come and go. They deliberate about Florian, who slumbers. Says Janicot:

> He dreams of aspiring and joy and colour and suffering and unreason, and of those quaint taboos which you and he call sin, as being separate things, not seeing how all blends in one vast cup. Nor does he see, as yet, that this blending is very beautiful when properly regarded, and very holy when approached without human self-conceit.

And the faces of Michael and of Janicot, in Florian's half-slumber, merge and blend into that of his father who is gently prodding him awake—this father whom Florian was not to understand for many years yet. And this father advised him to submit, without dreaming, and without demanding too much beauty and holiness, to face the fact that the universe is entirely uncommitted to us one way or the other. To do this is the great lesson which, when mastered, is wisdom. Yet "this always smiling father" of Florian assumes that "there is a Someone who is our neighbour, in His high place, and that I think His notions also should be treated with respect." And in spite of his glib advocacy of the lesson of life, he was "under so many graces, an uneasy and baffled person." Thus, *The High Place* is one more variation of the theme adumbrated in *Beyond Life*.

One of the major figures dominating the twentieth-century literary scene in France is André Malraux. Malraux has approached life as a philosophical man of action. There seems to be considerable affinity between his approach and Cabell's, and this approach is, perhaps, the sanest, most mature and adult approach seen for some time. It is the natural product of eternal man intensified by the extremes of the twentieth century. Malraux himself almost qualifies as a Puysange: the family of Malraux were shipbuilders at Dunkirk for three centuries; his grandfather, "a fierce little man," quarrelled with his local church and for twenty-two years attended Mass kneeling outside the door in storm and sunshine. Malraux has been described as a religious man in search of a religion. In spite of accusations of cheap atheism, this description may be pinned also on the author of *Jurgen*. Like Hemingway, Malraux has gone to scenes of action to see the soul under incendiary as well as spiritual fire looking for "the honour of being a man." In the Biography, this is the quality at which the gods laugh but which they envy as they laugh. In *La Condition Humaine (Man's Fate)*, Mauraux explains his inability to believe. "Certainly there is a higher faith: that proclaimed by all the village crosses. It is love and peace is in it. . . . I will never bow to ask of it the peace to which my weakness beckons me." This is precisely the predicament of Jurgen before the throne of Koshchei's God. As Malraux sees these things, the real defeat is acquiescence, to accept one's place and be shut up like a dog in a kennel, to be reduced to scuttling about like a beetle on a bonfire. All Cabell's writing is the record of this struggle as man elevates his knowledgeable, and therefore doubting, romanticism against the stagnant and the commonplace. For Malraux, man is as great as his defiance. The impulse to defy derives from his desire to attain something beyond and outside himself; this desire and its pursuit provides the release from man's estate. As Cabell has shown, in effect it does more than this. It changes man's estate. For as long as one pursues all that is symbolized by Helen, one will never be "the creature of use and wont, the lackey of prudence and half-measures." Jurgen spoke for all the champions of universal Poictesme when he said:

> Oh, all my life was a foiled quest of you, Queen Helen, and an unsatiated hungering. And for a while I served my vision honoring you with clean-handed deeds. Yes, certainly it should be graved upon my tomb, "Queen Helen ruled this earth while it stayed worthy."

In Jurgen's case "that was very long ago," but in Cabell's case it has been for a lifetime. The Biography itself occupied almost thirty years (1901–29), more than the time that Gibbon was enthralled from his limited conception of October 15, 1764, until, between eleven and twelve o'clock on the night of June 27, 1787, in his garden room in Lausanne, he was both released from slavery, and forced to say goodbye to his lifelong friend *The Decline and Fall*. In Gibbon's case it was the story of a civilization; in Cabell's, of man himself, but the subject is the same.[3] Out of the ashes of Rome rose the Phoenix of Europe; Florian, in this everlasting relay race, takes over from his father and hands on to his son. This son, eventually, became American.

13: *Gallantry* and *The Certain Hour*

> "Drunk as David's sow!" said Pawsey, "and 'im in
> the hactual presence of 'is Sacred Majesty!"
> "In the Second April"

Gallantry contains some of Cabell's finest stories. These stories, quite apart from anything else, make most enjoyable reading.

---

[3] The above was written before gaining access to the Storisende Edition, in the note to Volume 18, of which Cabell writes:

> I now complete my design, of writing the Decline and Fall of the Life of Manuel . . . I may now contratulate my deliverance from a long and laborious service . . . this . . . brief Author's Note was written a bit over a century and a half ago, by one Edward Gibbon.

They are, in fact, first-rate entertainment. But they have, too, their significant place in the Biography. In *Gallantry* the Cabellian saga moves forward to 1750, to the time when George II was permitting "Ormskirk and the Pelhams to govern England, and the Jacobites had not yet ceased to hope for another Stuart Restoration." Of this period and of the Pelhams, G. M. Trevelyan writes, ". . . Henry Pelham and his brother the Duke of Newcastle, the greatest boroughmonger England ever produced. They may be said to have reverted to the traditions of Walpole, in an age when these traditions were ceasing to be enough." Their rule extended from about 1748 to 1756. Dr. Johnson's *Rasselas, Prince of Abyssinia*, which expresses exactly one aspect of Jurgen, was to appear in 1759. Thus the choice of these years for the period of *Gallantry* is another illustration of Cabell's care for detail. For, while it was still an age of Walpole, an age, as Cabell describes it, "of Parasitism," Walpole's traditions were no longer enough. So there existed precisely that clash between ideals and reality which forms the inner drama of the Biography. In all probability Cabell's choice of this period was carefully calculated and included some such considerations, but it may well have been partly instinctive, for he is very much at home in the age which seems to have supplied the style for his own Dumbarton Grange, Virginia.

The stories comprising *Gallantry* were first published in 1907, but some were written much earlier. The earliest, "The Ducal Audience," was written in 1901 and appeared in *The Smart Set* in March, 1903; the second story, "Love at Martinmas" appeared in the same magazine in August, 1902, but was also written in 1901. "Heart of Gold," written in November, 1902, was first published in *The Smart Set*, in February, 1903. "Simon's Hour," the first story and one of the best, appeared in *Ainslee's Magazine* in April, 1905. "In the Second April" is also one of Cabell's best and this was printed in *Harper's Monthly* in 1907; it stands as the seventh in *Gallantry* and is closely associated with the sixth, "April's Message."

I. R. Russell has stated, "In this book Mr. Cabell first discovered that Dreamland known as Poictesme."[1] The revised version is full of the perpetuated spirit and concerns of Manuel and Jurgen; the geographical background ranges from England and France to the even more tangible and recognizable Poictesme and Noumaria. The scenes change naturally and easily and with a clear ring of the bell of enchantment. For example, from "In the Second April":

> . . . the great Duke of Ormskirk is now going to pay his respects to George Guelph, King of Britain, France and Ireland, defender of the faith, Duke of Brunswick and Lunenburg, and supreme head of the Anglican and Hibernian Church. And tomorrow Mr. John Bulmer will set forth upon a little journey into Poictesme. . . .
>
> Thus it came about that, five days later, arrived at Bellegarde (from Dover), Mr. John Bulmer, kinsman and accredited emissary of the great Duke of Ormskirk.

Nevertheless, Poictesme is not the dominant setting by any means. It is always there in the background and it is often the foreground, but *Gallantry* is not primarily about Poictesme.

The stories have been very carefully revised—there is as much difference between *The Eagle's Shadow* (1904) and *Straws and Prayer Books* (1924) as between *The Two Gentlemen of Verona* and *The Tempest*. Yet the child is father to the man, and the title of *Gallantry* is itself an epitome of all the outward actions even of the maturest of Cabell's heroes or champions. These stories show how Cabell converts into more secular form the theories put forward in *Beyond Life*, the more etherialized versions of which appears in such works as *Chivalry*.

The revised version of 1922 has a valuable introduction by Louis Untermeyer, one of Cabell's most understanding critics. He allows no prevarication at all about the visionary and romantic nature of Cabell's inspiration, and the result, as totaled by Untermeyer, is definitely positive. Yet Untermeyer has no illusions about these victories in Cabell's books, victories which

[1] I. R. Russell, *Revised Bibliography* (Philadelphia, The Centaur Bookshop, 1932).

might so easily be mistaken for defeats. And he notes the outstanding quality which, in itself, belies the self-affirmed weariness and boredom of many of Cabell's gallant worldlings, from Ormskirk to Florian. "Even this *Gallantry*, the most candidly superficial of Cabell's works, is alive with a vigor of imagination and irony."

The quotation preceding the *Gallantry* of 1922 is:

> Half in masquerade, playing the drawing-room or garden comedy of life, these persons have upon them, not less than the landscape among the accidents of which they group themselves with fittingness, a certain light that we should seek for in vain upon anything real.

This sentence from Pater's works has much significance, which has been well expressed by Untermeyer, who notes:

> . . . how subtly this volume takes its peculiar place in its author's record of struggling dreams, how, beneath a surface covered with political finery and sentimental bric-a-brac, the quest goes on, stubbornly and often stupidly, in a forgotten world made suddenly animate and as real as our own.

It would not do to leave Untermeyer's introduction without mention of its conclusion:

> . . . Cabell is not as much a masquerader as he imagines himself. . . . None but the poet, shaken with the strength of his vision, could cry today "It is only by preserving faith in human dreams that we may, after all, perhaps some day make them come true." Poetic consciousness is the key to the complex and half-concealed art of James Branch Cabell.

Untermeyer justifies his connection between the prophet and the artist by joining Cabell's professed desire "to write perfectly of beautiful happenings" to a reminder that "poetry, to which all literature aspires . . . is . . . the image of perfection, the light of disembodied beauty toward which creation gropes." "Prophet" is not quite the right word, perhaps, for Cabell does not wave flags, and his sword and lance are more often directed at other targets; perhaps, after eliminating its synonymous meanings, "seer" would be better, in the sense of "one who sees"—at least, a little further than the tumblebug, and at most, to the pattern glimpsed by such as Einstein, the Oriental mystics, or the poet of *Murder in the Cathedral* and *The Cocktail Party*. The vision behind Cabell's endeavors, together with his sense of external beauty as seen in his appreciation of natural, artificial, and womanly form and design, do indeed indicate the poet. Yet the poetic drive within the artist must be compounded equally of feeling and thought, of heart and head. In the long run, Cabell appears to emerge as an intellectual with a fundamental streak of poetry rather than as a thoughtful poet. During the earliest years, the scales tipped in favor of the emotions, of poetry diminished in stature by sentiment; in the middle years, the scales were just about even (there are undiluted passages of verse, in recognizable hexameters, absorbed into the form of, for example, *Figures of Earth*); later, during those years when many of Cabell's characters insisted that they themselves were "retired poets," the intellect tended to predominate, although Cabell's work owes its stature to the lasting retention of the fundamental poetic streak.

In his "Epistle Dedicatory," again to Mrs. Grundy, Cabell defines the nature of his gallant. He must accept life's pleasures leisurely and its inconveniences with a shrug; sin and sin again, yet honestly repent on each occasion and "he will consider the world with a smile of toleration, and his own doings with a smile of amusement, and Heaven with a smile that is not distrustful." With a quotation from Thackeray, (with whose attitude in *Vanity Fair* Cabell has much sympathy), Cabell proves the rightness of his refusal to deal in white heroes and black villains to clear-cut cheers and hisses. Thackeray, for some reason, had been unable to find, in "that dreadfully selfish time," anybody living irreproachably. In addition, Cabell states his intention to present his comedies of gallantry according to the correct conventions— that is, by dialogue and yet more dialogue, with intrigue and intricate plots involving rapid "ferric and verbal" cut and thrust, with the briefest of stage directions. To *these* conventions he conforms with pleasure.

The stories are presented as acts of a drama, and are complete with prologues, spoken often by the leading actress on behalf of the author, in accordance with the traditions of eighteenth-century drama as they were molded by Dryden and the Restoration dramatists. The subterfuge is perfectly executed. Because the spirit of the Biography permeates the talk and action and gives them deeper meanings, the dialogue rarely descends to the merely clever; thus a chief danger when recreating the artificially brilliant is overcome. These stories are much more than swash and buckle. An examination of the two stories "Simon's Hour" and "In the Second April" may illustrate this. "Simon's Hour" is the first story; it sets the tone of the book in much the same emphatic way that the story of "The Sestina" does in *Chivalry*. The dramatis personae are "Lord Rokesle, a loose-living impoverished nobleman, and loves Lady Allenby; Simon Orts, Vicar of Heriz Magna, a debauched fellow, and Rokesle's creature; Punshon, servant to Rokesle; Lady Allenby, a pleasure-loving, luxurious woman, a widow, and rich." The scene is the Mancini Chamber at Stornoway Crag, Usk, and the time March, 1750. Lady Allenby, who appears in several of these stories, is a slightly more powerful, if rather less subtly brilliant, reincarnation of Congreve's Millamant.

> She was tall for a woman. Her hair, tonight unpowdered, had the color of amber and something, too, of its glow; her eyes, though not profound, were large and in hue varied, as the light fell or her emotions shifted, through a wide gamut of blue shades. But it was her mouth you remembered.

To such a person, appears Simon Orts, clergyman. Simon Orts is akin to Villon; his relationship to Lady Allenby is that of a former lover, dispensed with in face of greater wealth. As a natural consequence, he went to the dogs. This is a situation so recurrent in Cabell's writing as to suggest a biographical significance, a connection as between "the dark lady" of the sonnets, and Beatrice, Cleopatra, and Cressida. This may be impure fancy; nevertheless, such a situation featuring a "good-for-nothing jilt" is frequently the heart of the most powerfully felt of Cabell's writing. Lady

Allenby has much of that womanly ingenuousness which destroyed Marlowe's draft of "Hero and Leander" in the short story "Porcelain Cups," which equates so effectively man's ruthless imagination with woman's ruthless cunning. Lady Allenby is now, many years later, the guest of Simon's master, Lord Rokesle, in this isolated "sea-washed scrap of earth." Thus the ingredients, barely stated, are of blood and thunder. The dialogue soon makes them more than that as Orts observes of the reason of his late visit:

> The Cloth is at any rascal's beck and call. Old Holles, my Lord's man, is dying up yonder, and the whim seized him to have a clergyman in. God knows why, for it appears to me that one knave might very easily make his way to hell without another knave to help him.

Of what like is this man of God?

> A small, slim anxious man . . . always fidgeting, always placating some one, but never without a covert sneer. The fellow was venomous; his eyes only were honest, for even while his lips were about their wheedling, these eyes flashed malice at you.

The dialogue is nervous, with the flashing incisiveness of forked lightning as it illumines this sombre scene at Stornoway Crag. The atmosphere is of the suppressed and smoldering defiance of a worm turning as Simon rises to his hour.

The point of chief significance here, perhaps, is that Cabell stakes all on the appeal of a clash between ideals and self-seeking. Admittedly, the action and plot are skillfully designed and conveyed; the characterization is excellent and well individualized. Yet the story stands or falls on the underlying significance of the central situation, which is that of an ageing down-and-out once more rising to the demands of his youth, the lackey of use and wont against the taskmaster of his mature lifetime. Simon Orts does this for the jilt who initiated his decline and who, he knows, is still inherently worthless. Thus, again these strange compelling forces that contend everlastingly within the minds of men reappear in the trappings of gallantry even as they stirred Manuel, Jurgen, Osmund Heleigh, and Florian as we move steadily forward through the centuries.

There are sundry very important touches that make the main theme solid and substantial. The Vicar regains a measure of grace even as did Samson, by one final burst of strength that succeeds because the preceding mental victory has already guaranteed that strength.

> "You are a dead man, Vincent Floyer, for the powers of good and the powers of evil alike contend against you. . . .
>
> Great ends may be attained by petty instruments, my Lord; a filthy turtle quenched the genius of Aeschylus, and they were only common soldiers who shed the blood that redeemed the world."

Simon, possessed again by a vision, becomes again a man. This is the pragmatic basis of Cabell's thought.

Another feature echoes the theme dealt with at novel length in *The Cream of The Jest*, a theme hinted throughout the Cabellian cycle of men and women. The Lady Allenby is portrayed, finally, as little more than a beautiful slut.

> . . . You are a widow, rich; as women go, you are not so unpleasant to look at as most of 'em. If it became a clergyman to dwell upon such matters, I would say that your fleshly habitation is too fine for its tenant, since I know you to be a good-for-nothing jilt. However, you are God's handiwork, and doubtless He had His reasons for constructing you.

Simon, in fact, still loves this woman even as Jurgen was still stirred by the amateur professional that was the Countess Dorothy in the final "moment that did not count." Yet Simon does not fulfill his hour primarily on her behalf—she is only the incidental means by which he returns to himself:

> "The woman's right, my Lord. There is such a thing as manhood, Manhood!" Simon Orts repeated, with a sort of wonder; "why, I might have boasted it once. Then came this cuddling bitch to trick me into a fool's paradise. . . . Oh, I am indeed beholden to you two! to her for making me a sot, and to you for making me a lackey. But I will save her from you, Vincent Floyer. Not for her sake"—Orts looked down upon the prostrate woman and snarled. "Christ, no! But I'll do it for the sake of the boy I have been, since I owe that

boy some reparation. I have ruined his nimble body, I have dulled the wits he gloried in, I have made his name a foul thing that honesty spits out of her mouth; but if God yet reigns in heaven, I cleanse that name tonight!"

As witness Spenser, Milton, Donne, and Smollett among many, the overwhelming desire for beauty can react against ugliness with the bite, snap, and snarl that is the defense of the sensitive as well as the attack of the unfeeling. Self-respect (Milton's "self-regard") is only vanity legalized, or vanity is only self-respect gone wrong. So Simon regains his self-respect. And by elevating one kind of conduct at the expense of another kind, Cabell is committing himself to the exaltation of right against wrong, even if, in the process, he conveys their ambiguities. This is presumably why Louis Untermeyer observed that "Cabell is not such a masquerader as he imagines himself to be."

When Simon tells the Lady Allenby how to leave Stornoway, he recommends that, disguised as himself, she stagger.

"Punshon will expect something of the sort and he will not trouble you, for he knows that when I am fuddled I am quarrelsome. 'Tis a diverting world, Anastasia, wherein . . . habitual drunkenness and an unbridled temper may sometimes prove commendable,—as they do tonight, when they aid persecuted innocence!" Here Simon Orts gave an unpleasant laugh.

So Simon, "This way and that dividing his swift mind," acts out the contradiction between his ideals and his awareness of things as they are. But although the woman is incidental to the redemption of Simon, their relationship renders this redemption yet more substantial. For to what is she escaping? Merely to her flatterers, her gossip and her cards. And yet both have the feeling that her betrayal of Simon when they were young was the turning point, the consequences of which steadily converted possible paradise into certain hell. And this, too, is a constant feature of Cabell's attitude toward the relations between men and women: and being so it is a moral attitude, for it implies the belief not only that the sins of the fathers are visited upon the children but that "it has been given to us to distinguish between right and wrong" and that we gain or lose in accordance with our ability to live life logically and according to conscience. This attitude appears in many of Cabell's stories, including "Simon's Hour"; it is the heart of the novel *The Cream of The Jest.* As late as in *Special Delivery* (A packet of replies, 1933), there is an autobiographical "letter" to a former object of love which states that had they really made a common effort to be what they ought to be things would have been different—reducing the law of happiness to will and logic. This is expressed not as a statement but as a feeling aided and abetted by clear moments punctuating obscure years. In "Simon's Hour" this attitude is expressed in the final words between Simon and the woman who had molded his life by an act of youth.

" . . . I think that I rather hate you than otherwise, for you remind me of things I would willingly forget. But, Simon, I wish we had gone to live in that little cottage we planned, and quarrelled over, and never built! I think we would have been happy." . . .

"Yes," said he, "we would have been happy. I would have been by this a man doing a man's work in the world, and you a matron, grizzling, perhaps, but rich in content, and in love opulent. . . .

Is this attitude constructive or merely sentimental? Robert Browning has expressed it exactly in his short poem "Youth and Art":

It once might have been, once only . . .

Each life's unfulfilled, you see;
It hangs still, patchy and scrappy.
We have not sighed deep, laughed free,
Starved, feasted, despaired,—been happy. . . .

This could have but happened once,
And we missed it, lost it for ever.

Browning, a born fighter who lived his art to the full, put this attitude to the test when he took Elizabeth Barrett to Italy and, by the power of his spirit, renewed her life, making it, according to *Sonnets to the Portuguese,* "rich in content, and in love opulent." It is an attitude that is full of feeling but much more than sentimental.

At least one other feature in "Simon's Hour" deserves mention. This concerns the relationship between Simon and his master, Lord Rokesle. Manifestly they hate each other; certainly on Simon's part, contemptuously on the part of Rokesle. Yet there is something more. This something embodies a bond or link which, in spite of all the misery and degradation experienced by Simon, still represents a kind of subterranean love by Rokesle for this man who is the devil's protégé. It takes the form of a grudging admiration which obliges Rokesle to cross words with Simon as, for the first time in his life, equal to equal. The closing scene of the story testifies to this feeling, a feeling which is constantly reproduced between Calbell's fictitious "enemies" even when they kill. As this strange force winds its ambivalent way in and out of human relationships in life, so in the Biography it underlies the surface actions. Even when these actions are the voice of a malignant destiny the bond is still felt. Sometimes the bond itself becomes the voice of destiny as in "The Certain Hour"; the outcome is then much happier.

This double relationship, which leads to so many duels, is seen at its best, perhaps, in the affair of John Bulmer, Duke of Ormskirk, in "In the Second April." John Bulmer, in many ways, is one of Cabell's best figures. He seems to have the author's special fondness.[2] He is a likeable but shrewder and more capable Falstaff with the bombast restrained for greater inner enjoyment of the pageant before him. He is successful and skilled in the cunning ways of intrigue and diplomacy. A lover of good food, good wines and interesting women, he can yet yield to romantic impulses which, in their consequences, restore his youth. Although he finds that the temptation to be picturesque is almost irresistible, he is the most worldly of realists. When he ventures forth to save his damsel in distress and is stabbed in the back by a treacherous bystander, he does not sink to the ground bewailing his lapse into naïveté. Underneath, he has a shirt of Milanese armour. This is against the rules but, more often than not, so is success, and John

[2] In the note to Volume 9 of the Storisende Edition, Cabell "confesses" to "a real liking for Ormskirk."

Bulmer continues to enjoy his escapade as a knight of honor protected by his belief that "sincerity is a devilishly expensive virtue."

Ormskirk has an easy grace that makes him at home in rogues' company; the Duke of Puysange, descendant of Florian, is an old enemy of his. He is also ambassador for France and was present at the signing of the second Treaty of Dover which, according to Cabell's version,[3] ended the Stuart hope of further French aid, gave England peace at home, and in India, simplified matters, if only for a while, for Dupleix. The dialogue between Jean de Puysange and Ormskirk clearly displays Cabell's ability to sustain wit and yet advance action. For Ormskirk requires a wife and wishes De Puysange to select one from the first families of France. As De Puysange observes, ". . . warfare being now at an end, it is only natural that you should resort to matrimony."

But John Bulmer is more than a lightly drawn figure of fun. He is to attend a ball at which will be the King, "a tipsy, ignorant old German debauchee," who will make "fat-witted jests at which Ormskirk would apishly grin and applaud." And the Duke of Ormskirk, "splendid in black-and-gold," pauses, alone in his dwelling, to ponder his mood of "curious lassitude, this indefinite vexation." He soliloquizes:

> The real tragedy of life is to learn that it is not really tragic. To learn that the world is gross, that it lacks nobility, that to considerate persons it must be in effect quite unimportant,—here are commonplaces, sweepings from the tub of the immaturest cynic. But to learn that you yourself were thoughtfully constructed in harmony with the world you were to live in . . .—eh, this is an athletic blow to human vanity.

Yet, in spite of an advancing belly and a receding hairline, the daily round and common task must go on even if the end is no more than that of tumbling tumbleweed. Nursing this ever-cooling heart, bridges must be built, wars fought, Empires won and lost,

---

[3] Although artistically thè point is irrelevant, Dupleix was in India at this time, the Treaty of Aix-la-Chapelle was made in 1668, and the Treaty of Dover (including Charles' unofficial arrangement which made him a pensioner of Louis XIV) was made in 1670—some eighty years too soon for this story.

the kettle boiled and lawns weeded. John Bulmer is to be married.

> De Puysange has had it in mind for some six months, I think. . . .
> Yesterday he knew from the start that I was leading up to a proposal
> for his sister,—and yet there we sat, two solemn fools, and played
> our tedious comedy to a finish. *Eh bien!* as he says, it is necessary
> to keep one's hand in.

So much for the debit side. However, according to De Puysange, this sister is "Beautiful as an angel, and headstrong as a devil." In the list of dramatis personae she is "a woman of beauty and resolution, of a literal humor." The Duke of Ormskirk suddenly recalls how he would have reacted in days gone by—and he decides for one more bout of knight-errantry rather as a more active equivalent of a letter to the *Times*. So, later in the evening, in a manner not altogether approved of by his vallet Pawsey, he informs his king that he is for a little journey into Poictesme.

Thus it is that, blithely enough in spite of a corpulent forty-five, the Duke of Ormskirk, *incognito* as his own emissary John Bulmer, arrives at Bellegarde-en-Poictesme, where the grass is always green and the sun upon the leaves. Here are truly amazing happenings including sword fights in forest glades, maidens in distress, and cunning wit-fights between the friendliest of ruthless enemies as John Bulmer, to his own astonishment, falls genuinely in love in this second April. Cabell both has his cake and eats it as he retains the naïve romantic framework of events and upon this builds the substance of his insight. For the expected is spun dramatically into the unexpected; characters reveal new facets and depths in this dance of dervishes upon which John Bulmer has embarked as the sensible and ageing elements within him combat with the revitalized "sparks and smalle-flamings." And always he "considers . . . Heaven with a smile that is not distrustful." His relationship with Heaven is one of Cabell's clearest fictional versions of his theory in *Beyond Life*. It is expressed when Bulmer meets his appointed wife and, of all things one might say, falls in love at first sight. How does Cabell take this difficult artistic hurdle? The great Duke of Ormskirk

. . . was puzzled. For there had come to him, unheralded and simply, a sense of something infinitely greater than his mind could conceive; and analysis could only pluck at it, impotently, as a wearied swimmer might pluck at the sides of a well. Ormskirk and Ormskirk's powers now somehow dwindled . . . and even the woman who stood before him; trifles these: and his contentment spurned the stars to know that somehow, this woman and he were but a part, an infinitesimal part, of a scheme which was ineffably vast and perfect.

This unheroic hero continues with the dance, with a mocking demon inside him who twists his tongue into jest when he is most serious, and who, at least in this and probably in more, echoes the author, who diverts his reader's attention with a false prosaic footnote neatly misplaced at the center of a dramatic climax— this hero who plays at life, forever posing as if for a portrait. Until he is jerked at last into sincerity and "In the Second April" becomes a moving episode from what is presented as a tragic farce, a predicament called life. John Bulmer, who had "always bungled this affair of living," comes once again to himself and to grace. For once again he obeys his inner god, echoing Tennyson's "Cursed be the social lies that warp us from the living truth!" Truth is beauty and by his presentation of such deeds in such a way even Cabell can be accused of aiding and abetting that good which is recognizable, in fact, of persistently exalting that good in all his writings. That he does full justice to associated uncertainties only makes for greater interest and verisimilitude. But at the center is always the exaltation of an idea; the idea governs action for and against it, in proportion to the characters' possession or loss of this living truth.

So these stories reveal Cabell's lifelong interest in these lifelike matters. John Bulmer is another outstanding example of the application of the author's theories of art and life, theories stated, for example, in the chapter "The Contemporary," in *Beyond Life*. This sums up, precisely, the conception embodied in and illustrated by the behavior of the Duke of Ormskirk. Cabell maintains that art should deal with humanity:

... and about the strivings of that ape reft of his tail ... (who) feels himself a symbol, and the frail representative of Omnipotence in a place that is not home ... ready to give all, and to die fighting, for the sake of that undemonstrable idea.

Thus saith the romanticist drawing his conclusions not only from the bricks and mortar but from the designing board in the inner office itself.

"In The Second April" ends in a welter of violent action, a violence made all the more effective because it is coldly calculated and impartially expressed. This detachment and understatement make the cruelty in man strike home all the more:

> He kicked the steward in the face two or three times, and Guiton, his countenance all blood, black in the moonlight, embraced the brigand's knees and wept. Presently (Achille) Cazaio slowly drove his sword into the back of the prostrate man, who shrieked, "O Jesu!" and began to cough and choke. Five times Cazaio spitted the writhing thing, and afterward was Guiton's soul released from the tortured body . . . . Then John Bulmer leaned upon the parapet of the Constable's Tower and called aloud, "Friend Achille, your conduct disappoints me."

That the reputation for this sort of thing went to such as Hemingway is presumably because writers like Hemingway deal in contemporary settings and with colloquial dialogue. Hemingway, like Yeats, uses violence to an artistic end but to no greater extent than does Cabell, who captures by it all the monolithic and heartrending cruelty of a universe which so easily seemed indifferent. It is in the face of this indifferent universe, and with the nagging knowledge that he may mean nothing, that the Duke of Ormskirk, like all Cabell's heroes, postures. He does it so magnificently that the happy ending is inevitable in this first-rate comedy of gallantry.

So it is that the negative and contradictory aspects of life are treated logically and made things of beauty and truth as they are threaded together on a cord of affirmation which is at least hypothetically positive. The author weds his romantic vision to his realistic reading and the resulting blend, as complicated as life, fulfills T. S. Eliot's requirements to the full. For this reading is nothing if not entertaining; unlike much by his contemporaries it is always well wrought. In spite of the author's despondent doubts and jesting denials, the vision that is the mainspring of the reading and its rendering aids in the acquisition of wisdom. Therefore—dare it be said of the author of *Jurgen?*—it is edifying in the best possible sense, for wisdom reveals more about the life around us; this life being what it is, such a revelation should always be conducive to an appropriate awe, particularly among guardians of public morals.

"Lord, what a deal of ruined life it takes to make a little art!" This observation, made by a re-creation of Shakespeare in "Judith's Creed," may stand as the hallmark of *The Certain Hour*. This contains, again, the neat number of ten stories, published in 1916. "Olivia's Pottage," the earliest and written in 1907, was accepted by *Harper's Monthly* in October, 1907; "The Lady of All Our Dreams" appeared as "The Dream" in the *Argonaut* in November, 1912; and "The Irresistible Ogle" in *McBride's* in October, 1915. "A Brown Woman" and "Balthazar's Daughter" were written in 1912, the latter appearing in *The Smart Set* in 1913. Thus, although not revised later, they were some of the latest to appear in the magazines. In these stories Cabell uses a number of genuine historical figures and re-creates them as examples of his undying "artist." These figures include Shakespeare in "Judith's Creed," Robert Herrick in "Concerning Corinna," William Wycherley in "Olivia's Pottage," Pope in "A Brown Woman," and Sheridan in "The Irresistible Ogle." Some resistance may be felt to having one's conception of these figures dictated in fiction like this. But, in the main, these stories succeed, certainly in demonstrating Cabell's view of the connection between life and art. And this is perhaps the chief value, here, of *The Certain Hour*, that it shows quite clearly that Cabell is an author who, whatever he says or does, does not regard art merely as an escape.

The Certain Hour is preceded by a lengthy "Auctorial Induction" in five sections. The first of these establishes the object of the book and the remainder deal with the literary state of modern America. This book deals with "the struggle of a special temperament with a fixed force." The special temperament is that which "desires to write perfectly of beautiful happenings" and the stories show how these special temperaments respond to the challenge of a certain hour, an hour wherein these artists must put their values to the living test. Of the numerous preliminary poems and quotations, the following is not least in importance:

> These questions, so long as they remain with the Muses, may very well be unaccompanied with severity, for where there is no other end of contemplation and inquiry but that of pastime alone, the understanding is not oppressed; but after the Muses have given over their riddles to Sphinx,—that is, to practice, which urges and impels to action, choice and determination—then it is that they become torturing, severe and trying.

The above quotation is at the beginning of the book: the last story concerns the notorious John Charteris, who "accepted defeat and compromised half-heartedly with commercialism." When such a passage as the above is linked, not merely with those qualities exalted in *Chivalry* and *Gallantry* but with the chapter "Sundry Devices of the Philistines" in *Jurgen*, it seems clear enough where Cabell's sympathies rest and that, in his case, the Charteris that is in every man was kept fairly well under artistic control.

In "Judith's Creed," the creed is responsible for the sunnier outlook that reappears in the final plays. Shakespeare, in midst of writing *The Tempest*, observes:

> I never knew a wicked person. . . . Undoubtedly short-sighted people exist who have floundered into ill-doing; but it proves always to have been on account of either cowardice or folly, and never because of malevolence; and, in consequence, their sorry pickle should demand commiseration far more loudly than our blame.

This forecasts the final conclusion about the tumblebugs in *Jurgen*. It is this conception within Cabell himself that appears to justify his view that art is not a branch of pedagogy—there is no such thing as intentional wickedness, only shortsightedness penalizing clearsightedness. Thus, spite, for instance, is only the outward expression of the inner discontent consequent upon lack of fulfillment. The artist is less spiteful or wicked, as a rule, because more fulfilled or, at least, more occupied by this desire to write perfectly of beautiful happenings. In his induction to the book, Cabell writes:

> For a man of genuine literary genius . . . possesses a temperament whose susceptibilities are of wider area than those of any other.[4]

And that it is the artist who of all people reflects his times not only in his writings but *in his personality.* As final evidence of Cabell's connection of art to life he writes of this inborn desire:

> To disregard this vital longing, and flatly to stifle this innate striving toward artistic creation, is to become (as with Wycherley and Sheridan) a man who waives, however laughingly, his sole apology for existence.

This particular will o' the wisp is best pursued in what, for any critical appraisement, is the dangerous quagmire of *Straws and Prayer Books.* However, this induction deals, already in 1916, with Cabell's approach to this urge to write perfectly of beautiful happenings. It is this urge, then, that we should accept as Cabell's definition of his impulse to create.

He extends this definition with another statement:

> Literature is made up of the re-readable books. . . . Therefore, in literature a book's subject is of astonishingly minor importance, and the style nearly everything.

It is always advisable to listen to what a writer says about his art and also, on occasion, to believe him. This applies even to Cabell, who delights in saying usually the opposite of what he means. But how is *this* statement to be understood? As H. L. Mencken understood it, when, in his introduction to *The Line of Love,*

---

[4] Compare Wordsworth's definition of a poet, in the Preface to the *Lyrical Ballads,* beginning: "He is a man speaking to men . . . endowed with a more lively sensibility, more enthusiasm and tenderness, who has a greater knowledge of human nature . . . ."

he concluded, "Content, with him, is always secondary"? It is submitted that this statement must be interpreted in the light of the remaining context. This context deals with the habit of contemporary writers of dealing with so-called "vital" themes such as feminism, corrupt politics, or white slavery, in other words themes which appeal not to thought but to prejudices. Cabell makes a very good case for the temporary appeal of such themes. He quotes Gautier's "Tout passe—L'art robust seul a l'éternité." And what constitutes this art? When Cabell observes that "a book's subject is of astonishingly minor importance," he would appear to mean that it need not be contemporary or "vital," that truth can be captured in the action of any people at any time. The literary status of any writer must ultimately depend on his ability to speak to all ages; this means that he must deal not with today's headlines but with those things which, even if they change in form, are unchanging in their nature.

> Some few there must be in every age and every land of whom life claims nothing very insistently save that they write perfectly of beautiful happenings.

Before writing perfectly it is necessary first to choose the happenings. This choice necessitates not a haphazard selection but a selection based on some principle or order, governed by logic or feeling or both; in other words upon some philosophy or vision of life which is, for the selector, truth. Conversely, by an analysis of these happenings which a writer has selected, can be elicited the vision or philosophy which prompted the selection.

Cabell's truth consists partly of happenings which illustrate the attitude that nothing is good or bad but thinking makes it so. At the same time, these happenings serve his vision, as summed up in the conclusion to *Beyond Life*, which implies that some thinking is good and some bad, that is, some is constructive and some destructive. That Cabell's vision or philosophy is not easily ascertained partly explains his long neglect and misplaced notoriety. As he himself notes, "In our present flood of books, as in any other flood, it is the froth and scum which shows most promi-

nently." A concern for style is an integral part of a good craftsman's approach to his work; the satisfaction that this brings is
the reward for labor—just as, in Cabell's mythology, the Author
should be pleased when he finds he has produced a good artist.
But a home is built to be lived in, not merely looked upon, and it
is by the measure of the life in his writing that the artist himself
is to be measured. *The Certain Hour* provides abundant evidence
to support the contention that Cabell's art is not simply fine words
pleasantly arrayed but that it is compounded of the tears and
laughter of hard and bitterly won experience ground in the mill
of suffering and checked against intensive thought.

14: *Something About Eve*

> *But he who takes refuge*
> *Within me only*
> *Shall pass beyond Maya*
> *He and no other.*
> —Bhagavad-Gita

Cabell's wide-ranging mind has embodied much from the Hindu
attitude and thought. In fact, his works seem quite clearly to illustrate the whole sequence of development of the person who goes
as far as it is possible to go on this earth, at least in the west. For
example, in the Bhagavad-Gita there is the following:

> ... there are four kinds of men who worship me: the world-weary,
> the seeker for knowledge, the seeker for happiness and the man of
> spiritual discrimination.

> *Certainly all these are noble:*
> *But the man of discrimination*
> *I see as my very Self.*[1]

One of the conceptions fundamental to Hindu religion is that if
the spiritual discrimination is sufficiently purified on earth, then
that person's spirit will remain united with the overall greater self

[1] Bhagavad-Gita.

and not have to be reborn to undergo again the process of struggle and purification. Manuel, it may be recalled, in *Figures of Earth*, found himself again at the Pool of Haranton where he had started. Ghandi often expressed the hope that he would not be reborn, although, paradoxically enough, he did not read the Bhagavad-Gita until he was a student in London.

Cabell's works smack, at first, very much of the world-weary, superficially in *The Cords of Vanity* and *The Eagle's Shadow* but more significantly when featuring those bored gallants of the Restoration. In many of his short stories during the years 1900–10 we meet heroes enwrapped in the world-weary pose, from John Bulmer and his compatriot Gaston de Puysange, to the even more polished later example in *The High Place* (1923), Philippe of Orleans, "whom people called Philippe the Debonnaire," and whose words of greeting to Florian were:

> "So!" said the minister, when they had embraced, "so, they tell me you have married again, and that you killed your brother this morning. I am not pleased with you, Florian."

Yet, already, Cabell's gallants possess abundant complexity and curiosity; in *The Cream of the Jest* and *Jurgen* the gallant heroes are very much in search of knowledge, Felix Kennaston journeying back in search of himself, and Jurgen experimenting with all aspects of knowledge in search of justice. Manuel, in his comedy of appearances, pursues happiness but attempts to find it externally, in action and material wealth. Now with *Something About Eve*, in Gerald Musgrave we meet with the man of spiritual discrimination. He is intent on going directly to Antan and spiritual fulfillment. Cabell's imagination spans both the East and the West in such a way as to reveal the latter by the former and even for the most exacting logicians and social scientists. He does this by remaking and juxtaposing those recollected experiences which, in their initial forms, constituted a revelation of a total pattern of inter-relations. As Cabell observes in the author's note to *Gallantry*, when telling of how Horvendile (who controls the life that originated in Manuel) emerged from Francis Vanringham:

Nor does it matter that I may not understand the origin of the long drama of the life of Manuel, nor who guides it to what end. . . . For it is so with my own life, and with the life of every person who is not too utterly an addict of the drug called use and wont. It is so with all human life, which everywhere is bound in by transient superficies behind which moves perceptibly the unseen and the inapprehensible.

Thus here—against the entire trend of his time—the Virginian succeeds in seeing synthesis even in this most complicated and entangled age of analysis. And this sense is a religious one. It is universal in its philosophical embodiments, but by finding in the total scheme a Neoplatonic place for woman, it becomes essentially Christian, a fact which befits peoples who are in the main active rather than contemplative.

Something About Eve is thus one of Cabell's most substantial works. It combines the episodic complexity of *Jurgen* and *The Silver Stallion* with the chronological unity and simplicity of *Figures of Earth*. Everything is here: the constructional care and use of drama, the establishment of that primordiality which illustrates the spiritual principles of all life, the irony, the color, the warmth of feeling, and the chill of thought. There is even sex. *Something About Eve* may well illustrate the farthest reach of Cabell's flight into outer space, the farthest revelation of his imaginative searchlight into the darkness. Perhaps this explains, at least in part, his observation in the author's note written in September, 1928:

> Yet one discovers, in looking over the hundreds of reviews accorded to "Something About Eve," a fact which seems mildly disconcerting . . . that no reviewer, and so far as I know, not any reader, evinced the least glimmering of perception as to what was the book's theme and object.

This is, perhaps, an inevitable penalty of achieving a spiritual synthesis in an age of intellectual analysis. Also, Cabell observes that "to the immature minded any reference to sexual matters is impressive beyond its rational weight."

Something About Eve was begun before 1923 but refused to take satisfactory shape. Consequently the manuscript was burned in the spring of 1925 and Cabell—after "regrounding" himself, be it remembered, in *Straws and Prayer Books*—turned to create *The Silver Stallion* and *The Music from Behind the Moon*. But Gerald Musgrave, red-headed like Horvendile, continued to haunt the recesses of Cabell's mind and spirit until, in July, 1926, he insisted on forcing his way out. Cabell found both his Cayford Cottage like Maya's and "that Gerald Musgrave's life history had become very easy to write. There was, now, no difficulty whatever about it: and the tale flowed onward without any stop." It is hoped that Kerenyi and Jung have helped us to see why. Cabell states:

> I do not assert that this is the best of my books: but I am sure that, after the first false start, "Something About Eve" is the story which I wrote with the largest portion of ease and zest.

This book must rank alongside *The Cream of the Jest, Jurgen, Figures of Earth*, and *The Silver Stallion*, all illustrating Cabell's tendency to alternate, in individual works, the episodic with the chronological in his structural technique. In this way he combines, in the total coverage, breadth of experience with depth of significance. His craftsmanship is at its best; the insight and maturity reveal themselves as effectively as in the author's notes to the works in the Storisende Edition where Cabell, relaxed in the confident strength of his perfected ability, achieves, with apparently fluid ease and never-failing freshness, the highest level of his performance. In dredging himself in *Straws and Prayer Books*, Cabell brought up much muck and poison, but this had been largely purged in creating *The Silver Stallion*. As a consequence there is less emphasis on the negative side, on disenchantment, here; but the intellectual realism expresses itself in a much more stark treatment of sex. In fact, Cabell is almost as realistic as life in his portrayal of something fundamental to life. But, as always, this treatment is completely absorbed into the general texture of the tapestry and its chief significance is spiritual. This treatment is brutal in its acknowledgment of the less romantic attributes of love but in such a way as to reveal the true stuffing of life. By recognizing intellectually these facets of sex, Cabell raises the status of his affirmation—and it amounts to affirmation—of the spiritual in love and life. Thus he justifies his romanticism by being as objective as a scientist. But, unlike so many of his scientific, realistic, objective contemporaries, Cabell forges ahead to complete the circle of his conceptions, to round out his awareness; he does this not by sacrificing intellect but, on the contrary, by a greater application of it in his observation of the continuity and inter-relatedness of all action and animation. Hemingway's work seems to illustrate how contemporary literature is just about the opposite of Cabell's. Hemingway never seems to give us a completed story in the sense that he creates a complete circle of cause, action, and conclusion. He consistently shows us a predicament and then leaves us in it—this is life, this facet contained in this predicament, whether it is the sense of bewildered loss at the end of *Farewell to Arms* or the shock of horror at the nature of blindness in his late short stories "A Man of the World" and "Get a Seeing-Eyed Dog." There is brutal acknowledgment of life and what it can be as seen in these splintered fragments but there is no synthesis, nor resolution, nor unity, nor even, perhaps, satisfactory catharsis. The reader—already in a predicament—is handed another one. This is not to belittle Hemingway's achievement and craftsmanship, which, in their way, require the acutest of observation and creative discipline. But, by comparison, perhaps Cabell's achievement emerges as not less, in its sentimental escape from everything harsh, but as much more. Because, while Cabell too, sees the stark and brutal and ultimately unknowable, he possesses both the intellect and the sense of organic structure to perceive and remold these experiences so that they constitute a revelation of the workings of the whole universe. His myths deal thus with man and the gods, with the earth and the stars, with the whole web of creation. Hemingway deals simply with certain local aspects of man's twitchings in the web. This is the justification for Cabell's mythic symbols: only these can take us to the heart of creation; for all our science and objectivity, this heart—

its cause and purpose, if any—is still a mystery to us. Dealing with most of these symbols, Edwyn Bevan (in *Symbolism and Belief*, London, 1938) observes:

> Of one thing I am sure: that the question I have raised regarding the elements of symbolism in our religious conceptions takes us to the very heart of the religious problem.

Perhaps only the symbols of genuine myth can make the remote immediate.

It may be, then, that the theme of *Something About Eve* is life, and its object, man's attempt to find fulfillment. Life, in this aspect, is regarded as primarily and essentially subjective; fulfillment is seen as the satisfaction of a spiritual want. The hero in *Something About Eve* is a cultured, or at least cultivated, man who if alive in all his senses is capable of perceiving this spiritual want and of doing something about it. The process is represented by the familiar means of a journey or pilgrimage from the flesh, in its limited earthly environment, to Antan, a land where resides that which will supply the want. Along the route there are various obstacles and diversions capable of distracting the hero from his journey toward a goal that he feels is there but cannot even fully define or be sure is actual. And he is so constituted that he cannot reach it anyway, though he hopes in succeeding generations more nearly to approach it. Thus Cabell constructs the means for showing what is, in effect, the real essence of all human history. Horvendile states:

> You travel, Gerald, on the road of the greater myths. Such myths do not perish speedily. And, besides, nothing is true anywhere in the Marches of Antan. All is a seeming and an echo: and through this superficies men come to know the untruth which makes them free.

On the foundation of his imaginative perception of life, as revealed in the various stages of the journey, Cabell builds his rational and ironical framework of dialogue and action. A major source of distraction and, indeed, of diversion, capable of producing loss of power if not of desire, is woman, as Gerald Musgrave travels on his "woman-haunted way." So while domnei can enlarge man it can also diminish him. In the end, Gerald must journey alone with his imagination upon the Silver Stallion which everyone wanted to take away from him—if he is to reach Antan.

As Eve was the instrument of Adam's downfall so are the series of Gerald Musgrave's opponents' varieties of the original Eve. The first is Evelyn Townshend in Lichfield. Gerald Musgrave, illicitly involved with her, is freed from his body and its awkward entanglement with Evelyn Townshend to follow the doubtful road to Antan (on the newly christened stallion Kalki[2] given him by Horvendile) to meet and displace the Master Philologist. The Master Philologist seems to possess, among other things, that word which was in the beginning which became flesh and expressed such poetic if unscientific things as grace and truth. Gerald finds that he himself is Lord of the Third Truth and he hopes to acquire from the Master Philologist the exact nature of this position. In other words, as one very much in touch with reality, Gerald knows that we copulate and die but, as one who seeks spiritual fulfillment, he desires to know if this is all. He feels that there must be something more as betokened by his undertaking this journey instead of simply enjoying himself with what was already available in that "unforgotten mortal world in which any conceivable young man could live very royally, and with never failing arder, upon every person's patrimony of the five human senses." In approaching his own kingdom then, Gerald controls himself.

The portions of this work are so divided and arranged as to symbolize in the versions of Eve—Evadne of the Dusk, Evasherah of the First Water Gap, Evarvan of the Mirror, Evaine of Peter's Tomb—the various temptations of the senses that can constitute diversionary cul-de-sacs and alcoves branching off the main road. While humor preponderates in brilliant, flippant, and irreverant dialogue there is a steady undercurrent of seriousness—as apparent and substantial here as in any of Cabell's writings. This accounts

---

[2] Kalki is one of a number of symbols taken over by Cabell from the Hindu. The Oriental Kalki is a white horse, the incarnation of which will bring the god with gleaming sword who is to restore the world to its primitive purity and make men's minds as clear as crystal (cf. verse at the beginning of *The Silver Stallion*).

for the very moving poetry which underlies the playfulness. The seriousness embodies the very immediate and personal decisions that the hero must take, ranging from sex to the half-earnest acknowledgement of the Protestant Episcopal Church. This is a rather reluctant and bantering acknowledgement echoing the chapter in *The Cream of the Jest* entitled "Evolution of a Vestry-man" and a recurring feature of the works. It is not going too far to compare this conception of Gerald Musgrave with that of the much-married author of the nuptial scenes of *Paradise Lost*, not to mention the early Latin poems, that is, with John Milton's conception of the role and significance of chastity. Beneath all the surface exploitation of sex in all its many aspects, there is this deeper awareness which subordinates it to the spirit and its requirements. In the author's note to *Straws and Prayer Books*, Cabell observed of the "now obsolescent ideals and virtues" of the Biography:

> It is true enough that "Domnei" exalts womanhood beyond our present-day, more prosaic beliefs, and that "Jurgen" upholds the austere and straight-laced and temporarily unpopular doctrine that a married man had best remain faithful to his wife; just as it is like-wise true that "Something About Eve" depicts a later Galahad who sets an example in the way of male chastity such as not many of our younger gentry as yet under seventy-five are inclined to follow nowa-days; and true also that "The Silver Stallion" pleads frankly . . . for the sustaining faith of old-fashioned religion. Yet these volumes touch upon many other matters; the spiritual message . . . is not wholly priggish.

But the absence of priggishness should not be interpreted as an absence of a very real and lasting spiritual significance, a significance inherent in the best literature of modern Europe, and ancient Rome and Greece, in the religious works of East and West (and remember the Song of Solomon), in the modern philosophy of Bertrand Russell, in the ancient ones of Greece, in the Koran, the Bhagavad-Gita, in Confucious and in Tao and in Buddha, in fact in everything created by those who have thought and felt at all intensively, about creation. These eternal, consistent, and consecutive cycles of "romanticism" or rebirth of spiritual synthesis must always be punctuated by periods of further analysis, rationalization, psychic readjustment, the autumns of the sear and yellow, followed by frozen winters of bewilderment. In this present winter of reasoned confusion, Cabell anticipates the spring— either that, or the hydrogen bomb.

But, in the end, the Western seer must always come up against the ultimately unknowable. While Gerald successfully enough copes with the series of most enticing Eves and their compatriots, finally he is defeated by himself. Yet in the meantime, what a magnificent struggle. Perhaps the music is at its finest in Chapter XII, "Confusions of the Golden Travel." Gone now is the playfulness, the ingenious banter. Here Cabell emerges in full and sonorous strength, "sage and serious" like Milton's Spenser in a relatively rare and direct revelation of the very marrow of the author's being. The writing is at its best: everything amalgamates to make this a chapter which may compare justly, indeed proudly, with anything produced by any people, ancient or modern. Gerald steps through the Golden Mirror of Caer Omn. Upon this act he enters successively a long line of beings, legendary, mythical, historical and fictional, who all constitute representations of the many aspects of the spiritual theme of the Biography. First was Prometheus, from whom all arts have come—"he who after he had discovered to mortals so many inventions had no invention to preserve himself":

> He suffered for the eternal redemption of mankind, the first of all poets, of those makers who delight to shape and to play with puppets, and the first of men's Saviors. And his was a splendid martyrdom, for the winged daughters of old Ocean fluttered everywhere about him in the golden Scythian air.

There is no doubt or prevarication about that. The figure and predicament of Prometheus merge into those of Solomon— "There was no power like Solomon's." But, even as Solomon "turned from these transient things to drunkenness and to the embraces of women," nevertheless, "always the undrugged vision of his mind regarded the fixed will of Heaven, 'These things shall pass away.' " And Solomon passes into Odysseus, who "was still a poet, making the supreme poem of each man's journeying through an everywhere inimical and betraying world." Cabell is by no means presenting merely the white contrasted with the black of life's experiences. Here, again, is clear evidence of his conception of the multiform nature of these things as Odysseus emerges in Judas, another rebel against the will of Heaven, the will to destroy men through the medium of life. The iniquity of Judas was supreme; "it was man's masterpiece in the way of iniquity, it was the reply of a very fine poet to Heaven's proffered truce after so many aeons of tormenting men causelessly." In reversing the conventional emphasis, Cabell drives, arrestingly and originally, to the heart of man's earthly situation. Judas yields to Nero, who was enslaved by the naked beauty of his own mother so that "from the loveliness of none of his poems, could he get happiness and real peace of mind." Nero is superseded by Tannhäuser, who, amid the acclamations of the damned in the Horselberg, was troubled by Heaven "with doubts and with premonitions, even with repentance." Villon follows, "who was still so fine a poet" as well as another victim.

> For time ruined all; time was man's eternal strong ravager, time was the flail with which Heaven pursued all men whom Heaven had not yet destroyed, ruthlessly.

Then an example, the favorite of both Cabell and Marlowe, as the centuries-long saga expresses itself through Johan Faustus. In this illustration, Cabell interweaves his own activities as a Virginian necromancer, for Faustus:

> . . . was a poet who worked in necromancy, his puppets were the most admirable and lovely of the dead. Presently he was restoring through art magic even those lost nineteen books in which were the secrets of all beauty and all knowledge and all contentment, the secrets for which Prometheus had paid.

This series of world-centered figures, historical, mythical, legendary, illustrates those principles inherent in the spiritual grounding of the Biography. In doing this, the Biography becomes also an expression of the classical, classically expressed. The supreme embodiment is still beauty, the beauty that is Helen's, and Faustus reappears in Don Juan Tenorio, who had the heart of a poet "which is big enough to be in love with the whole world." Don Juan, swaggering gallantly to his doom, encounters a rider and steed of stone. The rider is Manuel. Don Juan, clutching the horse about its neck, becomes that rather frightened Jurgen at the end of *The Silver Stallion,* as he looks up at the symbol of the life-force, the "dumb and staring effigy of a big man in armor":

> It was the bungled copy and the parody of a magnanimous, great hearted dream that he was grasping, and yet it was part of him, who had been a poet once, but was now a battered old pawnbroker, for in some way, as he incommunicably knew, this parodied and not ever comprehended Redeemer and he were blended, and they were, somehow, laboring in unison to serve a shared purpose.

Jurgen steps back from the statue, "that carved fragment of the crag of Prometheus," out through the frame of the golden mirror to become both released from its magic, and the shape of Gerald Musgrave on the road that all the others had traveled, the road to Antan. Poor Prometheus, poor all of them, poor all of us . . . but it is a fine thing to have Cabell, for once, emerge in his true self—even as he must do this through all his antecedents.

After this, perhaps the profoundest piece of synthetic creation in all his writings, Cabell again dons the cap and bells and avoids all danger of priggishness. But the clowning is at the same high level of performance; the comedy matches the tragedy. In these chapters (XV and XVI) the repartee is inspired and cannot be considered piecemeal. The essentials that comprise the two truths, in this comedy of fig leaves, are treated with truly Aristophanic candor, if it is remembered that Aristophanes was a friend of Socrates. Mention should be made perhaps, of one small chapter (XXI), "They That Wore Blankets," which shows the marvellous detachment of a writer who, in fact, is far ahead of his era both in apprehension and performance, as he makes irony of the very stupidity, lack of perception, and small-mindedness in general by which he was greeted. The wearers of the wet blankets discuss the art of Horvendile:

> I quite agree with you. Nobody admires the merits of our esteemed confrère more whole-heartedly than I do. It would be merely silly to deny that he has weakened his always rather wishy-washing magic potions by too frequent blendings. It is impossible to ignore that his magic has become a cloying weariness and a mincing indecency. We are forced to acknowledge that Horvendile is insincere, that he very irritatingly poses as a superior person, that he is labored beyond endurance, that he smells of the lamp, that his art is dull and tarnished and trivial and intolerable, but, even so, we ought also to admit that he does as well as could be expected of anybody who combines a lack of any actual talent with ignorance of actual life.

This equals the detached urbanity of Ecclesiastes, of Montaigne, of Sri Krishna, as what was no doubt ugly enough in the flesh becomes remade into a thing of beauty—and, thus, of joy—in the spirit expressed through art.

This is not the only time that Cabell climbs from the profounder level of the irony which sees the contradictory duality of good and evil to the sharper but less profound level of the satire which deals with their perceptible singleness. Often he combines the two as a form of musical counterpoint. He does this when Gerald reaches the cottage of Maya of the Fair Breasts on Mispec Moor. For with Maya, and her cottage and Mispec Moor, there is a certain recognizable affinity with the reality of good solid middle-class citizens about their daily business and their nocturnal pleasures in any one of the large number of fascinating and so very beautiful towns that help man, through commercialized industry, to bring the psyche to fulfillment in environments in which there is so much with which the psyche may correspond. Past the cottage runs the road to Antan; Antan is within relatively easy reach and requires of Gerald, a god, the Fair-haired Hoo, the Helper and Preserver, the Lord of the Third Truth, the Well-Beloved of Heavenly Ones, only the final spirited effort which would cap all his other achievements. But Maya, about her house-work, is unimpressed; furthermore, while she darns her stockings, she weaves her spell—and Gerald's visit extends and extends until it is as long as a lifetime.

The last third of *Something About Eve* concerns this stay upon Mispec Moore as Gerald talks with the myths, and gods, and poets who pass by toward Antan; he lives in increasing content with Maya, who gave him rose-colored spectacles and is at her best on Sereda's Wednesdays. Gerald regarded with indulgence and pity his predecessors in Maya's affection, "those beguiled men whom she had converted into domestic animals." And Kalki, too, is turned out to graze with "those docile geldings that had once been knights and barons and reigning kings," animals now not dissatisfied with "their transfiguring doom." So the entry into Antan is postponed, and postponed. The humor and banter are consistently gentle now. Maya makes Gerald an eight-year-old son, who arouses in Gerald "a tenderness which came appreciably near to being unselfish." Thus he continues to linger. Until, on one occasion, while Kalki was grazing just like an ordinary horse, Gerald sees someone else riding on a Silver Stallion toward Antan, a handsome youth dressed exactly in the manner of the Gerald Musgrave who had first met the Sylan in 1805. This young man does not even notice Gerald nor hear his greeting but rides un-hurriedly on, without hesitation, toward Antan. So Gerald ob-serves his youth pass by and stands there "feeling unwarrantably snubbed, and blinking behind his rose-colored spectacles."

Only the book itself can do justice to the intricacy and ingenuity of the planning of the various symbols and their interaction as Maya becomes again that Keleos Koleros which Gerald had wor-shipped after all, as his offspring (after revealing further reaches of the unknown) mounts Kalki, goes towards Antan and, for Gerald and his generation, destroys it. Gerald, the interrogative pronoun, as he fails to enter Antan and loses both his wife and his child, announces that it is the mission of the "Lord of the Third Truth, howsoever he may palter or struggle against his doom, to destroy that which he most loves." As the theme moves full circle to acquiescence in Lichfield and the triumph of the Two Truths, Gerald reoccupies his now aged body and observes:

> I, who have left the Marches of Antan forever, have bought free-dom from the ever-meddling magic of the Two Truths. . . . I have bought feet too old for errancy, ears that are deaf to the high gods, and to the heart stirring music of great myths, and to the soft wheed-ling of women also, and I have bought eyes too dim to note whether or not Antan still gleams on the horizon.

But, even at this moment, a younger Gerald Musgrave filled with confident high hopes, is just setting off for Antan.

The verisimilitude of Cabell's symbolic interplay may be fur-ther attested to by the similarity between the "downfall" of the Lord of the Third Truth and the downfall of Adam. But whereas Milton's Adam deliberately chose to share Eve's guilt even though the act which produced it was initially entirely hers, Gerald's downfall is essentially different in its origin. It is not, simply, that he was distracted from Antan by the witchery of Maya; in fact, she repeatedly told him to go to Antan, and *she* did not want his Silver Stallion. While this was, in one sense, the one way to en-sure that Gerald remained, her attitude throws the responsibility for his action ultimately back upon Gerald. As Cabell observes in his author's note:

> What detained him, when there remained no impediment be-tween him and his goal, I would suggest to have been, perhaps, his own nature. Here are the woman and the child and common cor-dial human living: yonder in Antan is but ambiguity. . . . Man—being what he is,—requires no persuading to remain where love at-tends him.

Cabell adds that while Antan is the home of all true poets, no man is entirely the poet and Antan can make no appeal to these con-siderable parts comprising the husband and the father. In any case, failure as a poet means greater success as a human being. Thus Cabell rationalizes. Indeed the enemy may well be within, and in the end, perhaps, it must be stronger than all as it becomes increasingly reinforced by the weakening flesh. Yet, for each new generation, Antan beckons, and in the sum total, humanity edges toward it: even as it struggled from the waters onto the land, so does it strive to pass from the earth to Antan. Perhaps that is really all that can be said. Yet the relationship between Gerald and Maya certainly constitutes "The Cream of the Jest."

15: *The Cream of the Jest*

La vie: c'est la femme que l'on a;
L'art: c'est la femme que l'on desire
—Jean Dolent

This volume united Poictesme with the present day, for the hero is Felix Kennaston, resident of Lichfield, U.S.A., in the twentieth century. The book was in growth from 1911 but unpublished until 1917; it appears to have been extensively revised and added to in 1922, as indicated for example by the chapter "Of Publishing," which embodies the autobiographical experiences leading up to and consequent upon the publication of *Jurgen*.

> So Felix Kennaston saw his dream vulgarized, made a low byword; and he contemplated this travestying, as the cream of a sardonic jest, with urbanity.

The attempts to find first a publisher and then some readers brought Cabell the friendship of Sinclair Lewis, who (as a publisher's reader) first rejected this work but later became its advocate; of Guy Holt for Robert McBride & Co.; of H. L. Mencken, who published a long and favorable article about it in *The Smart Set*; of Joseph Hergesheimer; and of Burton Rascoe, literary editor of the Chicago *Tribune*. What with one thing and another, Cabell was in danger of becoming not only that rare thing, a consummate artist, but that even rarer thing, one with an audience. As Cabell observes in his note to the Storisende Edition of *The Eagle's Shadow:*

> . . . Chicago had taken up polite letters in a really serious way. For some six months, did the literate of Chicago thus debate whether I was an unjustly neglected author or a posturing imbecile.

But it was not until he could be accused of being "lewd, lascivious and indecent" that anyone took any real notice of him. *The Cream of the Jest* "very soon appeared upon the marked down counters."

This book deals, less abstrusely than usual in some ways, with the standard Cabellian themes but with more autobiography. The very nature of the way in which Felix Kennaston takes to literary creation, rather as a duck waddles from the mire only to move easily and gracefully upon the pool itself, is significant. In real life Kennaston is something of a social failure, not very prepossessing or likeable, except when with every lady of his choice except his wife: in build, he is "a fat pasty fellow," rather like John Bulmer. Chapter XXVII, "Evolution of a Vestryman," amplifies the views on Christianity expressed in *Beyond Life*; Chapter XXIV, "Deals with Pen Scratches," foretells of the dispiriting perceptions in *Straws and Prayer Books* not to mention the puffed pigeons of pride and the mirror of self-conceit which add up to that vanity which is the life-source of all male activity (fame being the spur). Such chapters merit detailed analysis for appreciation of the neatness with which the smallest portions of Cabell's work dovetail into each other to enlarge the Biography.

An important theme is the relationship between Kennaston and his wife. As *The Observer* (London) stated, in 1923, "Mr. Cabell could probably put originality into a sonnet on a royal christening." This is indeed so but the object of this glance at *The Cream of the Jest* is to attempt to clarify further the true nature of Cabell's attitude toward his material. In many things has he been misread—

> *Men Who Loved Alison* is beautifully written and all that, but, exactly as the *Tucson Pioneer* said, it is really just colorful soapbubbly nonsense.

So says Kennaston's wife Kathleen who has not yet had time to read her husband's book about which everyone is talking.

Cabell's supposed attitude toward woman and marriage has been bandied about as so much commercial garbage. What is, at least the approximate, truth?[1] In *The Cream of the Jest,* Cabell reproduces in his own way what is, in fact, an ancient attitude not necessarily to be associated with the promiscuity, legal or otherwise, of the " 'twenties."

Felix Kennaston lives in Lichfield. He acquires a piece of a sigil which, on being regarded in the right light, transfers Kennaston into Horvendile, the puppet-shifter, who accompanies Ettarre, daughter of Manuel, up and down the ages in search of the meaning of Kennaston.

> His life until this had been in the main normal, with its due share of normal intimacies with parents, kinsmen, friends, a poet's ordinary allotment of sweethearts, and, chief of all, with his wife.

Nobody understands him of course, any more than they understand each other. Kennaston, whose capable wife is admirably suited to him, has never regretted his marriage; it is just that she no longer means much to him. Or is this a fallacy? And is the situation in *The Cream of the Jest* a little more complicated, even more profound? For, in the end, the sigil turns out to be nothing more, nothing less, than the top of a jar of his wife's cosmetics— this magic symbol which meant for its possessor the key to beauty and adventure. Through the sigil, Kennaston evades the drabness of provincialism. He embarks upon a quest for beauty which takes him deep into the realms of imagination and enquiry. And what does he find? He finds not only many ironies of history, fate, and folly but also the central philosophy of *Beyond Life:*

> Everywhere, it seemed to him, men had labored blindly, at flat odds with rationality, and had achieved everything of note by accident.

But Kennaston, asking always, "Why is a Kennaston?" finds that "the race did go forward; the race did achieve; and in every way the race grew better." This protoplasm had moved through fish to frog to reptile to mammal, the puppets being ever reshaped into better shapes "until amiable and shatter-pated man stood

[1] These hypotheses may now be verified by Cabell's autobiography, *As I Remember It* (R. McBride & Co., 1955).

erect in the world." And man himself, at the beck and call of the demiurge, blindly moved like the fish and reptile "toward unapprehended loftier goals."

But just as men's lives came to seem to Kennaston like many infinitesimal threads woven into the patterns of human destiny, so Kennaston grew to suspect that the existence of mankind upon earth was but an incident in the unending struggle of life to find a home in the universe.

In the chapter "Evolution of a Vestryman," Cabell or Kennaston considers, in one of the finest passages of analytical followed by synthetic thought in his writings, at least part of that "all" which was shown to and so shocked Jurgen in the forest.

There was to be found nowhere in inanimate nature any approach to symmetry ... to his finicky love of neatness the universe showed on a sudden as a vast disheveled horror.

As opposed to this, nearly all living things do struggle toward something like symmetry—order, proportion, and true balance.

Kennaston had here the sensation of fitting in the last bit of a puzzle. Life, yearning for symmetry, stood revealed as artist. Life strove toward the creation of art. That was all life cared about. Living things were more or less successful works of art and were to be judged according to art's cannons alone.

We have seen how closely art, for Cabell, is related to life: Kennaston glimpsed an artist-God whose studio was the universe but whose work was man engaged as a puppet in an eternal romance. And, as Kennaston sees it, the plot of this romance began with Eden and reached its climax at Calvary because of the "surpassing beauty of the Christ-legend. No other myth compared with it from the aesthetic standpoint." The artist-God's sense of pathos, of beauty and of irony could have had no other result. The life of Christ, then, would appear to represent the product of the highest art; by his life he revealed the nature of the artist-God so the "cannons of art" would seem to have the closest connection with the Christian way of life as seen in the mythical or historical figure of Christ.[2]

It may be objected that this may make at least a theoretical Christian of Kennaston but not necessarily a practicing Christian of Cabell, creator of lewd Jurgen. Kennaston is frequently a spokesman for Cabell, and there is additional evidence. In *Straws and Prayer Books*, there is a reference to H. L. Mencken which says "and it was with an eye upon Mr. H. L. Mencken that Kempis compiled the *Imitation of Christ*." H. L. Mencken was one of the "six most gallant champions" to whom was dedicated *Figures of Earth*. The closeness of these associations, which are outside the fiction, would seem to be enough to illustrate that Cabell's pursuit of beauty is inextricably intermeshed with the pursuit of truth and that truth is contained within the distinction, clarity, symmetry, tenderness, and urbanity seen in the life of one Jesus Christ. Associated ambiguities only add to the complexity and so enlarge the beauty.

Thus we appear to find confirmation of the positive heart of Cabell's art and its impulse as expressed in *Beyond Life*. His attitude is truly a religious one in the best sense, the Socratic sense, of the word; that is, in the practical embodiment in his work of enquiries about things supernatural tending to a deeper and fuller appreciation of life, tending also toward the symmetry that is good and away from the chaos that is devilish. But, as Cabell realizes, it is just possible that his Kennaston may be wrong. So another spokesman has the final word in this episode as Harrowby states:

[2] Compare the reasoning of Oscar Wilde about this *De Profundis*—not the flamboyant Oscar Wilde of the salons but the Oscar Wilde who, garbed as a convict and handcuffed, had stood amidst the gathering sneers, jeers, smears, and leers of the populace on the center platform of Clapham Junction in the afternoon of November 13, 1895. His observations include, ". . . wherever there is a romantic movement in art there somehow, and under some form, is Christ, or the soul of Christ," and "Christ's place is indeed with the poets. His whole conception of humanity sprang out of the imagination and can only be realised by it," and, "If ever I write again . . . there are just two subjects on which and through which I desire to express myself: one is 'Christ as the precursor of the romantic movement in life'; the other is 'The artistic life considered in its relation to conduct.' "

The fatal fault, sir, of your theorizing is that it is too complete. It aims to throw light upon the universe, and therefore is self-evidently moonshine. The Wardens of Earth do not desire that we should understand the universe. . . . So . . . I must decline to think of you and me as characters in a romance.

A man consists of many parts. Nothing is good or bad but thinking makes it so but some kinds of thinking are better than others. The kinds that are better are those moving constructively toward symmetry not negatively toward nothing. Kennaston does move toward a conclusion while Harrowby merely reaches negation. Both are parts of Cabell and both represent major themes in all his work—the chivalric as against the gallant, the aspiring as against the cynic; yet it is that part represented by Kennaston—the philosophy and the vision—which predominates, which is the essence, which is, in fact, the Biography. Harrowby, with all he stands for in Cabell's work, is integral yet not of the essence.

The vision is the heart of the matter, but Kennaston reaches it through the sigil which is the lid of a jar of his wife's cosmetic, that is, through his wife's attempt to make herself more beautiful, to withstand time, to amend reality even as Kennaston's art may be his cosmetic. And Kennaston sees his wife anew, as when young in the garden between dawn and sunrise—for they are the only ones who remember at all that time. Thus she holds the sigil and is the key to Ettarre after all—the tangible embodiment of what he pursues and knows to be intangible because, like the youth which bred it, it is transient. And yet only through her can he return to it. In considering these matters, Kennaston "touched mystery everywhere":

> My vocabulary and my ink went to the making of the book's Ettarre: but with them went Kathleen's youth and purity and tenderness and serenity and loving-kindness toward all created things save the women I had flirted with—so she contributed more than I.

Cabell does not use pathos lightly or frequently. Perhaps this explains, at least partly, the effect of the simple, unspectacular yet dramatic death of Kennaston's wife. Kennaston's last words to her were a mumbled platitude as she went upstairs and, while her husband followed a magazine story through the advertisements, quite peacefully she died. The incident grips with a hand of ice and brings us suddenly and benumblingly to a dark void. The sigil had taught Kennaston:

> that it rests within the power of each of us to awaken at will from a dragging nightmare of life made up of unimportant tasks and tedious useless little habits, to see life as it really is, and to rejoice in its exquisite wonderfulness.

The song becomes a symphony with all the wonder of the life cycles of the eel and salmon or the migratory routes of the swallow and the wild goose. Kennaston is the spokesman who most represents the positive side of Cabell which is here given full rein to move toward its conclusion. This conclusion is faith. Yet there is always Harrowby, who, with his own feet on the ground, offsets Kennaston as he finds his logical explanation for all the miracles. But even Harrowby makes grudging concession. After showing how Kennaston had "muddled away the only life he was quite certain of enjoying, in contemplation of a dream," Harrowby reflects:

> it is in this inadequate flesh that each of us must serve his dream; and so must fail in the dream's service and must parody that which he holds dearest. . . . Thus . . . we play false to the dream, and it evades us, and we dwindle into responsible citizens.

Even Harrowby could not help regarding Mr. Felix Bulmer Kennaston, who is all men, as a parable, as Harrowby concludes "that it is only by preserving faith in human dreams that we may, after all, perhaps some day make them come true." And it is Harrowby the cautious who comes forth with this, even as it was Charteris the sceptic who came forth with the creed in *Beyond Life*. So perhaps it is not, now, too fanciful to accredit these "beliefs" to the author himself; for these "beliefs" are the life which animate these figures of earth and they could come to them only from their creator.

The Cream of the Jest is literature embodying the author's philosophy; this philosophy is expressed as a vision qualified by doubts. It is tempting to describe the vision as a lighthouse and the doubts as the surrounding rocks and shoals. But it should be remembered that Cabell is an artist; as such as he does not necessarily set out primarily to throw light upon the universe but merely to write perfectly of beautiful happenings. In the outcome he achieves a composite of many things, including entertainment, and wisdom—which is where the philosophy and vision appear; but nothing is known for certain, as Cabell makes only too clear by his qualifying doubts, except that this composite is a thing of beauty. Nevertheless there are varying degrees of beauty and it is submitted that Cabell's is of the highest order, not because of the words alone but chiefly because of their meanings. Cabell is not a gadfly to the Athenians but these meanings are, in the sum total, remarkably celestial all the same. And, whether we like it or not, this seems to be the one quality we insist upon in any literature we regard as classical.

The frame to which all this is the picture is the marital relationship of Kennaston and Kathleen. The fact that this relationship contains the most moving portions of the book suggests that this subject meant much to the author. So, when all is admitted about the freedom of the attitude of Kennaston, and even of lewd Jurgen, his real views concerning "adulterous affairs" become surprisingly conventional. Kennaston, the artist, can continue his search for Ettarre only through the sigil possessed by his wife, the most long-suffering of his companions in the garden between dawn and sunrise, a garden where the moments of lordly youth become, even as they did in that other Dream in "Athens, and a wood near it," something of great constancy.

16: *The Lonesome Pine*

Its major theme I take to be . . . the doctrine cf our own world's Author. . . . I believe that the Biography . . . does summarize, in tolerably correct proportion, the main elements of our average human living.

Author's Note to Storisende Edition of
Straws and Prayer Books.

As the trail nears its end it is necessary, in this age which can leaves nothing alone, to face up to *Straws and Prayer Books.* This volume of "diversionary" sayings is the epilogue to the works which deal with the decendants of Manuel who was a redeemer. Major works—syntheses flowering from the analysis in *Straws and Prayer Books*—were still to come until, in 1929, Cabell drew the saga to a close when, once again dealing neatly in round figures, he was exactly fifty.

Writing from Cayford Cottage, in 1929, Cabell noted for the Storisende Edition of *Straws and Prayer Books* that it:

> strives to make clear the causes which, to my opinion, underlie and prompt the playing of every artist in letters. It, in any case, tells you what prompted me to write the long Biography of Manuel. The thing was done for, and in an especial sense, my diversion.

Thus Cabell, a genuine maker of genuine myths, illustrates the organic nature of his art. Far too realistic to deceive himself over his motives, he confirms Aristotle's views on the role of art as constituting catharsis for the creator—Cabell created to please himself. This meant activity which ensured his spiritual growth. Cabell was being true to *himself* not to appearances. This is why his art is so much more sound, cohesive, and satisfying than most modern literature, which, in possessing less introspective insight, becomes muddled in its motives and identified with all sorts of journalistic matters of the moment. Even then it often treats them inartistically because the inadequate introspective insight is matched by an equal inadequacy of thought and craftsmanship regarding externals. Hence the gargantuan gaucherie of writers like Thomas Wolfe. This does not mean that the artist, in grounding himself, in getting to know himself and in representing or revealing artistically the struggles of his psyche for growth, is escaping reality or is not of immediate and contemporary significance (however historically remote may be his symbols). On the contrary, by being thus honest with and true to himself, and topically undistracted, the artist, in proportion to his sensitivity and intelligence, being most representative of his era in his personality (he has to out-Herod his era), has most to offer that era if it wishes to remain spiritually alive. In other words, Cabell's art contains outcomes capable of reorientating man among modern doubt and confusion. Cabell, paradox as this is—because he, least of all, desired to be a prophet—is at the forefront of the taboo-breakers; he has, by the interaction of the ingredients in his created world, revealed for us the interaction of the prime Creator's ingredients in our world. In organically enlarging his own spirit he reveals a universal spirit. By the extent and power of his imagination, impelled by his feelings and steered by his thought, he has again revealed further reaches of the unknown in a way acceptable even to the modern intellect. Hegel and Sartre are reconciled.

In *Straws and Prayer Books* Cabell attempts to pin down, like so many butterflies and moths on a page, the beliefs which led to the Biography: he examines what prompted him to his life's work. As one who is a thinker he has the disadvantage of approaching this matter intellectually instead of emotionally. As a consequence he forges on through all the faiths and creeds and prejudices of the problem writers, the prophets, and the propagandists (however genuinely admirable and possibly "right" they may be) to doubt and despair. Frequently he is, as well as difficult, disagreeable to the taste and smell. And he seems to know this and to throw it at the reader as part of the truth about life and all of us—we are allowed to escape nothing. Only by outdoing the realists can romance justify itself.

> Man is, they say, the only animal that has reason; and so he must have also, if he is to stay sane, diversions to prevent his using it.

The eighteenth century has acquired the title of the Age of Reason. The number of its major figures who went insane or near it is surprising—from Swift, Johnson, and Collins to George III.

The prefatory quotation to *Straws and Prayer Books* is from Pope:

> Behold the child, by Nature's kindly law,
> Pleased with a rattle, tickled with a straw. . . .
> Scarfs, garters, gold, amuse his riper stage,
> And beads and prayer-books are the toys of age.

Using this, rather than the vision of *Beyond Life*, as his guiding light, the following becomes a normal conclusion:

> Pure reason . . . reveals out of hand that the main course of daily living is part boredom, part active discomfort and fret, and, for the not inconsiderable rest, a blundering adherence to some standard derived from this or that hearsay.

There follows the inevitable opinion that the artist is one who plays solely to divert, not even others primarily, but himself, as life's half-frightened playboy. Hemingway was once introduced to a crowd at a Mexican bull-fight, not as a writer or an artist but as "An American play-boy." This was greeted by thunderous cheers. On this occasion, Cabell was with the crowd. But energy must come from something. This something may be want of wealth which produces a businessman; it may be another kind of power which produces a dictator, a president, or a prime minister (who may be only dictators limited by lesser dictators); it may be beliefs which produce the great churchman (who also acquires wealth and power); or this something may be the desire for beauty which produces the artist (who, like Marlowe, becomes more powerful than potentates). At this point, Cabell's attitude comes very close to Dreiser's, for this something may be decided by the glandular system and general physical design and so be a matter of compulsive necessity.

It is on this basis that Cabell examines his beliefs. He leaves no stone unturned and there are repulsive things beneath nearly all of them. The emphasis is almost constantly on disenchantment and the causes thereof. The tone is bitter with an almost morbid desire to feast upon these causes as the hyena, when wounded, will consume its own entrails. Life is placed upon the operating table and the mind probes hither and thither with cold and apparently dispassionate, slightly weary, detachment. By comparison with this display of logical and impartial analysis *Madame Bovary* appears a newssheet of a bomb-throwing anarchist. At its worst, art is the diversionary toy of the childlike if not the childish—poor Nicolas de Caen seems most out of place now, with his prayer books and chivalry. A woman, far from being a manifestation on earth of Heaven can, at best, provide a moment's interest by her personal anatomical variations from her predecessor and successor. The person for whom she provides the interest has achieved all he ever desired—and does so over the body of a boy now full of leprosy and dwelling in ashes. The pot at the end of the rainbow is gold indeed but its discoverer is Midas. There is a weariness upon this world of Elfhame, where art is no more than an illusion and, like Socrates, we know so much that we know we know nothing. For a moment, art becomes a refuge and —crime or otherwise—nothing more, as Jurgen sees again that "all" which left him alone and shaken as with an everlasting ague. These chapters in *Straws and Prayer Books* are the cries of one not spoilt and peevish, but hurt and disappointed, because all that glittered turned out to be no more than gold. As Anavalt approaches the Queen of Elfhame, as he comes to the end of the trail, he finds she is, when not faced squarely, hollow and only as thick as paper. When properly regarded she is a lovely and most dear illusion:

> He kissed her. He was content. Here was the woman he desired, the woman who did not exist in the world where people have souls. The Elle maid had no mortal body that time would parody and ruin, she had no brain to fashion dreams of which he would fall short, she had no heart that he would hurt. There was an abiding peace . . . wherein no love could enter, and nobody could, in consequence, hurt anybody else very deeply . . . there were no longer two sides to everything, and a man need look for no reverses.

And the tragedy, which *Straws and Prayer Books* expresses throughout, is that this attitude, too, is wisdom. For the constant theme, on which many chapters ring many variations, is that only the young die good.

Yet there is another attitude which, like cheerfulness, keeps breaking through. On one side, the artist is seen as an anchorite who, with perseverance and the right ideas, converts a rubbish dump into a garden. At best, this garden may be shared, between dawn and sunrise and at any other odd moments which recall this period, by his wife or other temporary associate with sigils and the eyes of Ettarre; at worst, no other person but the creator can ever gain admittance. And the garden has a marked, sometimes overwhelming, tendency to revert to a rubbish dump as the weed-killing propensity weakens or blight invades the blossoms. But, with diminishing resources, the gardener must continue, and this he knows for certain. And there is always the possibility of a head gardener around the corner. In the chapter "Celestial Architecture," speaking of the Author or artist-God, Cabell writes (Charteris has been dismissed and the author speaks through these essays in the first person):

> He still seems to me the likeliest creator, upon the whole, to have fashioned . . . the wholly incomprehensible world we live in. . . . And essentially, I find, I still believe in Him, with a faith that undermines and goes deeper than mere reason because it was developed in me earlier. . . . Men have discovered no firmer hope than that, in defiance of all logic and of all human experience, something very pleasant may still be impending, in—need I say?—bright lands which are in nothing familiar.

It is perhaps now quite unnecessary to add that there are many statements in *Straws and Prayer Books* which contradict this notion flatly. One must attempt to pick the statements which, in their sum total, are most conducive to symmetry.

Cabell takes pleasure in the fact that he has most successfully disguised or concealed himself in his work. This may well be right, up to a point. For he is detached as few "dedicated" artists are detached from what they say. Whether his desire to write perfectly about beautiful happenings is in order to divert himself, or whether this "desire" is the carrot dangled by the Author before all artists to persuade them to pull his load, a man is what a man does, and the Biography, as he himself insists, is Cabell's main achievement. It is itself a deed, but it is also comprised of countless actions. The deed and actions are selected according to a logical pattern to make for symmetry. The logical pattern is the philosophy, vision, and doubts; these are the man even when he is the man behind the masks. The philosophy and the vision represent, at the least, attractive ideas (but, again, it is significant that it is these particular ideas which are attractive), at the most, a hypothesis which the author would most like to be true. The doubts and denials are concrete facts illustrating, not only the dangers of dogmatism but the extent of the author's desire to comprehend. This desire is really the inner one, clothed outwardly by the desire to write perfectly. Owing to the strength and penetration of his intellect, Cabell has pushed his inner desire beyond say, the evolutionary certainty of Meredith, (although Cabell's vision depends on an evolutionary principle), the drawing room equanimity of Jane Austen, the patriotism of Whitman, the modern mythology of Henry James (in many ways the nearest realistic equivalent of Cabell's symbols), into the cold, bleak area of a self-knowledge, which, if they perceived it, none of these artists has so fully expressed. Cabell has expressed something of it even in his earliest work; in his later works it becomes increasingly dominant. The positive romantic affirmation of the vision which concluded *Beyond Life* and was the core of *The Cream of the Jest*, battles throughout with the realistic doubts of self-perception. In *Straws and Prayer Books* the doubts well-nigh eliminate the vision; the self-knowledge almost makes mockery of any philosophy. Yet *Straws and Prayer Books* ironically enough, is the book with what is, perhaps, the clearest admission of religious faith, as in the chapter "Celestial Architecture." And no hero of the Biography could ever tell a lie that was merely profitable. Why should this be such a standard feature of their behavior? Beauty is truth which is a *pursuit* of goodness, even as Socrates pursued it in face of the same injustice that puzzled Jurgen. Thus, moral considerations—which are very different from moral conclusions —permeate the Biography and animate the figures in proportion as they possess them and are compelled toward beauty, which is symmetry, which is perfection—as it was at Jerusalem.

PART FOUR

THE LATER WORKS

17: *Their Lives and Letters*

Cabell's later writings consist essentially of five trilogies. The first trilogy is entitled *Their Lives and Letters*, and it stands as a prologue to the later novels while a second nonfiction trilogy is called *Virginians Are Various* and acts as the epilogue. The first of the trilogies of novels is *The Nightmare Has Triplets*; this comprises *Smirt* (1934), *Smith* (1935), and *Smire* (1937). The second is *Heirs and Assigns*, consisting of *The King Was in His Counting House* (1938), *Hamlet Had an Uncle* (1940), and *The First Gentleman of America* (1942). The third and last trilogy of fiction is called *It Happened in Florida*, and is composed of a history, *The St. Johns* (1943), and two short novels, *There Were Two Pirates* (1946) and *The Devil's Own Dear Son* (1949). Closely associated with and yet not exactly of these compact units of threes are a number of critical essays and interpretations concerning Cabell's contemporaries such as "Joseph Hergesheimer: An Essay in Interpretation" (1921), "Some of Us: An Essay in Epitaphs" (1930), and "Of Ellen Glasgow" (1938). There is also a fine essay dedicated to the cause of Cabell's fame, John S. Sumner, Agent of the New York Society for the Suppression of Vice. It is cruel in the tradition of Augustan satire, very funny, and well-enough entitled "Taboo" (1921).

The development and literary status of these later works are significant. After completing the Biography, Cabell omitted his first name; in a special sense, he is a different person and his art reflects this fact. It is rather as if his writings prior to 1930 took him toward Antan while those after 1930 betoken a reluctant but steady withdrawal. This is not to say that Cabell's art goes to pieces on completion of the Biography—far from it. Nevertheless he does seem to be like Napoleon returning from Moscow, although he fights every inch of the way, frequently halts for stubborn rear-guard actions, and even at times—as in *Heirs and Assigns*—makes recognizable if temporary advances. The nonfiction remains consistently superb. This last fact may be the clue to the total development. Cabell's earliest writings dealt with contemporary life and more satirically with people and personal relations as in the first novels and short stories. Then he plunged into an ironical treatment of the relations between men and the gods as he produced his best works culminating in Gerald Musgrave's "camping" on the very borders of Antan. Now, Cabell deals increasingly again with the satiric; he gradually abandons the depths of irony even as he begins to move again toward the present in time. His last novel, *The Devil's Own Dear Son*, deals, however unusually, with contemporary Florida. It was published in 1949, the year of his first wife's death. He had met and married Priscilla Bradley Cabell in 1912 and in 1913 he published *The Soul of Melicent*, the first work of novel length in which Cabell found himself as an artist. His last prose deals in memoirs covering, of course, the twentieth century up to 1955. Thus it may be said of Cabell that as he started, so does he return. The spiritual cycle or circle is complete and closes at the point of both departure and return. This accounts for the sustained pungency of the later works even as they are less profound and, on the whole, less moving. Where Jack London was cut off in narcissistic prime, where Sinclair Lewis tended to lapse into the sentimental when going beyond the satiric, where nothing remained to Hemingway but to intensify the horror of his predicaments, where Faulkner's studies of decay may be too specialized for a lasting general audience, where most of Dreiser's work is a topical and colloquial representation of disintegration, Cabell has completed the full circle as demanded by Eros.

The subconsciously rooted human instinct for aggression and self-destruction has had very full play indeed during the first half of the twentieth century. On the last page of his study *Civilization and Its Discontents* (1930), Freud notes how man may now pause, in face of his ability for complete self-destruction, and the last words of the study are:

> And now it may be expected that the other of the two "heavenly forces," eternal Eros, will put forth his strength so as to maintain himself alongside of his equally immortal adversary.

This statement is helpful not only because it reveals Freud expressing himself in terms of myth, but because it seems to offer additional confirmation for the contention that fuller understanding of Cabell may well ring down the curtain on twentieth-century realism as surely as the preface to the second edition of Wordsworth's *Lyrical Ballads* likewise did for the Age of Reason. Further support for this viewpoint may derive from the fact that where the reputations of all too many modern artists tend to suffer at the hands of psychological assessments, the very opposite seems to be the case with Cabell. The artist, prophet, or seer, is foremost: he is at the summit of human effort; he is the spearhead of man's advance into the unknown. Behind him come the intellectuals, rationalizing and producing objective and scientific data. Perhaps Freud and Jung have been the scientists nearest the summit or spearhead: they have most rationalized in that area between the known and the unknown in the trail of the foremost artists who have dealt in worthwhile syntheses and not simply fallen back on objective analysis for want of imagination. It may not be right to say that Jung's intellect is greater than Freud's but Jung seems to have possessed greater feeling or compassion, so that, in the total application, perhaps Jung has made more imaginative use of his data. Consequently, where Freud tended to reduce all to the life force or libido within the individual, Jung was able to go beyond the individual to relate man to cosmic organic workings. Jung did this by concentrating upon world-wide myths. He was thus able to enumerate more comprehensively than Freud the compulsive forces within man, forces which not only prod him on but which dictate the very nature of his inventions as seen supremely in the case of Prometheus and his fires. Much may be made of all this in the remainder of the twentieth century. Meanwhile, Cabell will grow in stature, as only he has so fully kept ahead of them all. In doing this through myths he has given us a unique opportunity for examining the human psyche in its very latest stage of evolution. A psychological study of his writings would be invaluable. And there is little likelihood that he would suffer from this, even as he illustrates his metamorphosis of the gods. Such a study should be undertaken only by the generous minded, for we approach truth only in proportion as we think generously—a little fact which is encouraging in itself, suggesting, as it does, that somehow generosity is an attribute of universal creation even though it can certainly disguise itself effectively enough externally.

The matured and skilled intellect that produced the author's notes to the Storisende Edition carries over directly into the prose works and is apparent in *Their Lives and Letters*. The first of this prose trilogy, *These Restless Heads*, was completed in July, 1931. The title is taken from Marlowe and the book is subtitled "A Trilogy of Romantics." It consists of a short story dealing with Prospero after he releases Ariel and returns to Milan, then with direct personal reminiscences and reflections, and finally with a short story as an epilogue about one Thomas Learmont. Prospero's story tells of what is, in effect, a betrayal by Prospero of his imaginative gifts as he turns from art to politics. The reason for this betrayal is lack of an audience (although Caliban had provided "the advantages of contemporary criticism"), but there is an additional reason, which echoes the ideas in *Something About Eve*. For Prospero reflects on the fifteen years of his prime, a prime spent upon creative magic but at the cost of all human affection except "the cool charity of old Gonzalo," at the cost, then, of any "talent for human living." So lack of an audience and loneliness causes Prospero to relinquish his magic and return to the splendors of comfort, wealth, and men's deference. He practices common sense and he conforms as a good executive "with sound views as to agriculture and finance and the problems of sewerage," so that his realm prospers in arms and in commerce. Prospero has every reason to be pleased with his new creation, the Duke of Milan—every reason except one. This consists of what he sees in mirrors:

> He noticed that in mirrors he found the sage and calm figure of an all-victorious prince, but that this admirable figure regarded him with the bright, the slightly malicious, and the contemptuous eyes of Ariel.

This discovery rather upsets matters and there is not much that Prospero can do but have another glass of wine. Yet never can he escape those "sane and implacable eyes which remained lightly amused"—until he dies, that is, on a fine March morning and with proper medical attention. Yet some talk of a small boat that puts to sea that spring, accompanied by the right winds and escorted by the right sea-nymphs, carrying—it is said—the incurable artist "through the dawn of yet another new day" back to "the beauty and the nonsense of his Island."

In his introduction to *These Restless Heads* Cabell observes that it is "a cohering trilogy which concerns itself...with one main theme and with one protagonist." In the second part of the book Cabell takes up the account in his own person, day and place. This second part occupies most of the book and shows Cabell as an essayist in the very finest manner of the classical tradition. Language betokens the individual or the people as they develop from the unconscious infantile state to increasingly conscious awareness of subconscious motivations. Thus Cabell's writings can remind one of Addison and poor Richard Steele (very much a prototype for Cabell's gallants as seen in Steele's fine gesture of garbing the bailiff's men as footmen for a last bankrupt party while regarding himself as never so well attended), of Johnson and Goldsmith, of Lamb, De Quincey, and Hazlitt; yet with Cabell there is a more mellifluous economy of expression and his intellect is often more incisive. Thus he directly links the Virginian tradition with a heritage of thousands of years of profound and intense intellectual endeavor. The second and most important section of direct reflection moves forward lightly on the wheels of personal reminiscence, of the postman, godlike in his dispensation of providence, of the mail itself—a standard theme of the later writings—and of the proposed visit of a young novelist, a visit which enables Cabell to discuss literary genius. The chapter entitled "Rewards of Economy" indicates the sources of scenes and people in Poictesme as they originate in Rockbridge Alum before it was bypassed by a faster way of life.

> The ballroom of the Central Hotel after nightfall would still be, I knew, peculiarly like that Hall of Judgement wherein Jurgen conversed with young Guenevere. . . . Here was the lawn upon which Jurgen had won back to his never-aging dream of Dorothy la Desirée. . . .
>
> Upon the farther side of Bratton's Run I came again to the patch by which Florian de Puysange had ascended to Upper Morven; but me it conducted to the boulder beside which the same Florian had kindled his tiny fire in the gardens of Storisende.

Here seems to be useful evidence not only for the Promethean significance of such as Florian but also for the identity between Cabell and his creations. He strings his reflections upon the thread of the year's seasons and an important section is entitled "Near a Flag in Summer." Here the irony and satire intermingle to show clearly his oceanic sense of eternity as he brings men's antics into timely perspective. Even as he is engaged, childlike, in making myths, Cabell is accompanied by the prattlings, childish, of this flag. Honor receives Falstaffian considerations; patriotism is seen, with Johnson, as the last refuge of a scoundrel. Yet the compulsions behind these attitudes are fundamental not only to humans but to Cabell's own created characters; these compulsions molded the deeds in Poictesme, as they do the deeds of the followers of all flags. Thus, while Cabell certainly avoids dealing with the externals of contemporary life, he nevertheless puts his typewriting fingers right on the pulse of that life and renders it in eternal form.

In illustrating this, Cabell actually discloses the true creative propensities of the myth-maker as established scientifically by such as Jung. In the chapter entitled "Practical Matters" Cabell writes:

> . . . the practiced author develops a highly specialized subconsciousness which decides for him, far more happily than he can do, the theme and the general outline of his writing. . . . It tacitly picks out for him, I think, if only he possesses the intelligence not to meddle here, such tasks as will be truly and profoundly to his liking. Like a well-trained butler, it brings up from the cellarage of the subconscious, without any ostentation, a vintage in all ways suited to the known tastes of the master of the house.

This bears directly on our understanding of the organic nature of artistic creation, seen at its clearest in that form most subject to the bodily constitution, in myths, as the writer sublimates his physical lust for life symbolically through the spirit rather than the flesh. Consequently it seems worth augmenting this evidence in the prose by quoting from Cabell's personal correspondence. In a letter dated February 12, 1958, he notes:

> From childhood I have been interested in mythological stories; and I yet have the Greek and Roman ones and the Russian skaski I was enjoying in 1886. I daresay a large deal of these volumes remained in my subconsciousness.
>
> But when it came, some years later, to the writing of books about imaginary countries, my usual course, I believe, was to make up their mythologies as I went along, so I thought; and then while I was completing the book, to consult various volumes of folk lore, in my sizeable collection thereof, which almost always suggested changes and additions in what I had first written.

This piece seems to fit the jigsaw puzzle very well. The subconscious was from the beginning, well stocked with an assortment of universal symbols. With the years of experience and insight came rational discernment confirmed and strengthened by introspective analysis, the "founding" in the preliminary prose essays; then came the natural outpourings of this same discernment and discrimination clothed in the symbols that were either ready and waiting or contrived for new meanings. The process of perfecting and polishing embodied changes in accord with what was felt or what was seen logically to be better as the process was carried consciously to its conclusion. Thus Cabell's art offers confirmation of Malinowski's description of myth as "not a mere tale told but a reality lived . . . an original, greater and more important reality through which the present life, fate and work of mankind are governed." Cabell, who refused to listen to the flag flapping "Look at me! look at me!" yet wrote always in its presence at the beck of "that daemon who in some sort both serves and controls my endless typing." This section ends with a consideration of Cabell's cosmos as he observes:

> . . . upon the national flag which waves over all its unseen towns and fortresses (wherein nonsense reigns, wherein beauty yet endures) one would discover ramping a silver stallion.

This, too, is as it should be, for the paramount symbolism of the horse is the life force or Freud's libido, or yearning, as it appears in all mythologies and is very clearly shown in Shakespeare's *Venus and Adonis*.[1] In Poictesme it signifies the most economical expenditure of energy in the orderly pursuit of beauty: most flags, which also betoken the life-force, signify a chaotic pursuit of aggressive expansion leaving trails of ugliness. But perhaps the silver stallion will fly longest as it slowly overcomes the serried rangs of all the rest. Unless, of course—as is implied in a number of Cabell's books including *The Silver Stallion* itself— man turns out to be an experiment that failed, through lack of that generosity necessary for understanding. So Poictesme has a very good flag and one under which Manuel was not the only one to die as Eros does eternal battle with Ananke.

[1] Jung notes on page 308 of *Psychology of the Unconscious* later entitled *Symbols of Transformation:*

The hero and the horse appear . . . [as] the idea of humanity with its repressed libido whereby the horse acquires the significance of the animal unconscious which appears domesticated and subjected to the will of man.

This is the exact use of Kalki as rendered in *Something About Eve*, where it does, in fact, become domesticated as soon as Gerald desists from his journey to Anton. It is useful to note also the saying (quoted in the London *Observer*) of a car manufacturer, that nothing makes a man feel more like a knight on horseback than driving a good car.

As autumn supersedes summer, Cabell writes not of the flag but of Aesred, Our Lady of Compromise and Conformity. He dives yet more deeply into those pools whence he acquired his life-giving myths. These chapters are invaluable for their illustration of his attitude toward this material and his saturation with their substance. The prose, which is already intellectually of the first order, suddenly becomes imbued with the power of the Biography as, in Chapter XXIII, Cabell touches again the essence of vital concerns, like conformity and compromise: "In the mythology of Poictesme there was, save only Koschei the Deathless, none more mighty than Aesred." Of this passage Cabell notes, "All which is quite the approved style wherein to handle this theme, and employs with discretion the dear old decadent phrasing." Cabell identifies conformity as a subject common to at least English and American writers.

> Everywhere I detect writers of every degree pointing out with unexplained animosity . . . that the habitual conformity can be neither candid nor rational.

Cabell, with ironic perspicacity, turns the tables on this attitude and, in effect, produces a literary parallel to the findings of psychology about the best form of sublimation as far as the artist is concerned. The writer must take himself seriously and cherish the notion that what he does is important even if all reason proves the opposite. Still do all writers continue to rage rebelliously against the cohorts of Aesred and still in the outcome are they doomed. Brilliantly does the author unfold his conceptions of the value, the usefulness, the inevitability of the triumphant march of mediocrity and conformity in all walks of life. Cabell shows us just what can be signified by a simple prosaic box of matches—as each match is traced to its mythological source and all the cohorts of Aesred are employed to deliver them from Finland to Virginia. Even as infantile man delighted to quell the first fires have these matches been rendered impotent by a rainfall. Aesred is supreme. Or is she? Where there is Aesred so also is Ettarre. Here again does Cabell's prose become fine music:

For Ettarre teaches that the ways of conformity are wise but ignoble; that the respect of the dull witted and of the cowed is an honor somewhat incriminating; and that her secret knowledge, if only we could master it, may yet lead some of us, among dim byways, toward that unique land in which one may live, perhaps, with more competence. Even in the ambiguity of that half-promise she lies, no doubt; but she remains wholly lovely.

So Cabell still continued with creative writing to experience the "baseless contentment" which was so preferable to the wisdom of Aesred.

As autumn yields to winter, Cabell draws his reflections to a close, a close that illustrates the origin and strength of his best fiction. He surveys the recurrent theme of all fiction from the old tale of Prince Asuga to the story of the traveling salesman. The essential outline is, "the human hero must leave that which is familiar, to journey upon a quest." Jung has confirmed this by illustrating the origins and nature of the compulsions within man which predetermine that he should do this and that he should seek precisely that Helen of Jurgen and all the other heroes whose wives nature has decreed shall be only partial substitutes or partial embodiments. Meanwhile, "there is but one fable which holds true everywhere. The man goes upon a journey: that is all."

The epilogue is a short short story of how an ageing maker of half-magics refused the invitation to return to the land of faery, and, on account of his age, decided to continue as a well-thought-of citizen. Albeit his also remains one of "these restless heads."

The second work of this trilogy, *Special Delivery* (1933), contains, in the form of replies to the letters authors most often receive, a series of reflections more immediately personal than the middle portion of *These Restless Heads*. It may be said that where the first book of the trilogy deals with Cabell's art and attitude in general, *Special Delivery* deals with himself and his ideas most personally, while the third book, *Ladies and Gentlemen*, deals more specifically with the sources, the archetypes, of his own mythology. Thus each volume of this trilogy fills in details of related personal aspects of Cabell's attitude and art, as the earlier prose essays of *Beyond Life* and *Straws and Prayer Books* do for his thought and philosophy.

These prose writings also provide, although not to such profound depths, germinal analysis from which came later syntheses. For example, many of these ten replies touch satirically upon the nature of Virginia, the U.S.A., and modern life everywhere in the west, a nature to be dealt with more substantially in the first of the later fiction, particularly *Smirt*; likewise out of the letter to Hamlet in *Ladies and Gentlemen* was to emerge the full-length treatment in *Hamlet Had an Uncle*. There is a very sharp edge to these letters even as there is in most of the later writing, as the urbane impersonal irony yields to observations closer to the present in time and in person. After all, Cabell's position was so clearly unique: here is a civilized writer with mind and heart fully attuned to skills and concepts immortal who was free to express himself to the fullest of his range. Where so many were producing more marketable goods, here was the genuine artist cast in the mold of the ancients but with full command of the present. Not often has this century produced such a coincidence of circumstance and ability in letters. Cabell looks from Olympus upon the antics of his own era and a fine spectacle is finely portrayed—not by the usual topical means but through the gaze of eternity. In ten letters or essays, Cabell directs his attention to numerous facets of life as represented by the writers: a schoolgirl, a would-be author, a reviewer, an established female novelist, an enthusiast for culture, a young lady prepared to give all for her career, a questionable character from England, a religious writer, and an old love. One way or another these writers all enable Cabell to comment on pretty well every major feature of modern life. But even as he becomes caustic he does so with the attitude of Ecclesiastes. At the end he turns his attention to himself and produces perhaps the finest Roman writing in the collection—"Odi et amo" quoth Catullus as Cabell says the same of his "unsought correspondent."

The following may be regarded as representative and as dealing with aspects useful to an understanding of Cabell's motives. "The Breast of the Nymph" is the second letter; it is addressed to the young would-be writer who has asked for a guide for the future in a "pathetically brisk, and forthright, and business-like and moonstruck letter." This letter causes Cabell to reflect on the situation in Virginia when he himself was asking this same question, for his own intent to become a writer was firmly and clearly in his mind from about his sixteenth year. Wealth was not his aim, and Virginia was not likely to have satisfied it had it been, for Virginia wanted only the fulsome flattery of the spoken word, the more loudly spoken the better. Jerusalem was a fair maiden but Babylon was otherwise:

> The leather-lunged congressmen and the braying senators she took into her bed of love, and they defiled her with loud platitudes: she doted also upon divers retired, but not at all retiring, Confederate veterans, whose voice was as the voice of asses. To the roaring of wild pastors she hearkened amorously. All these had bruised her teats so that her breasts might nurse the young no longer. With all these never-idle talkers Virginia had played the wanton in a little corner, in the plashed mire of her stagnant backwater, saying, Speak to me of my pre-eminence!

So Cabell had only the "blind and very strong instinct" to write: but it was enough. In this essay, too, appears the literal version of what in the fiction is symbolized by Ettarre; this concerns the instinct which expresses itself as a compulsion to make things out of words. It is the sight of beauty, glimpsed during youth, not comprehended and certainly never grasped, that harnesses this instinct as Ariel to Prospero or flame to Prometheus. The poet

> has seen, somehow, what Swinburne, in one rare moment of lucidity, has called "the breast of the nymph in the brake."

Cabell notes that the poet

> has seen this but as a gleaming beheld only in part and only for the space of a heart-beat—a space wherein the beholder's heart did not beat at all, but faltered between terror and worship and longing.

The poet differs from ordinary mortals in that while they become sensible and grow down he remains sensitive and grows up. But another point emerges here which seems to indicate the difference between the artist of the unconscious, the myth-maker, and what might be described as the artist of the conscious, the one who deals with his own time as a reformer as well as as entertainer— as Shaw and H. G. Wells (who, after all, formed a climate of opinion for many years), the later Zola, and Upton Sinclair. While noting that the creative writer is one who does not forget the glimpse of beauty which entranced him, Cabell believes also that the writer must remain if not childish yet forever childlike, at least inwardly, and certainly in so far as he must not undertake any logical analysis of art's justification. The poet is born and fulfills himself by "making" in accordance with the demands of an instinct. As Cabell sees it, there can be no more logical justification for art than for any "other high matters, such as religion, or a sense of honor, or the institution of marriage." Here we must beware of his perverse irony, his ability to damn with faint praise, his tongue in his cheek, his delight in tying ideas up into bouquets which hide his meanings:

> Age and experience will teach the considerate to distrust every exercise of human intelligence, and to observe that life is made livable only through a wise choice of delusions.

Yes, but for the choice to be wise requires at least some exercise of intelligence. As it is just prevarications such as these which have done much to label Cabell as an escapist, perhaps it is advisable to look more closely at these statements to see if any primary principles can be discerned. He refers to high matters such as religion, honor, and marriage, and relates his derogatory remarks to his view that there can be no logical justification for art. Now place these observations alongside his comments in the author's note to *Straws and Prayer Books* about his major writings:

> "Domnei" exalts womanhood beyond our present day, more prosaic beliefs, and . . . "Jurgen" upholds the . . . unpopular doctrine that a married man had best remain faithful . . . *Something About Eve* depicts a later Galahad . . . "The Silver Stallion" pleads frankly . . . for . . . old fashioned religion.

Thus these themes deal with religion, honor, and marriage, and they constitute however unpriggishly, the spiritual messages of Cabell's literature.

These would seem, then, to be the delusions chosen to make life livable. Wherein lies their wisdom? The answer seems to be much more than a simple reduction to morals, although it may embody moral discrimination. The delusions which make life livable are those which make for integration, even if it includes such sinful things as divorce, spiritual instead of theological self-sufficiency, and withdrawing from one's neighbors as well as loving them. Integrity is involved, too: not only is courage needed to retain illusions but their retention supplies courage. Thus art deludes after a "handsome and comfort giving fashion"—life is made more livable or more enjoyable. We are brought nearer to that happiness for the pursuit of which a new world was made.

Is there, in the extension of the legend of a redeemer—as illustrated in *The Silver Stallion*—any further connection between life and literature? Throughout the English-speaking world a myth of a redeemer is perpetuated and, however slightly, man seems to have been elevated at least to the point that policemen now carry our clubs for us. The leaders or men of action have had much to do with these developments, but always the seers have been near. Is it too much to say that we are more civilized or, at least, that there is a little more equality before the law because of the ideas of such as Sidney, Raleigh, and Spenser—poets who were also prime men of Elizabethan action perpetuating the legend of a redeemer—of Cromwell's secretaries, Milton and Marvell, redesigning a kingdom even while creating its greatest myths, as did Vergil and Homer; do we not see the bridge from old to new in the distribution of Tom Paine's Jeffersonian *Rights of Man* by Burns, Shelley, and Blake, as these principles of life live on for those who can choose their delusions wisely? And, in so far as Gerald went East to find them for his journey to Antan, are not these principles universal? Yet they have emerged as revelations not explanations, making Cabell sound in his acknowledgment only of that insistent instinct for "the breast of the nymph"

—the spiritual equivalent of that physical desire implanted in man which harnesses him for all his endeavors and achievements even from his first inventions of fire and speech brought about by the sacrifice or repression of the incestuous impulse residing like a dynamo in his unconscious. Perhaps this tirade should be concluded in Cabell's own words:

> Nor do I mean to speak further of the matter. For this is, I admit, a matter with which the ordered life and the slowly gathered wisdom of man's race have no concern, and of which human reason may well doubt the civic and economic worth . . . but the eyes of young men have seen this matter and they stay perturbed.

"For Rhadamanthus Smiling" is directed to one of the judges of Hell, in this case a reviewer whose significance may not be eternal. "A Study of Sincerity" is a fair estimate of much popular literature if only from the point of view of the analysis of style as it illustrates the tools of Cabell's own writing equipment. In "Art, Beauty and Balderdash," Cabell again grapples with that view which insists on identifying the artist with the martyr and the seer: any American, Cabell notes, when dealing publicly with aesthetics,

> . . . must justify "art" upon some altruistic or moral ground. . . . He must rank the artist somewhere between the seer and the martyr, and yet suggest too that the artist's labor has kinship with the public-welfare work of the local Chamber of Commerce. He must always ignore the fact that the artist pursues his art, in chief, because . . . "he likes to."

It is hoped that enough has been said here to clarify at least some of the ambiguity as Cabell steps in and out of the shoes of the Tumblebug. "A good book is the precious life-blood of a master spirit," said Milton. Cabell has been molded by the company of many such master spirits even as all humanity is molded by the company it keeps. If we *are* evolving, someone must represent it. Yet, admittedly, that is no reason for ignoring that the artist too is compelled by the self-interest of enjoyment or what Freud calls the "pleasure principle."

The essay "Mirror and Pigeons" is one of the wittiest of this series and well does it treat that attitude which, on the eve of Dunkirk, forbade tank exercises on the downs of southern England because such activities would ruin the gallops of nearby stables. Yet, if dullness and mediocrity reign supreme, they do so universally. "Liturgy in Darkness" sustains this humor and offers a direct illustration of the author's attitude toward organized orthodox religious rituals; this illustration shows in action the ideas about this which permeate the earlier essays and the fiction as Cabell goes to church:

> Half visible grave persons shake hands with me in the gloom. They remark with needless significance, that they are very glad to see me here. Dozens of handshaking persons thus remark solemnly, one by one, that they are very glad to see me here. . . . When we reach the church door I shake hands with the rector and I tell him, in the same earnest tone, that I am very glad to see him here.

Yet, as always, behind the facetiousness there is an optimistic profundity. Here is the direct personal rationalization of such as the chapters in *The Silver Stallion* dealing with the god Donander playing with a world in the temples of which people like insects beseeched him for his mercy even as he was about to destroy them to make something better:

> From the deep dark we cry out to a wisdom very far above our blunders, to a strength above our feebleness, and to a kindliness above our spites, our lewdness, and our busy hatreds . . . we cry out rather hopefully for compassion, upon the firm ground that creatures so pitiable deserve compassion: and we are certain that omniscience can hardly miss a point so plain to mere common-sense. Hearing, He must heed, in mere logic.

Even if there is no such power, and life is the consequence of the chance playings of a dumb devil, still is it "the assured part of wisdom, I think, to believe in a wholly fine and a wholly noble deity," if only on the grounds of "when ill, take treatment." Thus we seem to have that emotional core which is the dynamic source of all the intellectual striving for understanding even though consequent insight sees both sides of every question and imaginatively embodies them in its paradoxical and perverse fiction.

The last letter, except for the address to himself, is to one who was an old flame. Ruthless is Cabell's depiction of the unmercifulness of time, cruel in its ravages; abundant evidence is here of the precision or realism of Cabell's observation. Here too is, perhaps, part of the reason for his artistic pursuit of Ettarre:

> But thirty years ago—then there were goddesses. All earth was populous with divine girlhood. And its dear possessors came to you unworthy; they came one by one, as philanthropists, ungirdled, yielding without parsimony an opulence of well curved and fair colored charms; they came, in those remote times, as fondly as Venus came to Anchises, as alertly as Diana might approach an Endymion who had no least present thoughts of sleeping, or as daintily at Titania came to Nick Bottom.

This may represent the high water mark of this writing while the best may be Cabell's equivalent of Shakespeare's review of the ages of man, seen in "Art, Beauty and Balderdash," where he lists the "great commonplaces of (man's) life here as a thinking animal."

In the third book of this prose trilogy Cabell's writing maintains its high level of wit and intellect. It consists of a prologue which deals with the writer's situation in any society, and with twenty "letters" to figures who are mainly the sources for the many incarnations that make up his own mythology. *Ladies and Gentlemen* is one of the most important of the later works as well as one of the most enjoyable.

All these letters are marvelously suggestive and are all relevant not only to an understanding of Cabell but to understanding in general—Jung's answer to both belief and disbelief. The most immediately relevant appear to be as follows: the prologue, which "treats of writing without tears"; the first letter, "To Penelope, the Daughter of Icarius"; the fourth letter, "To Egeria, the Fond Huntress"; the eighth letter, "To Sir Galahad of the Siege Perilous"; the ninth, "To Hamlet, King of Jutland"; the eleventh, "To

Lord Timur the Splendid"; the thirteenth, "To Dr. Johan Faustus
. . ."; the eighteenth, "To Mr. John Wilkes Booth"; and the twentieth, "Which Deals with a Pawnbroker."

Part of the prologue appeared in the *American Spectator* as did parts of a number of the letters, notably the thirteenth. In this prologue, Cabell considers the standard view which bewails the lot of the artist in a society that lacks understanding; by reversing the usual approach, he illustrates that the artist who demands rewards from his society is not an artist, that real artists keep silent because "they happen actually to be artists, whom their art contents in its own special, illogical, and high fashion, and upon whom an innate form of insanity acts as a cordial." The letter to Penelope, the wife of Odysseus, is the first to contribute to the unfolding of a viewpoint fundamental to Cabell's conception of life:

> A quaint outcome it seems, that, although the Odyssey has been regarded from countless standpoints, the tale . . . actually is . . . the history of a man's strong and allsurmounting love for his own wife.

Penelope emerges as a calm and capable housewife, repelling the suitors even as she accepted gifts for their board and lodging, as she awaits with confidence the return of the wanderer. Odysseus "wept as he embraced his beloved and true wife" and was greeted by Penelope with cool affection. Penelope, in fact, is the archetype of all the wives in the Biography, of Niafer, Lisa, of Madoc's Ettarre and of Maya in *Something About Eve*. All are perpetuated even through *Heirs and Assigns* to the wife in "The Devil's Own Dear Son." If the man goes upon a journey, Helen is at home at the end. This is precisely in keeping as illustrated by Jung, who shows the reasons for the dual pursuit of Helen and Penelope. Out of the motivation of this dual pursuit and in proportion as man sacrifices carnal gratifications—as Odysseus avoided Circé, or Gerald his Eves—does man approach Antan. So Cabell's insight is sound and profound as he identifies the source of male motivation and casts it in mythic mold, showing us here the beginning and the end of all journeying:

. . . she has her own deep wisdom, denied to golden Helen and unguessed at by any wanton Sirens, that wisdom through which Penelope creates and rules over the quiet afternoon of each lucky man's living. . . . Affably, gently, and implacably, she converts the egotistic and self-reliant hero into the sedately contented husband.

For the wandering intellectual there is allocated Penelope; for the wondering man of action there is Egeria. If Penelope controls the beginning and the end for the seer, Egeria controls the middle for the statesman or leader. Egeria, the Fond Huntress, is the woman in the background, the power behind the throne, the woman who, without a vote, controls the legislation. Egeria it was who gave up godhead to devote herself to the advancement of Numa Pompilius and the creation of Rome. Finely does Cabell trace her descent and influence through the ages. There emerges the author's conception of the innate childishness of the masculine mind (cf. Hitler's dance on the occupation of Paris) as compared with the finely balanced logic and impartiality of the feminine brain. Until at last "a third prince . . . had just started out, from over yonder in Poictesme, upon his quest of something or other," and once more Egeria, who introduces a semblance of order and common sense into male activities, went to the back of the king's palace, "and loosed one of your very finest dragons, to afford the lad a little harmless diversion." Behind the light touch of this treatment is the powerful hand of comprehension; we see the ever-interwoven threads of male and female that are the groundwork in the unfolding tapestry of life that is here spun for us.

The eighth letter, "To Sir Galahad of the Siege Perilous," is worth considering along with the eighteenth, "To Mr. John Wilkes Booth." In the special Cabellian manner both of these illustrate the workings of Christianity throughout the English-speaking world; that is, they deal with a force that persists, however ambiguously, to represent a major supporter of Eros against the dark tyranny that makes for the elimination of individual worth and freedom. Cabell is not a political writer. He does represent constructive human effort, and consequently, however inadvertently, he approaches the essential attitudes and forces behind peoples who claim to be Christian.

This eighth letter surveys the attitudes and deeds of Arthur from the days of the Romans to, it would seem, Tennysonian dissolution. In the early stages the fellowship lived and loved freely and contentedly enough, compromising where convenience required yet maintaining at least the semblance of law and respectability with renewed vows of honor and chastity. "Matters were already going quite well enough—upon the whole—in King Arthur's England." Then came the prophecy of that Galahad who "shall be the Best Knight in the World." With the Reformation came Sir Philip Sidney, Raleigh, Spenser, a host of warrior poets, and with this arrival of Galahad came the burden of the greatest quest of all for Arthur's realm, the quest of the Sangreal, "which is the secret of Our Lord Jesus Christ." For ordinary mortals the burden proved too great: of the fellowship only Galahad himself succeeded, the others being outrivaled to their ultimate dissolution.

> For outrivalled they were, very completely. Within a week or so, in fact, a few of them had straggled back to Camelot, disposed to laugh off the entire matter.

For these, there were always compensations, like other people's wives. Cabell seems to outline the rise and complexities of Empire as a compulsion which expressed itself as a truth and was found to be beyond the reach of most. The miracle of Sir Galahad had left "momentarily, a noble desire and a high aspiring, not utterly grasped by the mind." This produced, also, a feeling of not quite liking holiness.

> And yet one felt too, perhaps that absurd, young, beautiful, grave Galahad had found in life an exceedingly great treasure which one had missed, somehow.

Sensible people would leave ideals alone. Yet the old spirit of genial and broadminded compromise was weakened by the task set by the high ideals of Galahad. Stranded between pretensions and compulsions,

. . . the power of King Arthur crumbled, now that it was bereft of
the kindly aid of human humbug: and the treason of Launcelot,
the malignity of Mordred, and Gawain's lack of self control, all
combined to complete . . . the task which your unflawed virtue had
begun at Camelot.

Cabell observes that no safe moral seems possible. But this compulsion and this Christian example has had world-wide consequences; the example and the truth it is held to represent have
considerably restricted any dictatorial tendencies so that, willy
nilly, individual and national freedoms have been granted. The
children have left the mother and embarked on their more independent lives in the normal process of growth and without too
much squabbling. At least that is how we like to see it.

In the letter to Booth we see how this strange compulsion, still
garbed in the guise of Christianity, expresses itself in perhaps the
biggest of these children, the U.S.A. In this chapter, Cabell describes the evolution of the "Lincoln myth," that "invaluable
American possession." The irony here reveals the reality from
which he made his fiction. The assassination of Lincoln by Booth
is similar to that of the Duke of Orleans by Florian in *The High
Place*. The action of Booth is equated with that of Judas in *Something About Eve*, with the usual distribution of moral emphasis
again reversed so that the "betrayer" emerges as a poet, a creative
artist of the highest order because he has made, in the medium of
life, a myth of the greatest lasting service to confused people. After
indicating certain discrepancies between the actual historical facts
and the mythic versions attached to the figure in the temple in
Washington, Cabell observes of Booth:

None the less does this splendid myth, which you Americanized
with a pistol, well satisfy a great people's need; and it inculcates
steadily among us every one of the standard virtues, so that your
self-sacrifice has fostered both art and morals.

The myth itself is, of course, adapted from an older one as reflected
in the view that Lincoln was conceived by one higher than his

own father, a carpenter—born in a stable and killed on Good Friday. Cabell concludes:

> You gave us, in place of the dingy truth, a demi-god and a national messiah. But instead of that gratitude which you had earned, we have repaid with obloquy the most great of America's creative artists.

This is precisely the theme of *The Silver Stallion* and the growth of the myth of Manuel. Somehow or another this force, as embodied in this myth, must go on, but few have recognized so clearly and expressed so neatly that paradox which is its vehicle.

The ninth letter is to Hamlet, not the prince but the king. As Cabell indicates in *These Restless Heads,* as far as he is concerned and in spite of contemporary literature, Shakespeare and the Bible have not yet been ousted from their literary supremacy. Indeed, all his thinking can be traced back through the European-Roman-Greek line of continuous descent into legend and myth until lost in premythic mists when even Prometheus, the earliest Hamlet, went on all fours. This letter is, in fact, the germinal synopsis for one of the best of the later novels, *Hamlet Had an Uncle* (1940). Although Cabell does not, in the novel, concentrate on Shakespeare's Hamlet, we can see in this letter something of Cabell's thoughts about the earlier, portrayed by Saxo Grammaticus, and the Shakespearian. In the letter the two Hamlets are brought on the stage together and the procrastination of the latter is confronted with the habit of direct action of the earlier. Yet this is done in such a way as to imply fresh considerations concerning the Shakespearian. Do we, even now, fully understand Hamlet? It is worth glancing for a moment at the evolution of critical thought concerning the Black Prince. With all the respect due to Johnson, this thought does not really start until the nineteenth century. In evaluating our most imaginative artist, Johnson did surprisingly well for one who lacked an imagination. Yet it still remains that for him and his age the chief thing about *Hamlet* was still that the ghost was frightening. It was as natural for Johnson to think that Shakespeare had done no more than hold up a mirror to his age as it is for twentieth-century realists not to see that Cabell has been doing more than take photographs. With Coleridge the metaphysical approach is well launched. This continues through Goethe and Bradley to Dover Wilson. All these see Hamlet as a tragedy of the spirit, a spirit which, thinking too precisely on the event, is either incapable of decision or overwhelmed, being no more than a soul unequal to the performance of a great deed. Criticism beyond this has concerned itself with language to the point that, so minute and close is the examination of each tree that we forget we are in a wood at all—even though this may certainly be one way out of it.

The Coleridge-Schlegel theory regards Hamlet's as a tragedy of reflection where the excess of reflection or speculation leads to irresolution. This (the tragic enough culmination for Coleridge himself) is only a starting point for our understanding of the play. Bradley shows that Hamlet, among any other circumstances, is fully equal to his tasks as far as action is concerned. This seems self-evident from his actions concerning the letter carried by Rosencrantz and Guildenstern to England, even if Hamlet's return to Denmark was no more than chance. Bradley takes matters a step further by showing that the cause of the excessive reflection is the discovery of the true nature of the members of the court, in particular as expressed in what seemed the prostitution of his mother. Bradley regards the shock of this discovery as responsible for the horror, then the loathing, then the despair of human nature that besets the melancholy Prince so that, pondering on the value of all life, he delays to deal merely with that of Claudius. Thus does Shakespeare convert a simple and well worn theme of revenge into the classic document of man's perplexed enquiry into the purpose and nature of existence, and into human nature, its obligations and travails.

Dover Wilson, from his first kindlings in a railway compartment, spent a lifetime taking this play to pieces and revitalizing our understanding, but even so he observes:

> Shakespeare . . . never furnishes an explanation for Hamlet's inaction. All he does is to exhibit it as a problem . . . so that we may see every side of it . . . to draw our own conclusion.

But there is an explanation perhaps. In accordance with laws of withdrawal and return, to acquire understanding and then to impart it, Hamlet, resurrected and unbound, finally comes to himself, as explicitly acknowledged by Horatio, chorus as well as immovable rock of generous fortitude, when he clearly states "What a king is this!" on hearing of Hamlet's action over Rosencrantz and Guildenstern. While Dover Wilson recognizes Hamlet's return to sanity and his positive, sustained action, he seems to regard it as the consequence of approaching physical death as suggested by his reference to Hamlet's behavior over Horatio's Roman antics as:

> One more outbreak of the tremendous self that death has recovered for him.

But Horatio's earlier exclamation shows that Hamlet came to himself before being poisoned or even challenged to his final battle. Hamlet's age should be associated with the following words from Keat's preface to *Endymion*, that Keats whose letters again enshrine the thought of Hamlet and whose usefulness was again cut short:

> The imagination of a boy is healthy, and the mature imagination of a man is healthy; but there is a space of life between, in which the soul is in a ferment, the character undecided, the way of life uncertain, the ambition thick-sighted; thence proceeds mawkishness, and all the thousand bitters. . . .

Whoever listened to Horatio? Only this interpretation makes sense of the last part of the play and the military honors to one who was likely to have proved most royal.

Hamlet, it is submitted, is not a tragedy of the spirit but something much more terrible—a tragedy of circumstance. It is much more terrible because that which made Hamlet was unable to use him. This interpretation seems the only one that explains the fact that the last words of Hamlet, most independent of spirits, concern the notions of his neighbors. These last words bring us back to Cabell again because he uses them to precede his letter to Hamlet the King:

> O good Horatio, what a wounded name,
> Things standing thus unknown shall live behind me!

It has seemed worthwhile to indicate this conception of Hamlet because here appears to be direct literary evidence of the advanced nature of Cabell's thinking from the point of view of natural evolution building on what went before to achieve greater insight. By stepping historically back with his Hamlet, Cabell ridicules the interpretations that have presented the Prince King as the embodiment of vacillation rather than the central symbol of Christian, classical, oriental, eternal mythology seen at its intellectually most complicated.

The letter to Tamburlaine is interesting chiefly because it deals with the archetype of Manuel of Poictesme. Manuel began life as a swineherd. Timur or Tamburlaine began in almost the same manner:

> No city and no kingdoms, throughout the length of some forty years, had withstood successfully the assaults of the former sheep-tender.

Whereas Marlowe placed the emphasis on the self-sufficiency of Tamburlaine, the conqueror molding outcomes to his own will— a conception appropriate to an England on the threshhold of empire—Manuel receives much more godly aid in his conquest of Poictesme although he himself received all the praise and glory. Yet even though Cabell suggests that Manuel was the instrument of something else, there remains a real achievement in Manuel's actions even if he is only the vessel of predetermination—he is worthy of his role. So Cabell's version of a great conqueror is more complicated than Marlowe's; Manuel's pageant is more solemn in its implications of the ambiguities of human destiny, in the bewilderment within the man of great action even while the action is always immediate and decisive. The letter to Timur shows the ascent to supremacy with an ironic and yet valid comment on the graciousness of cruelty:

> To your adversaries likewise you remained constantly gracious, al-

lowing every besieged city two entire days in which to surrender and to become your property without further oppression.

Cabell's admiration for powerful action underlies his recognition of something more than moral issues. He admires, even likes, this despot just as—once Shakespeare has taken us inside the dilemma of Macbeth—we can no longer regard the Scot simply as a tyrant. Marlowe's lust for life tended to confuse his dramas; his latent sense of irony was never adequately developed beyond youthful satire and ridicule, however magnificently these were conveyed. Thus, as a young man, he sided with Tamburlaine when he was a despot overthrowing despots; but he became confused when dealing with the problems of Tamburlaine as a despot who was also the scourge of God. There is no such inherent contradiction in Manuel, and as this letter shows, the paradox of personal mildness and impersonal cruelty is resolved by this larger conception of necessity which governs Cabell's Tamburlaine as it does his Manuel:

> So did you live and prosper, quite incredibly; and develop into a shriveled, partially blind, nearly toothless, infirm, crippled, quiet, stout-hearted little old gentleman, who still rode continuously about Asia, huddled up on the back of a white stallion, winning battles half-absent-mindedly. It had become with you an obsession "to achieve glory and to found your dynasty."

Marlowe did not live long enough to resolve dramatically the contradiction between greatness and goodness—censorship was not his only difficulty in that problem. Cabell, from essentially the same starting point, has shown how greatness is goodness if only because it perpetuates what the instinct of the majority must believe in—the myth of Christianity. So Manuel, no matter what he does, actually becomes the scourge of God. Thus, where Marlowe's Tamburlaine could appeal only to and through fear, Manuel's fame was eventually spread by love not only to the extent that organized religion represents that force but also, here and there, among disinterested individuals and the young.

It is natural that Marlowe, a young poet speaking for a country at the beginning of powerful and aggressive growth, should appeal strongly to an America now similarly situated. Tamburlaine was the strong man of action unfettered by the qualms of conduct. Manuel derived naturally from this embryo, but with the additional skill and insight of centuries of general intellectual endeavor as well as additional years of Cabell's personal experience and thought. Thus Cabell was able to create a much more unified conception: even if the intensity of Cabell's poetry is less, it is longer sustained and much more intellectually profound. Marlowe, whose flight was cut short, went higher and more brightly but Cabell was longer on the wing and went further. And a chief point that emerges from this letter is that legends of any kind are perpetuated only by the poet.

If Achilles through Tamburlaine becomes Manuel, Odysseus through Faustus becomes Jurgen. The descendants of Manuel and Jurgen inevitably have some of each in them—even as Manuel was frequently thoughtful and Jurgen, on appropriate occasions, acted very well. In his letter to Faustus, Cabell emphasizes the one thing which ultimately betokens the stature of his own achievement in the reincarnations of these figures of action and intellect. This one thing which is fundamental to all Cabell's art appears after he has traced something of the various attitudes and motives of the artists who have handled the myth of Faustus. After illustrating Marlowe's poetic instead of pedantic rendering and Goethe's "pedantic" understanding of the philosophical mind, Cabell notes:

> For at bottom you wanted only, let it be repeated, knowledge. . . . It was permitted you to reflect, in the same instant that Mephistopheles was dashing out your brains, that these were the best stocked brains ever exercised by a descendant of Adam. You had found out the exact truth as to everything touching mortal life, including now the quaint pangs of its dissolution.

All the way through the centuries of the Biography the quest is spiritual, and therefore intellectual, rather than carnal, just as it was with Faustus, who was something more than a tenor cast "as an elderly nincompoop who gave up his soul's salvation in order to seduce an underbred working-girl."

This twentieth letter is a particularly fine one. It clarifies considerably personal ingredients in the art. The letter is preceded by the following:

> We conceive the literal acception to be a misconstruction of the symbolical expression: apprehending a veritable history, in an emblem or piece of Christian poesy.

Cabell notes that Jurgen was a character always liked by him, along with "your father Coth, and Gerald Musgrave, and, within abrupt limits, Felix Kennaston and John Charteris." The abrupt limits may have something to do with a statement made much earlier, in *The Rivet in Grandfather's Neck*, that Charteris grew a moustache to conceal the shape of his mouth; always do we come to the core of character, likeable in proportion as it is, not necessarily Christian, but courageous and generous. Here is offered evidence of the manner in which Cabell undertook his myth-making in the interest of his psyche. In the unfavorable atmosphere of the South of the late nineties, youth dwindled into sedate mediocrity.

> But when once I had transferred into Poictesme the yet unconquered youngster whom I had known . . . thrived handsomely in a congenial clime. All his faculties found employment, of a sort more or less edifying; and he lived to the full of his nature—such, I concede, perforce, as that nature was. He became, in brief, you Messire Jurgen; and in this new incarnation he stayed, as thitherto, a person over whose doings . . . I had remarkably little control.

Here is confirmation, also, of Jurgen's traveling toward Penelope or Lisa until he was "again safely caught in the talons of a virtuous female." Cabell notes that Jurgen, most thrifty of romanticists, after feasting at "life's wide and prodigal table," saved up the most generally acceptable of his illusions for dessert. Lisa, like Penelope, transformed the egotistic and self-reliant Jurgen into a sedately contented husband. The book ends with a very fine palinode. This recantation should be taken seriously although it also seems to prove that, in retiring as a poet, Jurgen, for once, did not reflect his maker. It is worth giving in full, for the creative heart is here clearly shown as it beats with the pulse of long-gone Augustans, Elizabethans, and Gallic and native Romans:

Regarding the famed dead herein allied
In letters as in proverbs; ye abide
Concernless now, and heed not, in the grave,
How once ye postured—and thereafter died.

And yet, lest such epistolary flings
Rehearsing your lost lives seem flippant things
Devoid of grace and tenderness, I crave
Benignancy of you—queens, knaves, and kings.

Unite in pardon, if I utter aught
To mar your splendours; for indeed I sought,
Long and all loyally, with truth for guide
Even in my jestings, but to mar misthought
Regarding the famed dead herein allied.

Grant me forgiveness, if perchance I name
Lightly or rashly your yet-living fame
And smile upon your hurtless sins, which rest
Eternally beyond all care or blame.

Nay, ye will pardon me—but not that wide
Zoology of zanies who deride
Exaltedly such fribbles as would jest
Regarding the famed dead herein allied.

18: *The Nightmare Has Triplets*

Smirt, Smith, and *Smire* comprise Cabell's first substantial fiction after the completion of the Biography of Manuel. In *Their Lives and Letters,* Cabell had clarified many ideas about the causes and effects of modern life in general; many of these ideas were now to be presented in *The Nightmare Has Triplets.* He is still rather uneasy at finding himself outside Poictesme even though he symbolizes it by Branlon and occasionally re-enters it.

In *Smirt,* Cabell undertakes to depict a "real" dream in the mode of Lewis Carroll. Whereas all his previous books dealt with men's dreams, those dreams had been, in effect, artistic representations of instinctive racial desires. But what of the equally illogical nightly dreams also made by Miramon Lluagor? Cabell uses the technical method or machinery of a real dream and embarks upon a survey of modern life and letters. The schematic devices are devilishly ingenious. Using flippancy, irreverence, and the profoundest clichés of a reading public, Cabell expresses not only the essentials of modern living but also a conception which hints at age-old hypotheses amounting to a form of deism. Here Cabell's intellect is clearly paramount. There emerges both a satiric porprait of a life dominated by dullness and mediocrity and an astute rerendering of Cabell's long-held view of domesticity; both aspects are united by a treatment which hints at deeper hypotheses from reincarnation to a planned and ordered universe. In addition, balance is maintained by the acknowledgment, implicit in the name *Smirt*, of the artist who is not only subject to the dangers of hubris but frequently, in his innermost thinking, an "embarrassed booby." Smirt is rather like a more topical Jurgen. He meets the public at large and notes the workings of the gods as expressed in the daily headlines; he visits the gods themselves and the creator of the universe, who is the author of that best seller the Bible; he considers the magnificent lineage of the bluebottle fly and meets lost Arachne as well as other notable females who all have technical and spiritual as well as physical parts to play; in the end, even as a bluebottle fly, but with one important proviso, Smirt happily enters the web of Arachne, heroine of the lost legend which Smirt was to rediscover for her.

Smirt is most useful for illustrating Cabell's technical skill. There are eight parts, each of which is virtually a self-contained unit in its significance although carefully interrelated with the others structurally. It is in their interrelations that the craftsmanship can be seen. For example, the first part is dominated by Smirt's meeting with his public at large. Like Browning in *The Ring and the Book*, Cabell handles this meeting traditionally: the public consists of the butcher, the baker, the candle-stick maker,

Tom, Dick, Harry, Madame Quelquechose, Senora Etcetera, Lady Ampersand, Anon, and Mrs. Murgatroyd. They exalt Smirt, all speaking in perfectly modulated well-chosen language such as appears on the best book jackets: so, with adulation on all sides, Smirt, 'a supreme genius who is in every way superb and enviable," sets off on his wanderings as a Peripatetic Episcopalean. Yet he is still not quite sure if he is now a genius who dreamed that he had been a bluebottle fly or a bluebottle fly dreaming he is now a genius. This situation establishes a host of possibilities, including that one which gives structural unity to the whole work with Arachne's appearance at the beginning and at the end. The structural planning is intricate and important. For much of the impact upon the reader derives now from this planning as well as from the content. There is, perhaps, less poetry than before. The direct emotional effect is less but is augmented by the additional emotional significance which dawns upon the reader as these various overtones, particularly of the fly and the spider, are intellectually manipulated in the spinning of the book itself. The public at large suddenly reappears in Part III. At first they are still refined and appreciative:

> . . . the butcher said:
> "Smirt is in our midst. Polly put the kettle on. Never had I hoped to find among us that genius who depicts with such utter loveliness, such impish wit, and such tender humanity, man's endless searching after the golden dream which he creates for himself."
> "Pleased to meet you, Smirt," said the baker. ". . . Anyone with a soul to appreciate beauty will find in countless pages of your books that which no other living writer can offer."

When Smirt wishes to leave them, they change their tune, become angry and sing:

> ". . . Smirt, Smirt, he deals in dirt! We think, just now, that you are, finally, unimportant. You buzz about in your season of sunshine, over your filthy little fantasies, like a blue-bottle fly over cow-dung."

Thus Cabell keeps us aware of the strange undercurrent that he is weaving into the more obvious satire, like a layer of deeper music which gives substance, though the more sprightly and staccato upper notes are more immediate to the reader's conscious perception.

At the end of the first part, Smirt meets Arachne and informs her that she is an exile from romance but that he will restore her to her lost estate in the lands beyond common sense, swearing by the acumen of Sir Thomas Browne, the theology of Congreve, the trimness of Robert Louis Stevenson, the inclusiveness of Pater, the carelessness of Saki, and the "pleasant eddies, to the ampleness, and to the ultimate, the ineffable rightness, of every paragraph which was written by W. M. Thackeray." In aligning himself with his tradition, or part of it, Cabell adds "I refer also to the general content of my own works . . . ." It is these "seven great mysteries" by which Smirt swears to restore Arachne to her lost legend just as Cabell embodied his own wife in the many females of his art. On making this promise, Smirt goes to meet the "All-Highest," who appears much like George Bernard Shaw, although—or because—he has horns, and the hoof of a goat for a right foot. By means of a not entirely disparaging discussion of Shaw's art, Smirt illustrates that even a lucid free-thinker may not know all. Yet, on being explained all by the All-Highest, Smirt is shocked to find that the universe is operated with old-fashioned premeditation. The rationality of Smirt's response is significant:

> But this work of Yours, All-Highest . . . is government. It has a formal plan. It is rational. It involves the long ago exploded notion of a Personal Creator.

All this is against present trends in art and does not allow for irony; nor does it permit life to lack meaning. So Smirt gives his advice to the All-Highest before once again fleeing from the public at large to the devil, who completes the company of the All-Highest as a minor partner. Smirt continues to enlighten these antiquated creators of the universe by pointing out such inadequacies as lack of variety in the shaping of planets amounting to the fault of unimaginative repetition. Gradually is built into the fabric of this book the more topical representation of human nature; the All-Highest and Company, for instance, possess the relationships of earthly enterprises as well as the same stock jokes. Smirt dreams on. By his ancient grave he recalls a former marital relationship; he notes how his wife must be recognized by his future biographers "at my centenaries until time ends."

> "So do I cry out to you, my dearest, who have been dead now for a great long while, Hail and farewell!"

Thus Ettarre is again acknowledged as synonymous with, though distinct from, Seraide, Aesrede and Arachne. The various mirrors reveal the different symbols which yet emanate from the same source, constituting an enigma with many variations.

The Stewards of Heaven, who previously hovered omnipotently but largely by suggestion over the Biography, are here encountered in person as Smirt visits the home of the Shining Ones. The eternal city of Amit is splendid, but the Stewards, although all except the Divine Father had everlasting youth, are no more than glorified Rotarians.

> All were serene and handsome huge persons, and yet, as Smirt saw, they were impervious to humor.

In their sublime dullness, they had never laughed over anything that was not wholly stupid. They applaud Smirt, as did the public at large; they ask him the same questions asked in *Special Delivery*; speeches are given punctuated by "(Laughter)," "(Applause)," and "(Cries of No! No!)." Reports are made which account for the headlines quoted in the first part of the book as Hogith explained how he had that day split a French cabinet, displayed storm warnings along the coast and led worried mother to slay son and self—all being entirely routine work. Then the Stewards "drank out the evening as conscientiously as throughout the day they had worked" until they sprawled out in restful stupor. "Smirt only remained awake and alert in the eternal city of Amit." It is interesting, when a religion is thus logically extended, to see what those are like who make men in their own images. Smirt continues to enlighten the gods, demonstrating his romanticism to them and revealing its superiority over journalistic realism, until the Stewards embark upon a course of steady reading, in a library, upon Smirt's works:

> "Never had I hoped to find," said Och, "a genius who depicts with such utter loveliness, such impish wit, and such tender humanity ..."

Until Smirt, looking over the ramparts of earth, sees that the Stewards have eliminated all headlines and substituted the deeds of romance: "Everywhither rode abridged likenesses of Smirt upon magnificent quests." Smirt explores this romantic world but, while meeting with many adventures, including an almost realistic domestic scene with Arachne, he cannot find the lost legend of Arachne so returns to Amit, where he is the acknowledged master now of the Shining Ones. So the conception of *Smirt* is a large one; if it does not plumb the depths of sea-green mysteries so enchantingly as does the Biography, the wit and intellectual paradoxes contained herein are sharper and can still merge into poetry. As Manuel talked with Grandfather Death, so Smirt to Azrael:

> "Of all human follies," said Azrael, gently and meditatively, "I shall make an end by-and-by. But not as yet. Not even of you, Smirt, and your continual babbling. . . . The worlds take shape, the worlds swarm with life, and the worlds perish, as All-Highest and Company work out their design. And yet, from out of the wreckage of each world as it perishes, arises an odd sound, which is at once a taunt, a giggle and a questioning and a sneer. . . ."
> "That sound, my dear Azrael," Smirt explained, "is constructive criticism. It is the defiant answer which a small civilized minority flings back at the inescapable and poorly contrived doom of mankind."
> Azrael said, with some shortness: "That sound is Smirt. So long as that tiny sound endures, so long will you also endure in your flippant and feverish dreaming. But for no instant longer."

This seriously flippant extract restates the philosophy of *Beyond Life*. It may even be remarkably suggestive now that science maintains that about one hundred million years ago the dinosaurs were eliminated not only by the decrease in carbon dioxide due to the evolution of plant life but also by cosmic rays from an adjacent exploding star; that statistical odds border on the certainty that intelligent life exists on at least a million earthlike planets in the Milky Way . . . among which every two hundred million years or so a supernovae explodes. That Cabell may not be entirely alone may be seen from that rather surprising speech made by Faulkner when receiving the Nobel Prize on December 10, 1950:

> It is easy enough to say that man is immortal simply because he will endure; that when the last ding-dong of doom has clanged and faded . . . that even then there will be still one more sound . . . that of his puny inexhaustible voice, still talking. I refuse to accept this. I believe that man will not merely endure: he will prevail.

Cabell actually goes further than Faulkner because Cabell implies that one of the reasons that man must endure is that he already only too clearly "prevails." But Cabell's statement has a remarkable unity with Faulkner's in that Smirt lasts only while he endures in his attempt to prevail. Faulkner made his statement after referring to the need to return to "the old verities and truths of the heart . . . love and honor and pity and pride and compassion and sacrifice." If these words are considered in conjunction with Jung's reference to nihilism and associated with the need for feeling as well as intellect, then they justify the uniqueness of Cabell's art. Perhaps this is why Cabell noted, in conversation, that when he met Faulkner in Virginia, Cabell thought that Faulkner was "a young man who would develop."

So Cabell continues to present his ideas of an artist-God making worlds according to plan. But now the treatment is much more direct and less poetic, much more satiric and less ironic. Contemporary life is much more in evidence even if the evidence is largely against it; it is communicated lastingly as generalizations and abstractions are given impersonal labels where the contemporary would loose meaning later. And finally, of course, just like Felix Kennaston, Jurgen, Manuel, and Florian, not to mention Ormskirk, Smirt enters the web of Arachne like a bluebottle fly, demonstrating not only that the same creative style governs all

243

earthly life but that love is, as it was for Gerald, quite possibly supreme. Yet even if it traps the fly, the fly in this case has a safeguard. Whereas the actual spider could devour the fly at will, Smirt would have awakened on being thus endangered and Arachne, too, could no longer have existed outside Smirt's dreaming. Cabell thus enables Smirt to continue, if not to Antan, at least his irrational dreaming. For even as Smirt sets out to look for a little shop with which to maintain Arachne and her offspring he notes:

> The one thing which counts at all, my very dearest, is that the dreaming of Smirt—whoever Smirt may happen to be—still continues a while longer, just as irrationally as it began.

Smith is subtitled "A Sylvan Interlude," and it recaptures much of the sunny tone and atmosphere of *The High Place*. It is one of the later novels that most nearly returns to Poictesme in treatment and significance. If, on the whole, it is not so profound, it by no means lacks substance—everything is relative. Like *Smirt*, *Smith* has fifty chapters, but this time they are divided into six parts. The general background of *Smith* is the Forest of Branlon, which represents Cabell's art as a whole, into which he may go at will and over which he rules no longer, like Smirt, as a universal deity, but now only as Mr. Smith, a local deity. Smirt is betrayed by Arachne, and in his own shop, so that he awakes from that dream to find himself as Mr. Smith, a pedlar whose first encounter is with Charlemagne, who halts his army on the borders of Branlon to hear what this pedlar has to say.

In this work, set against this ever-near forest, are recounted the adventures of the offspring of Smirt's marriages made when searching for the legend of Arachne in the romances of *Smirt*. Volmar, son of Rani (the South Wind's third daughter and erratic queen of philosophers), is a more unruly Prince Hal who does not reform his ways yet never fails in the essential soundness of his rebellious nature. He thinks that his contemptuous mockery has deprived him of the scornful Sonia, but she, to have him, exchanges a kingdom for his smithy. There are constant echoes of the short stories in *Gallantry* and *The Certain Hour*, but the skill is now without flaw. These individual units make much more, once again, of plot and situation and express also variations on old themes. For example, the theme of *Something About Eve* is dealt with again in Part III, "The Book of Elair."

Cabell stands back from his portrait. Although filling in his standard ingredients with infinite care, he is much more open in his humorous asides concerning his myths; thus the spontaneity becomes much more self-conscious with the consequence that while almost mocking his use of myths he justifies his very good application of them just as, in *Gallantry*, Ormskirk derived pleasure from his romantic naïveté while making fun of himself. The technique is applied now to a much vaster field of learning and comprehension—in fact, to all that digested experience acquired since the early short stories. So while there is a return to action and intrigue, while Cabell still has his cake and eats it, the built-in implications signified not only by Smirt and Smith but by Branlon itself ensure a richer texture than that in the early work, though Antan itself is gradually receding and there is not the symphonic sweep of the Biography.

But if Cabell is dealing more now with humanity and his own art, seen from outside, he is by no means bereft of the profounder irony. The music, if slighter, is still melodious:

> Though Branlon be but a dream, yet Branlon is wonderful. It abounds in the superb improbabilities of myth, and at will I create to inhabit Branlon new myths also. These attend me, who am Lord of the Forest, and we make sport together in this wood. The entire effect is baroque and rococo, of course; my bucolics incline to the school of Chinese Chippendale. Yet this Branlon contents me.

Mr. Smith walks in and out of the adventures of his offspring, and Urc Tabaron plays a role akin to Horvendile's. While all the ingredients are here and while the use of the dramatic devices of the short stories ensure entertainment, Cabell frequently deals with the more superficial to produce a lighter laughter in this sylvan interlude. But not always. For example, in "The Book of

Elaire," Elaire requires a magic which will enable him to live with both the women he loves, Sonia, and the woman he seeks, Fergail. Cabell conjures up, in what is some of his finest writing, the resources of Heaven and then those of Hell:

> They replied to him reverently; but not wholly in words . . . No: for beyond their speaking was a not quite heard music, Elaire reflected. He seemed aware of a great sea of malevolent, and fierce, and lascivious music, like a sea that followed with high-hearted lustiness after a leprous moon and all the dear poison of the moon's cold corruption, a sea which agonized under perverse tides of moon-maddened ecstasies,—raising everywhere, beneath winds that had come out of worlds less innocent than ours, their proud waves of flashing and bitter and evil beauty . . . and the foul greatness of hell delighted him, even in the teeth of his sedate better judgement, by its horrifying magnificence.

But "neither good nor evil seemed able to help him."

Mr. Smith and others of his offspring move in and out of the different parts enough to provide a continuous strand. Yet the part about Clitandre, (Part IV) who is the son of Arachne, is really the era of *Gallantry*, with highwaymen, police (superbly funny ones in a rare incident smacking of burlesqued London Bobbies), cobbled narrow streets towered over by studded doors into thick walled castles surrounded by rickety timbered houses. The following incident outlines a theme much used by Cabell but forever fresh and original. It is that of the poet experiencing the true nature of feminine cruelty, witting or otherwise, as embodied in impurity. Clitandre speaks to Marianne as he turns to her "jewel littered dressing table":

> "And are these also paste, madame, like your beauty and your purring innocence, your modesty and your coy virtues?"
>
> She replied frankly, moved to an unaccustomed humility by the young highwayman's grief. "They are the gifts, Clitandre, of those yet other men who have descended this ladder."
>
> Ceremoniously the proud freebooter took from his finger a sapphire ring; and he dropped it among the many colored gems saying: "I must pay my toll, then with the sole trinket I have about me. I leave

also yet other gifts. For I leave, in this dreadful, gilded and brightly cushioned and sweet-smelling room, my youth and a poem not ever finished. . . . You have slain a great poet, my sweet," said Clitandre, "not knowing that which you did."

This re-echoes "Porcelain Cups" in *Gallantry* and Marlowe's attitude—curbed here—as well as the scenes between Hamlet and Ophelia, Troilus and Cressida; Cabell deals with it once more in "The King Was in His Counting House" in *Heirs and Assigns*. In this episode of Clitandre, Cabell springs this diabolical twist in the plot to produce an unexpected backlash in his dramatic machinery. So Smirt's sons turn out to be a drunkard, a fool, a thief, and a fraud—except Little Smirt, who, guided by the firm hand of his mother (which he carries with him), becomes an exemplary little scholar as Cabell draws another dream to a close. Mr. Smith has Tana, who is the only one who brings him contentment, although there is also a clock which marks off inexorably each tick-tock of human life and experience—except those ticks embodied in these particular and continuously ingenious dreams concerning the Lord of the Forest of Branlon.

Smire may be the best of this trilogy. Cabell completes his disengagement from Poictesme and deals, in a detached manner, with his own transition. While still meeting with the public at large, while still upon his eternal quest, he reflects a spirit of reconciliation and acceptance; this pervades the well-chosen material to produce a smoothly-flowing music that frequently echoes the orchestration of *Jurgen* in its sombre and majestic overtones. Where dialogue was later to diminish to ineffectuality, in *Smire* the loquacity is apt, very funny, and yet fraught with substantial meaning as Cabell in effect winds up his long personal, if fictional, versions and estimates. Yet the spirit of acceptance does not betoken compromise, and *Smire* offers precise confirmation of the essential ideas in *Beyond Life*. The reconciliation is with the gods rather than with the public at large.

Smire, reduced yet a step farther in his status, returns to various key episodes in literature and history: to Dido prior to the arrival of Aeneas; to Gabriel, who, in some slight embarrassment it seems, is about to arrange an immaculate conception; to the Almighty again; and to Moera, who, like Egeria, rules over all. Smire gives generously of his advice and guidance; he knows everything from how to tell a painter what is wrong with his picture to explaining the meaning of honesty to a statesman. Yet he remains modest in his persistent avoidance of *hubris*. Always the intellectual subtlety of dialogue and ingenuity of situation are underscored by the slow rhythmic sense of tragedy.

Here is abundant confirmation of the myth-making chemistry of Cabell's art. For example, in Chapter XXIV, "To the Public at Large," Cabell supplies a convincing distinction between realism and romance. In doing this he distinguishes between the copyist and the creator. We see how the poet, as the myth-maker, creates that which man desires and pursues while the copyist attempts to photograph and annotate that which actually is. Only the poets—Cabell includes Homer, Shakespeare, Shelley, and Milton, as well as Walter Scott and Conan Doyle—create.

> . . . the best novelist brings to us "des nouvelles," the "news," unaffectedly, very well content to be a journalist who is about the beneficient work of increasing our knowledge.

But the poet—the poietes, the "maker"—when his toil prospers, then makes for us a new world, evoking the implied claims upon reverence such as we grant always to the divine task of creation. This is in keeping with Coleridge's conception of imagination. To support the theory of the poet, the Hebrew "prophet" or singer, as one who leads, there is a casual but significant comment made by Smire in Chapter XXXVIII which is worth juxtaposing with these remarks in Chapter XXIV. Smire, with the help of Charon, is returning to life:

> "To me," said the dim ferryman, as he reached stiffly toward his black oar, "it is much like any other instant, except that never until this instant have I carried back any passenger to the world of flesh and blood."
>
> "But, naturally," Smire answered, with a shrug, "I would be the first here, as in yet other places."

So Smire stands on the ferry and smokes his cigarette, meditatively, at the prow. Thus Cabell, in this, the last of his wholly mythical works, creates and completes his metamorphosis of the gods as they adjust themselves to Smire's logical requirements.

Urbane Smire decides not to burden himself with a volcano, have his vitals gnawed by vultures, or undergo awkward surgery at the hands of Zeus; rather than oppose cruel and arbitrary use of authority, he finds a convenient moral justification in his converse with Apollo, so allowing the Aeneid to be written. Instead of becoming a rebellious immortal, Smire permits Heaven to weave its own sequence of human misery, and he does so with complete moral justification. In other words, in *Smire* is one of the best treatments of a theme long inherent in Cabell's works. This concerns the bungling of the Creator's "realism" as compared with true romanticism. Smire examines the Bible for the Almighty. He enumerates the precise statistics of Jared's genealogy: "and all the days of Jared were nine hundred sixty and two years; and he died." This, Smire maintains, is the truth "in point of fact" but not "in theory." For Jared lived not in these externals but within his own mind and emotions. The Almighty had bungled his representation by omitting Jared's dreams, the dreams which permitted Jared to endure the world that this Almighty had fashioned. Smire notes that poor Jared in his dreams,

> . . . arraigned You unanswerably. He exposed you as the crude bungler that you are. And in his dreams he builded a world far more beautiful and a vast deal more just than you have been able to contrive.

In theory, then, the Almighty has produced, while no doubt doing his best, only a shoddy and second-rate universe. The Almighty becomes sullen; then He resorts to indignation, that substitute for being in the right, but it is by no means certain that Smire forgives Him. So where Jurgen weeps, Smire is such that the Almighty is abashed. It is a valiant variation. The theme is still that of human suffering for all its brilliant bubble and squeak.

Other evidence of the way in which emphasis shifts in these

later works, to extend and amplify rather than alter, is provided in Chapter XXX, "In The Picture." In this picture Smire is wearing not the rose-colored spectacles of Gerald's Maya but spectacles supplied by the "Wrong Occulist." These spectacles enable Smire to see everything, and for just what it is. Smire is older and, as he looks again upon the picture—different from the Mirror of Caer Omm only in form, not in significance—he averted his eyes from the faults that he could now see:

> I loved and relinquished the phantoms seen to all sides of me, now, as my youth was unable to see them. Satan is truly an occulist worthy of praise for his skill, but poets prefer mediocrity guilded. They laud is as golden.

Distributing meters like largesse, Smire passes on to throw his diabolical spectacles away. Yet if, on doing this, Smire's observations are no longer merely objective, they are even more close and accurate. By looking at things properly—with heart as well as head—Smire sees the true and ultimate reality. Although he has renounced the opulence and prestige of Poictesme, while the magic of Branlon continues to diminish and elude him, the quest goes on unchanged, stubbornly, still productively and still with the same principles of motivation. Neither Smith, nor Smirt, nor even Smire had revolutionized history or reformed mankind. All lacked the necessary *hubris*. Yet as Smith becomes Smirt, who relapsed into Smire, their dreams still endure:

> And his dreams have their points, their benefaction even, inasmuch as to humankind they offer, in their own manner, distinction and clarity and beauty and symmetry and tenderness and truth and urbanity. That is not everything perhaps which mankind desires; the appeal, rather, is to virtuosi: and yet these are fine virtues.

Cabell first voiced them in 1918 and still they are fundamental in his art in 1937. Most authors are satisfied to communicate to anyone but not for anything did Cabell adulterate these virtues. Here is one case where the civilized has withstood promiscuity. As Smire leaves the now dumb phantoms of Branlon to return to flesh and blood, he is beset by this promiscuity speaking with the voices of contemporary criticism.

> . . . the nine spectres all screeched together, with thin laughter, saying,—
> "Now, but this absurd out-of-date creature is telling us, yet again, that the dream is better than the reality!"
> He said then: "To the contrary, I am telling you that for humankind the dream is the one true reality."

So still, and from this considerable distance, does Cabell pronounce from *Beyond Life*.

19: *Heirs and Assigns*

Heirs and Assigns appears to contain, not Cabell's last fiction, but his last substantial fiction. On the other hand, these three novels, *The King Was in His Counting House* (1938), *Hamlet Had an Uncle* (1940), and *The First Gentleman of America* (1942), may well be the best of the later fiction, the backbone of the writings after the Biography. In *The Nightmare Has Triplets*, Cabell was disengaging himself from Poictesme; he dealt with the familiar themes even as he gave them more topical treatment and made greater use of the dramatic devices of his earlier short stories. Still making magnificent use of myth (as in Elaire's farewell to Astrild, Chapter XXI in *Smirt*) to probe the profoundest possibilities of human feeling and meaning, precisely in accordance with the primordial mechanics of human motivation as illustrated by Jung, Cabell also gave increasing play to his intellectual gifts for satire, to embody pungently standard elements of modern American, indeed all Western life.

Much of *The Nightmare Has Triplets* grew out of *Their Lives and Letters*; much of the fiction of *Heirs and Assigns* may likewise be seen forming in the first of the later stories and letters. For example *The King Was in His Counting House* is essentially an enlargement of the first story concerning Prospero after he had released Ariel in *These Restless Heads*; *Hamlet Had an Uncle*, as seen, develops further the letter "To Hamlet, King of Jutland," in *Ladies and Gentlemen*. With these two of the three novels comprising *Heirs and Assigns*, Cabell finally breaks clear of Poictesme and the Biography, although he retains Branlon for convenient reference. And the Lord of the Forest of Branlon reappears in *The King Was in His Counting House*; his role can be fully understood and appreciated only in the light of the themes in the preceding works. In the third novel of this trilogy Cabell begins his last fictional phase, which unites his own lifelong interests more directly with national, topical, historical, and legendary themes, with the emphasis on satire, though neither the irony nor, indeed, the poetry is ever entirely absent. In *The Devil's Own Dear Son*, we are again in the America of the twentieth century.

In different ways, all three of the novels in *Heirs and Assigns* are excellent. After forty years of creative activity with words, Cabell here still displays versatility and variation in ever fresh forms, without appearing repetious The preface (dated 1935–38, St. Augustine, Florida) to *The King Was in His Counting House* states the theme explicitly. Where Cabell's previous poet-heroes, such as Jurgen and Gerald Musgrave, eventually relinquished their spiritual guests to relapse into domestication, in this work Cabell deals at length with what happens to the poet as he turns to his practical vocation rather as he might deal with the reign of Shakespeare's Hamlet had Hamlet conquered Claudius. Cabell notes:

> My theme hereinafter, under whatsoever trappings of the ironic, remains, as every instant, the growth of altruism and of social responsibility which makes civilized every human life.

All are poets in their youth, with the flourishing self-conceit and rebelliousness and self-sufficiency of the poet. But after boyhood comes "the marked respect for altruism" or, at least, the need to acknowledge the needs of others. Cabell describes this realization as "the supreme shape-giver of human character . . . the most dynamic of all strong forces in human life and in human civilization." It is most relevant to note in this work what is possibly the clearest statement of Cabell's implicit, if not belief, then certainly idea, of a force which uses humans in proportion to their usefulness for its own ultimately constructive ends. All whose characters do not develop to recognition of an acquiescence in the need to harmonize with these social forces are destroyed. Each character who dies ("excepting only chance-murdered Gratiano") does so "through a pursuit of some private interest which is at odds with implacable altruism."

Two characters illustrate this theme in excellent illustration of ingenious stagecraft and plot manipulation. These are Duke Ferdinand, afterwards King of Melphé, and Cesario, his poet-cum-successor son. Cabell observes at the end of his Preface:

> ... in the words of my final chapter, "Cesario becomes Ferdinand";
> and after his allotted jaunt into Branlon he accepts more or less
> quietly his allotted place in the social organism of flesh-and-blood
> Melphé: that is my story. It is the normal story of all mankind.

How does Cabell tell this story? He resorts to Jacobean material, placing his settings in Italianate fortress-cities with additional movements approximately in the areas of Corsica and the Balearics and moving in time to the early seventeenth century. He gives an authentic historical flavor to deeds and environment. Apart from a signed edition of 125 copies in black morocco, this work was published by Farrar and Rinehard, Inc., in only one edition, illustrated by Charles Child, though there was an English edition by John Lane, The Bodley Head, printed in England. Charles Child was one of the most appropriate of Cabell's illustrators. His black and white drawings emerge starkly but naturally out of the text, augmenting the flavor and characterization perfectly and much more adequately than is so often the case in the difficult matter of illustrations.

The setting, then, is the Italy of Jacobean drama, and the characters are in accordance. Of the males, Ferdinand, Cesario, the Sieur de la Forêt, who is "a vagabond scholar" (with hints, like Horvendile, of magic and predestination), and Lorenzo are chief; Hypolita and Hermia, Greek daughters of Shakespeare's Lysander, are central among the women and the general action. To begin with, Ferdinand, a minor noble, becomes the tool of a tyrant only to remove that tyrant and resume power over a consolidated kingdom over which he forthwith reigns rationally, peaceably, and with flourishing consequences for the populace and burghers if not the nobles. To do this, Ferdinand also is ruthless but in a disinterested and positive way solely on behalf of his "exorbitant mistress," the kingdom of Melphé. On behalf of his offspring, one of which seems to be legitimate, he pulls strings attached to thrones and papacies all over Europe. But eventually he needs a successor and the choice narrows down between Cesario and Lorenzo. Lorenzo receives his chance, or test, first, because Cesario has disappeared into Branlon.

Cesario's manner of doing this is worth considering. The second of the five parts of this work deals with "The Love of Cesario." He is a young man, poetically inclined, who falls in love with the Greek girl Hypolita. They seem both to be very much in love on the sunny island of Gratignolles, whose north shore faces Poictesme. Cesario composes poems to his love, and Hypolita says "I love all your poems." But on standing beneath her window under the stars, composing a poem to his love's truthfulness, Cesario observes a ladder lowered from this window and a figure ascending to it. Whereupon Cabell magnificently runs to the edge of mirthful melodrama even as he retains a hard core of real and tragic meaning. Cesario climbs the ladder and enters the room of his true love to meet the first real lesson of his life as he finds her offering her bare but generous hospitality to the Sieur de la Forêt. Cesario, too, divests himself of his clothes and his pretensions and participates in thrashing out the naked truth. He whips back a coverlet from Hypolita and considers her:

> He had loved this fair naked animal with an all-worshipful adoration such as, he now knew, he would not ever feel again, toward anybody.
> She said, without moving, and with a half-yawn,—"You dream too much, Cesario."

254

"In fact," he admitted, "I had dreamed of an unreal Hypolita who does not exist anywhere. . . . I did not serve briskly your hot needs."

The Sieur de la Forêt said: "I am male, she is female, my poor minor poet. You have reached the inevitable instant when the young poet discovers that every healthy young woman enjoys copulation, and that she itches for it just as ravenously as he does."

Hypolita said, gravely, "It seems to me, just the same, and poetry or no poetry, that when we have our clothes on, and copulation, as you call it, is not convenient we ought to pretend that doing it is not quite nice."

"Why?" says Cesario, who was much interested by the naked new Hypolita.

"Why, because to pretend that is more well-bred. It is more religious."

Cesario's situation, thus, is rather like that of a groom leading out of the church his young bride only to find her pause by a rear pew to exchange foul-mouthed witticisms with a—to the groom —unknown salesman. In this magnificently sustained and serious foolery the Sieur de la Forêt reveals the objectivity which gives the work its stature:

"We are agreeing . . . that since we are both naked here, at your bedside Hypolita, with the thick, rich, lecherous, harsh, ugly, juicy smell of you in both our delighted noses, there is no need to pretend that the mating of a man with a woman can have, in the eyes of any case-hardened deity, a more important, or indeed a more depraved aspect, than has the mating of a bull with a cow, or than a cock's treading of a hen. The spectacle . . . must be virtually the same in all three rump heavings. Are we to imagine that Heaven would so rigorously distinguish among buttocks as to bestow condonation upon one . . . and punishment on another?"

To this further blow the Sieur de la Forêt adds the observation that urbanity is a manmade virtue, man's only armor "against the wild finesse of his womankind and the great gaucheries of Nature." After being told, in effect, that everything is his fault for climbing into people's rooms at midnight, Cesario prepares to depart:

"But have you no jealousy?" says she; "and is it the part of a gentleman, to be leaving me here to be ravished by a naked man?"

"No," said Cesario, very quietly, reaching for his doublet; "but then I am no longer a gentleman. I am a poet; and I have been betrayed."

So does Cesario receive his education and acquire that ruthlessness and tenacity to hold to his purpose and to ultimate "usefulness." Hypolita, whose cunning is inevitably shortsighted, is ultimately destroyed by her pain-giving self-interest. For many years Cesario lives in Branlon. Lorenzo fails his test of administering power under Ferdinand. Cesario, recalled, acquires kingship and clear-sighted administrative ability—over the dead body of Hypolita as, likewise, of his youth. The intricacy of the weaving is on a par with the quality of the design.

King Ferdinand himself illustrates the actual nature of the administrative burden in the greater portion of the book, ruling with mildness and thrift" after "he had got to be a king through murder and thieving." Hermia, the positive to Hypolita's negative, becomes central to both Cesario and Ferdinand. The situation arising out of the various domestic relations of Hermia and Hypolita as well as the behavior of Ferdinand offer abundant humor, not always only melodramatic. Over all plays the sense of purpose or design as it is seen first by Ferdinand then, however reluctantly, by Cesario as they see beyond immediate self-interest.

Culminating many years of skilled application, the drama and dialogue are of Cabell's best. Characterization is individualized and at no time are characters oversimplified to black or white. The novel is an excellent, intact work of art in the best of Cabell's tradition of dramatic, meaningful storytelling, as characters are revealed in action which makes, as all action must do, for or against the common weal.

Hamlet Had an Uncle is a comedy of honor. Cabell had long been concerned with the dilemma of Hamlet; in this work he gives his own direct and full-length treatment of a problem at the heart of all his own writings—the consequences of that strange compulsion to action, which, when studied, seems akin to the folly of the pursuit of beauty in the contemplative poet. The setting moves to the period of Beowulf and the Vikings. Charles Child's illustrations again augment accurately the text, yet Cabell uses his material freely so that the trappings, armor, and speech are also of the Gallic and post-Renaissance period liberally intermingled with the Norse and Celtic. The intellectual ingenuity with which clues to the ultimate significance are planted is of the subtlest and must be watched for as carefully as at Elsinore. For example, the work is preceded by a short dedication to "The Forgotten Man":

> Here is your story steadfastly retold
> And freed of fancy, seeking nor to lend
> Music where music was not, not to mold
> Less frankly your remissions, but to mend,
> Even as you mended, error, and to hold
> Truth as you held it even to the end.

This acrostic tells us that the forgotten man is Hamlet—technically the historical Hamlet. But this dedication follows the quotation: "Even with the very comment of thy soul Observe my uncle," and is followed by the quotation, "Thus the native hue of resolution Is sicklied o'er with the pale cast of thought." Spiritually, it may well refer also to Shakespeare's Hamlet. "What is truth?" said jesting Pilate. Hamlet gave one answer, Claudius and Wiglerus another.

By the most adroit juggling with circumstances, Cabell contrives, on the basis of Shakespeare's play and its antecedents, an ironical comment on the nature of truth and the difficulty of perceiving and retaining it in the face of the ever-present wiles of "honor" as it becomes confused with self-interest and self-deception. To begin with, Hamlet has the more pronounced "madness" of the Norse antecedent Amleth; he has also the astuteness of Shakespeare's Hamlet, but it is acquired largely through the services of a familiar spirit called Orton, who at first seems to have a role akin to that of Horatio except that, rather than friend, he is philosopher and guide. In fact Orton is a wizard similar to Horven-

257

dile in the Biography, or to Urc Tabaron. Compare the significance of Cabell's Horvendile with Horvendile, father of Amleth, (in Saxo Grammaticus) and the symbolism of perpetuated "indestructible vital energy" to see how Cabell's choice of names is well made. With Orton's guidance, Hamlet makes his astute way among his elders as, in the early part of this book, Cabell builds upon the general outline of Shakespeare's version. Except that Hamlet is the offspring not of Horvendile and Geruth but, illicitly, of Fengon and Geruth. When Horvendile discovers Fengon with Geruth, Fengon is obliged to kill Horvendile, the whole affair being tactfully concealed by Wiglerus, a third son of the Danish king, whose daughter, Geruth, was married first to the Jutlander Horvendile then to Horvendile's murderer, Fengon, the father of Hamlet. Hamlet proceeds to take revenge for Horvendile, his supposed father but actual uncle, by killing Fengon his actual father but supposed uncle. Thus, already, "young" Hamlet is ensnared in the pursuit of honor as Cabell supplies a significant and neat twist to the Shakespearian version:

> Hamlet said: "This just and violent death is your fit reward. Now go your ways, lost soul of Fengon. Do you tell the great soul of Horvendile that he is avenged honorably."
> . . . In this pleasant vein of romantic irony, by killing his own father, did Hamlet avenge the death of his uncle.

Hamlet, in a magnificent display of decisive action involving a "fireside chat" to the populace beside the smoking ruins of the banqueting hall, becomes king with a speech written for him by Orton:

> He promised them a reduction in all government expenditures at once; and a balancing of the budget next year through the use of counterfeit money; and a more abundant living for everybody, now that pensions would replace taxes.

From this point forward does Cabell have an even freer hand with the action as all seems virtually original to him in the subsequent events. These involve Hamlet's return to England and political marriage to the daughter of Edric, a daughter already promised to the ageing but gallant uncle of Hamlet, the Dane Wiglerus. Eventually Hamlet divorces this daughter Alftruda for the Scottish warrior-queen Hermetrude, who accompanies Hamlet back to Jutland. Wiglerus, who loves Alftruda, notes now the opportunity this gives him; he states of Hamlet's action over Alftruda:

> I cannot in honor permit anybody to break an oath made to me. The big, sprawling young goat was explicit. "If ever my faith fails her," says he, . . . "then let my head answer for it." On that agreement I shake hands; on that agreement I shake worlds. Because of this cut-throat whore he has cast out Alftruda, into the gutter. Alftruda!

Although Hamlet's action at this point does seem out of character, he is somewhat justified, as he later makes clear. But this act nevertheless seems to be the turning point in his luck and endeavors—and Orton transfers his interest to Wiglerus.

Now, by what is revealed to him in Orton's magic crystal—a souvenir of Orton's youth which had been laid "for only three weeks in . . . water in which the first-born son of a king had been bathed, by an insane Baptist prophet, down in Palestine"—Wiglerus finds that he, Wiglerus, has become King of Denmark. This makes him, also, liege-lord to Hamlet, King of Jutland. Wiglerus defeats Hamlet and Hermetrude, depriving them of their possessions, and most of their followers, and trapping them in the lonely swamps of Vildmose. Now it is that Hermetrude reveals herself spiritually instead of, as is more usual with her, physically. Hamlet, deprived of fortune, makes his last speech which, because of his state of mind, amounts to a soliloquy:

> Honor . . . is a commandment written very plainly in the heart of each man that lives, if only he be brave enough to read it. Through cowardice he may come to ignore that writing, and . . . he may come by-and-by to erase it utterly. But when that happens, Hermetrude, the man is dead; and though his body may go on breathing, it is but the body of an animal . . . which continues to eat and to breed and to sleep, not discontentedly. But I will not die slowly in this manner . . . I will die with my manhood full upon me, as befits my brave father's son."

Thus Hamlet, without the guidance of Orton, reasons on the basis of a misconception. It is an interesting commingling of truth and falsity. Hermetrude considered it impractical.

> When she next spoke, it was about the true love which existed between Hamlet and herself. . . . She spoke gently and very nobly; and Hamlet replied with grave tenderness, quietly, in a sort of half-humble gratitude.

Then, with the help of Magnus the Skald, Hermetrude had Hamlet killed.

Thus Hamlet's uncle Wilglerus, the one who all his life had followed after pleasure, is left omnipotent and with Alftruda the former wife of Hamlet. And what does Wiglerus note?

> Human life seemed astoundingly casual; you could not find any meaning in it; but you could find in human life a quite ponderable amount of pleasure, through the exercise of continued tact. That, and that only, might enable you, for some while as yet to come, to eat and to breed and to sleep not at all discontentedly.

The colophon would seem to complete this by adding:

> . . . take pattern by the unwisdom of Hamlet in this discourse; who erred in that he loved over-greatly; and who, while others made lax cheer, continued sober and ardent; so that, where the more nimble wits of his fellows sought as much as they could to get pleasure and treasure, he accounted not anything to be equal to honor.

Poor Hamlet: what a fool *he* was—Shakespeare's greatest. As Cabell observes in his preface, "Should you ask for precision, the true Prince of Denmark proves to be Wiglerus." Wiglerus, Hamlet's Uncle, also held a kind of truth, horrible as it was, "even to the end." Thus this novel, like life itself, is devilishly contrived, to an extent that would give Shakespeare himself, not only entertainment, but food for thought. Here seems to be a lesson in American objectivity—a lesson cruel but apt—inso far as it was Wiglerus who retained the throne and "sentiment" which lost it.

These are but the bare bones to the body of the book as a whole and other aspects are significant for appreciation of Cabell's art in its later stages. For example, there runs throughout the novel an underlying symbolism playing upon the two themes of life and death. Death is well portrayed by Magnus the executioner, who is an artist on the subject of death even as Shakespeare's *Hamlet* went beyond immediate matters of human conduct to graveyard questions. This can be seen in Chapters XXII, concerning Ferbis of Ablach, and XXXIV, in which Magnus transfers allegiance from Hermetrude, who killed all lovers who did not conquer her in battle, to Wiglerus. An examination of these two chapters may help to show just how astute, profound, and ahead of his time was this psychological wizard. Chapter XXII recounts how "the young Lord Ablach" came to woo in marriage "Queen Hermetrude, who ruled over Pictland and Mel and some part of Berwick." Hermetrude comes to represent not only a humorous, wanton companion for such a Wiglerus, not only a cruel, scheming woman as she is in Vildmose, but the symbol of beauty and fulfillment sought by all youthful warriors—in exact keeping with Jung's theories of motivation in search for that transmuted mother-image which brings peace as well as ecstasy at the end of long journeys. The place where Hermetrude and Ferbis fight is a square covered with a cloak, white like a sheet to show the first fall of blood. A ceremony dedicates this area of sacrifice. Shakespeare's Hamlet sublimated the incestuous urge partly by spiritual assault and conquest of Ophelia—to succumb, later, to circumstance. Ferbis, strong but young and inexperienced, is mortally wounded. Note the poetry of this dialogue, chiefly iambics and anapaests:

> To you who have had all I had to give," said Ferbis, "I give what alone remains. My restive dreams and hopes and desires have now ended; they fall away from me, like frail grey ashes, in the flame of your beauty. I am at peace dear Queen; and I give praise to Heaven that I may quit this world seeing only what is most lovely in it and not needing any longer to think about anything else.

Magnus, the executioner with the timely ax, strikes off the head of Ferbis and notes:

Death is that harlot with whom all men must sleep at last. From that which is good and wise and pleasant this ugly harlot draws us away with her foul cunning. All beauty, all power and all honor must lie down in her ignoble bed.

Often in Cabell's art, the last moments of life are filled with distant birdsong. This is the case here and it is so again in *The First Gentleman of America*. On Ferbis' shield is a unicorn which is, according to Jung, "a procreative symbol of the Logos." Likewise Ferbis noticed, while kneeling in death between the strong legs of Hermetrude, "in the woods south of this field, a thrush was singing. Ferbis wondered if thrushes could be mating thus late in the year?" Jung, explaining the symbolism of birds in ancient world-wide myths, notes, "The bird probably means . . . the longing of the libido, the rebirth of the phoenix. The longing is frequently represented by the symbol of hovering. . . . This act signifies rebirth, and the bringing forth of life from the mother, and by this means the ultimate destruction of death." As with Elaire and Astrild in *Smirt*, and even more clearly in *The First Gentleman of America*, the bird hovers in the sun over water, the sun symbolizing the rise from the womb of the ocean in rebirth or everlasting or immortal life or "indestructible vital energy" as in Ahasuerus, in whom Jung traces a link with Christ and sun gods. This may indicate the depth and complexity of this art as it arises organically out of the source of all life in accordance with universal laws. In obeying these laws thus closely, Cabell ensures that his work is true and lasting.

More immediate aspects are discussed between this Magnus, artist of death, and Wiglerus, expert on love. Wiglerus maintains:

> . . . all written poetry is minor poetry. It at best is but an adulterated and very thin version of that poetry which poets alone know about, and can know about only while they are under the influence of being in love.

But Magnus is not to be denied:

> The poetry which is begotten by love . . . remains always lyrical. It is poignant perhaps; in any case it is brief. . . . So must I provoke

constantly the remunerative spectacle of death because to regard it inspires me with a rich ecstasy of terror . . . Over the unfinished career and the unfulfilled promise of resplendent youth my imagination has soared perhaps to its highest; and in soaring has struck unforgettably its most haunting note of pathos. "That question"—Magnus added with diffidence—"I may not presume to decide. It is needful that every great artist should leave to posterity the selection of his masterworks."

Yet Wiglerus has the penultimate word, which is as much as anyone could expect in dealing with Death:

The King looked at him intently; and the insane blood-lust of this furtive creature, Wiglerus thought, was quite horrible; even so, you could get profit out of it, by using tact.

As Shakespeare brought into *Hamlet* his theories on the nature and performance of drama, Cabell introduces—and much more relevantly—ideas on the nature and performance of poetry.

Many are the subtle meanings thus interwoven (including Hamlet's Promethean use of a bundle of kindling twigs) in *Hamlet Had an Uncle,*—perhaps Cabell's subtlest work. It is a superb imaginative representation of the death of Hamlet and the life of his Uncle, which gives lastingly to eternal mysteries the emphasis and imprint of our times.

The First Gentleman of America (1942) concludes this trilogy of inheritance. It also begins the last phase of Cabell's fiction, a phase in which he deals with semihistorical, legendary, and national material to present lasting traits of human nature in their more satirical perspective. Of this last phase, including this work and the trilogy following under the collective title *It Happened in Florida, The First Gentleman of America* seems the most substantial. So with this third work of *Heirs and Assigns* we see Cabell's last major novel. Just as he dealt first with semihistorical material in such as *Chivalry, Gallantry,* and *The Certain Hour,* as he approached Poictesme or Antan, so again does Cabell deal with the semihistorical as he withdraws from them.

The basis of *The First Gentleman of America* is the activities of the Spanish, French, and English as they endeavored to extend their possessions in America. Already in America were the Indians. Taking these two sides—the invaders and the invaded—Cabell presents his sardonic portrayal of the real and ostensible motives of human conduct as they went into the making of this new world in his comedy of conquest. Cabell establishes as his hero the Indian Nemattanon, who lives with the people of Ajacan in the northern neck of Virginia:

> In not any roadway of Ajacan did a black and yellow announcement of "Slow men working" epitomize cynically the activities of democracy.

Their god is Quetzal, son of the White Cloud Serpent. His origins are deep in indigenous folklore and mythology as Quetzal had come out of the heaven of Tapallan, bringing an infant child, to offer peaceful but firm guidance of a constructive kind to his people so that they flourished in crop development and in the building of good villages while avoiding wasteful indulgences in tribal warfare. Thus the son of the White Cloud Serpent ousted the former god of the Ajacan, Maskanako, who compelled to war and pillage in the name of patriotism. Then came the Spaniards, the French, and the English. Quetzal's infant Nemattanon is adopted by the leading Spaniard and introduced to the more civilized ways of Christianity. Cleverly does Cabell weave into his version the possibilities of Nemattanon and Menendez as interrelated in blood and destiny as, in fact, Nemattanon emerges as kin to the Spanish leader who educates him and gives him introduction to the sophistication of Spanish court life and ladies. But what are Nemattanon's final judgments?

> I have been much thrown with a superb throng of heroic and brave persons, and with a fair number of virtuous persons, as they went about noble labors, intrepidly, in obedience to the trumpet call of conscience, or of patriotism, or of religion, or of some yet other highly esteemed abstraction. They were all serving—so it seemed to me—the strong black serpent called Maskanako, whom my father put out of these parts for having incited magnanimity;

and because of this high-minded reptile's advice, the Spaniards and
the French, the Protestants and the Catholics, were embroiled continually, hating one another with an exalted heroism.

Each one of these untiring champions was bringing the very best
qualities of his nature to the service of mankind's most lofty ideals.
. . . And the results were oppression and misery . . . no less brutal
than witless.

Yet Nemattanon accepts the force of necessity which underlies
these enigmatic contradictions, as he foresees the future. He returns to safeguard his people as long as he can, leading them west-
ward,

> up into the Blue Ridge Mountains, and beyond Charlotesville, and
> so came to a well-sheltered pleasurable land like a hollowed-out
> crevice in the Alleghanies.

Here, he feasts any visiting Europeans and then kills them, thus
preserving the happiness of his people for a little longer.

As usual, Cabell embodies numerous elements which, in their
total, reveal humanity as not only deceiving but deceived. The
people are caught in this predicament—they struggle to reconcile
the compulsive force within them with their desire for self-respect.
The leader or Werrowance of the Ajacan has a role similar to
that of Ferdinand and his successor Cesario in *The King Was in
His Counting House*; yet even as the Spaniards slaughter and en-
slave in the name of an empty sepulchre, they likewise are valiant
men of action like Manuel. This can be seen from the editorial
note. Cabell has based this work on preliminary enquiries within
a large, and this time authentic, bibliography of history and legend.
Although in the note itself we again find his tongue in his cheek,
the work cannot be described as placing innocent Indians at the
mercy of evil invaders. Pedro Menendez is also a hero, or at least
a heroic villain. As we find in the editorial note:

> He believed alike in the existence and the all guiding wisdom of
> God; and he loved God utterly. It is that which nowadays makes
> Pedro Menendez incredible. And it is that which leads me into
> parading the fact that I in some slight degree have helped to honor

the memory of Don Pedro Menendez de Aviles. I admire the man profoundly; and I envy him.

Which is what one could say of Manuel also. By honoring the name of Don Pedro, Cabell refers not only to this book but to the fact that Cabell unearthed the coffin of Menendez from a junk room in the city hall of St. Augustine and had it given due prominence (as a tourist attraction) as it rested in state in the Chapel of Nuestra Senora de la Leche. In fact the note of humorous perception into human foibles which is the hallmark of this novel is caught clearly enough in Cabell's civic enthusiasm for the beauties of St. Augustine:

> I regard with a proper reverence, and with not more than a half-dozen reservations which stay civilly tacit, The Oldest House; whereas toward The Former Mansion of the Spanish Governors between the years 1597 and 1763 I cherish an almost proprietary feeling on account of the interest with which I saw it being builded during 1937.

With, presumably, no more reservations than had Jurgen before the empty sepulchre of Manuel in *The Silver Stallion*, Cabell's practical activities on behalf of Don Pedro included addressing the Chamber of Commerce. With what devilish innocence he must have harangued those innocent devils, the Shining Ones.

Mention should also be made of Nemattamon's return, after long absence, to his wife—a return which illustrates clearly and movingly the conception of the unbreakable and lasting quality of union between man and woman where that union is bound by love. This conception has been inherent in Cabell's work from the beginning, and here it can be seen at its strongest, with full mythic overtones, as a spiritual union which will outlast even physical dissolution. This is a difficult enough idea to convey artistically today, and the success with which it is communicated is a measure of Cabell's imaginative reach as well as of his craftsmanship.

Of the many brilliantly conceived and executed dramatic situations in these novels, one of the finest is in *The First Gentleman of America*. It concerns the unavoidable slaughter of the French by the Spaniards:

This was not, of course, an impressive massacre, as go our modern standards. . . . Yet in its tact and restraint and ease, and in its polite consideration for the persons who were being murdered . . . [it] appeared to excel.

The whole episode is fraught with symbolism. The chief symbol is that of a sea-gull settling on blue water. Gallant Ribaut, out-witted, goes forward to die.

He looked seaward . . . at a small seagull, which, at this instant, came out of the north. The bird, in its leisured progress, flew near the water; and the gull wheeled about, daintily, under the west wind's pressure. The gull's feet hung beneath it, very pink. It dropped weightlessly upon the surface of the water . . . and it raised again.

Then, very expertly, Ribaut was executed—but the bird signifies renewal of life as it hovers, descends upon and arises from, the ocean, source of all life, from the beginning. *The First Gentleman of America* thus transfers long-held conceptions into a more local medium. While the gods are still present, the emphasis has shifted so that this novel brings out much more sharply, with the more barbed and cutting edge of satire, man's cruelty, ridiculousness, foolishness, and grandeur in the presence of an unchanging dilemma.

20: *It Happened in Florida*

The St. Johns was written by Cabell in co-operation with A. J. Hanna at the request of Stephen Vincent Benét for the series en-titled "The Rivers of America." The genesis of this work is de-scribed in *As I Remember It* where Cabell notes the number of "grotesque persons who . . . had animated this memory-haunted river," and the book thereby becomes rather than a formal history a chronological pageant of these "surprising" people from the figures of Jean Ribaut and Menendez, who are featured in *The First Gentleman of America*, to Stephen Crane's widow. Stephen Vincent Benét, whose death occurred suddenly before the book's completion, acted as a referee between the collaborators. The chief value of this book, here, is for the light it sheds upon Cabell's development. Whereas in *The First Gentleman of America* Cabell was freely making use of facts, in *The St. Johns* he makes use of his facts very freely with the result that the book becomes a satirical pageant of human faults and foibles. Brilliantly the saga of history up, down, and around this river is used to illustrate again, but much more intellectually, the discrepancy between ethics and morals, the ostensible intention and the actual outcomes, of human behavior. Thus the book becomes a shrewd combination of wit, fiction, and historical fact illustrating, in a manner midway between Gibbon and Thackeray, vice and folly and misfortune. Yet, while the fun remains fast and furious, while the craftsmanship, the style, the execution, are excellent, profundity is now replaced by shallows, however sparkling. Yet the intention was probably not otherwise, and the aim probably fully achieved.

As a work of art, *The St. Johns* fulfills its purpose. That this purpose is a pageant of the grotesque seems to speak for itself. Certainly over such a full range of material the purpose could hardly have been other. Yet themes which Cabell had previously dealt with very differently are now represented more for their ridiculousness than for their deeper, if ironic, significance. For example, Audubon is treated rather ungenerously when it is recalled that his life seems that of a most courageous and determined artist overcoming what to most would have been insuperable difficulties including wading, chest-deep in mud, through Florida's swamps. In fact, in many ways, Audubon's behavior, attitude, and self-sufficiency constitute a major theme of Cabell's best works. In *Audacious Audubon* (New York, E. A. Muschamp, 1929) appears:

> At heart Audubon was a deeply religious man, but as one of his friends once declared "he knew nothing of the theology of the schools, and cared as little for it. . . ." And since there was about him no suggestion of sanctimonious unctuousness he made no conscious proclamations of his mission. But . . . Audubon believed that a sustaining Power more potent than any of the forces that resided within himself, had destined him to do those things for which he found himself equipped. . . . And so, inspired or deluded—one can-

not but wonder at times whether there really is much difference between the two words—Audubon met each new disaster . . . with unfailing serenity.

But in *The St. Johns* it is no longer the ironic portrayal of both sides of this problem of inspiration or delusion but the more superficial aspects of all human folly which receive the emphasis:

> It really does seem a distinct pity that all these strange rare birds should have been denied the pleasure of meeting John James Audubon merely because the captain of the *Spark* was not so tactful as to grovel before a Fellow of the Royal Society of London, England.

That Cabell is making freer use of his fancy may be illustrated by the following extract from *Audubon, the Naturalist* (New York, F. H. Herrick, 1917):

> Early in February, 1832, Lieutenant Piercy took Audubon and his assistants aboard the government schooner *Spark* at St. Augustine, and sailed for the mouth of the St. John's River, which he had orders to ascend in the interest of the Revenue Service. On February 12, when they had reached a point one hundred miles from the mouth of the river, the vessel, being in need of repairs, was suddenly recalled. Audubon, with two men, thereupon engaged a boat and attempted to return to St. Augustine across country, by a short cut to the eastward.

This reason for leaving the *Spark* seems to be supported by the following extract from a letter of February 24, 1832, from the Navy Department:

> I regret that the impaired condition of the *Spark* made it necessary some weeks ago, to order that vessel to Norfolk to be refitted.
> I have heretofore taken much pleasure in furnishing Mr. Audubon with credentials to the officers of the Navy . . . to furnish every aid . . . and shall be happy to afford any further facilities.

Similarly, in *The St. Johns*, appears a reference to Audubon's behavior as akin to that of a spoiled child sitting upon the floor screaming because the dessert was not what it expected. Yet

Audubon's account states that on leaving General Hernandez, with whom he had stayed for ten days,

> A wagon was sent out for our baggage and horses for ourselves were offered at the same time, but it was not my desire to give unnecessary trouble, and above all upon an occasion when I was glad to see the country in as much detail as possible . . . During the whole long stay with Mr. Bulow, there was no abatement of his kindness . . . one of the most deserving and generous of men.

This is not quite the picture Cabell paints. Furthermore, in *The St. Johns*, reference is made to Audubon's "much-enduring wife" —but so also, and in the same way, endured Penelope and Egeria. If these points are not matters of world-shaking consequence, they do seem to suggest that Cabell, while retaining full intellectual power, has moved to lesser concerns and more facile entertainment even if, considered impersonally and in the abstract, that entertainment has its full measure of satiric truth. That it does contain truth, even realism, may be attested to by a letter (dated December 11, 1943) from Cabell to Ellen Glasgow, in which Florida, it seems, was enraged by *The St. Johns* as a "libel upon Florida's heroic and spotless past."

Cabell's last two novels are slighter. Structurally they are clever and skilled, but the ingenuity does not include much of the substance or content. *There Were Two Pirates* (1946) tells, in the first person, the exploits of a Spanish pirate José Gasparilla off the shores of Florida as he attempted to accumulate enough savings to return to his beloved in Spain. Cabell uses "flash-backs" and a magic green stone which can release one from one's shadow, but the substance is slight for all the technical skill and the novel becomes no more than a pleasant pastime, although that, in itself, may be achievement enough. With *The Devil's Own Dear Son* (1949), the background is more topical in that it consists of a tourist home in Florida. St. Augustine again features prominently, but dialogue tends to extend and extend without real justification as we experience the life of an embryo Rotarian who journeys to the castle of his youth's dreams through a universe akin to Florida itself. The scheme gives opportunity for satire but—except in scenes among the devils who serve in a democracy under a chief executive called Satan—it is now a little too contrived, while power and spontaneity are slowly diminishing.

21: *Virginians Are Various*

> Of old the Hellenic race was marked off from the barbarian by being more keen-witted and more free from nonsense.
> —Herodotus

The three columns which make up this trilogy complete Cabell's writings by illustrating his place in the evolution of American and Western culture. European culture, with its classical foundations, must now interact with forces from Russia on the one hand and America on the other. Is it a question of Europe, as an extension of the classical, having to withstand the onslaughts of the barbarians? Will the barbarians dominate and destroy the cultural endeavors (various as these are) of thousands of years to the complete elimination of things spiritual? Or will the dynamic energies of the New World revitalize the old even as they become civilized, to the ultimate benefit of both? Cabell's art lies at the heart of this dilemma and shows how it can be satisfactorily resolved. In *Let Me Lie* he considers American Life in Virginia; in *Quiet Please* he deals with his own personal development within this framework; and in *As I Remember It* he illustrates more intimately the individuals who have influenced his art and himself. Emerson said:

> There is a correspondence between the human soul and everything that exists in the world . . . the principles . . . may be penetrated into within.

Just as within the individual there are forces making for integration and forces making for disintegration, or harmony and disharmony, or order and chaos, so within the community, the nation, the community of nations, the hemispheres and the world itself are these forces wanting to subordinate the state to the individual as represented by the majority, or the individual to the state, not necessarily represented by the majority. We can distinguish these forces only through our culture—a word signifying the state of cultivation toward fertile ground or barren ground. This is not the place to examine the ingredients compounded in the American melting pot except to hope that the outcome will be more than a mess of pottage. If we bear in mind Aristotle's advocacy of "all things in moderation" we may say that nearly all is chaff that is not of the spirit—this is not to deny Gerald Musgrave's final experiences and the very substantial validity of Penelope. Yet even this validity is substantial ultimately as it becomes spiritual. How, then, has Cabell resolved this dilemma? He enumerates the various ingredients that comprise the Virginia in which he was born and molded, and freed from, even as his freedom was achieved by the constructive illusions of this same Virginia as these illusions took him to their origins in England, Europe, Rome, Greece, and universal culture in general as he himself developed from the provincial to the cosmopolitan.

In *Let Me Lie*, Cabell deals in several essays with the backward-looking nostalgia of Virginia and South Carolina, with the golden age of plantation glories, of a freer and more gracious way of life which was to be ended by the one and only war acknowledged in those areas. He does this in such a way as to present, not only the humbug and self-deception inherent in Southern pretensions but, also, an admiration and a liking for the stubborn tenacity of conviction and purpose as illustrated supremely by General Lee's acceptance of the position of president of a "country-boarding school in a mountain village" at "the gaunt salary of $1500 a year," instead of exploiting a reputation to make a fortune. Thus emerges a clear, logical evaluation of Virginian romanticism, its inherent paradox—even as it appears in the Biography—of self-deceit, all producing the conception that "Mundus vult decepi" at the same time as "all goes forward towards something." One chapter, entitled "Published In Richmond, Virginia," illustrates provincial reaction to the "sophistication" of the writers of the twenties while the section dealing with Ellen Glasgow analyzes a Virginian who actually did become widely acknowledged as a creator of literature about Virginians if not for Virginians. But the significant thing is that eventually it is as a Virginian that Cabell emerges. Only there could he have been molded while young by, and in the atmosphere of, the illusions which he was later to present as hypotheses amended and then verified by evidence drawn from all times and places. At the end of this book Cabell shows this by connecting his own attitude, as a Virginian, with the words of Alfgar in the garden between dawn and sunrise:

> It may be that no man is royal, and that no god is divine, and that our mothers and our wives have not any part in holiness. Oh, yes, it very well may be that I have lost honor and applause, and that I take destruction, through following after a dream which has in it no truth. Yet my dream was noble; and its nobility contents me.

Contentment is happiness, and it is the pursuit of happiness in which not only Virginia but America and all other lands are engaged. As they approach it—by following the same dream—they will ultimately accord honor and applause to one who went ahead more rapidly by combining the old illusions with the new objectivity.

The precise manner in which Cabell did this may be seen in *Quiet Please*. This is a short work which contains information concerning the genesis and content of, for example, *The Nightmare Has Triplets*—much being reproductions of material already dealt with. The introduction is by Marjorie Burke, who seems to have acquired all of the Devil's own lucidity in *Smith*; this introduction is interesting for a definition of irony given by a visitor to Cabell called Dr. Fulg, who speaks with the perspicacity of Little Smirt when he states:

> Irony, Mr. Cabell, is the most distinctive of literary qualities and it is at the same time the most elusive of definition, since its essence is at its own paradox, whereby it expounds itself in a dualism.

Yet it is the last chapters, illustrating the evolution of a romantic, which are of most importance here. In these chapters Cabell treats the customs of the environment of his youth in a nonfictional equivalent of the early chapters of *Something About Eve*. When examining the early short stories such as "In Necessity's Mortar" and "Simon's Hour," it was wondered if Cabell had undergone some personal experience such as seems to have befallen Shakespeare with his Dark Lady who reappears from Beatrice to that Cleopatra who so strangely acquired black hair and a *pale* complexion, presumably for someone in the audience. In *Quiet Please* perhaps we receive the answer. Addressing himself when young, Cabell notes:

> You were twenty-one, in brief . . . before you strayed into the Garden between Dawn and Sunrise a large number of years before Jurgen had heard of this place, or you of Jurgen. There you encountered the original of Dorothy la Desirée. And that changed all. That was the primal cause . . . of your eventually . . . becoming my collaborator in a rather huge number of books.

This may be direct evidence of Cabell's transmutation of his own immediate experience. Note how the circumstances are such as to predetermine the art, even as with Shakespeare—or Melville, whose personal circumstances determined that he should live and then re-enact the mythical experiences essential to great art long before Jonah tackled the same problem. So here also we see how, as Cabell wrote, human life everywhere "is bound in by transient superficies behind which moves perceptibly the unseen and the inapprehensible." Cabell is grateful to that original of Dorothy because:

> . . . she dismissed that twenty one years old penniless youngster in order to marry a partially lame, age-stricken person (who, in fact, was well on in his thirties) with a substantial bank account. And I am far more than grateful for the enraged misery which the bewildered young man then faced.

Cabell made much art out of this misery and even the ruins were rebuilt. The experience appears to have armed Cabell's youth with the armor of promiscuity as the originals of many of his fictional heroines were put to the test and found wanton. But only his youth. For with marriage, as Cabell has frequently made clear even while acknowledging its uniqueness, came the "well-contented husband" caught "in the claws of a virtuous woman." With maturity came the style which was so well to communicate all Cabell's themes included that of *Jurgen*—that a husband had best be faithful to his wife, without being priggish about it. This style was not fully perfected in *The Soul of Melicent*, but it was in *The Cream of the Jest*, which Cabell here describes as "My own first book." We can see this attitude in the revisions whereby *The Soul of Melicent* became *Domnei*—the attitude which was so sorely mocked by the original of Dorothy la Desirée. Now, it is in the the loss of promiscuity as Cabell acquired maturity and distinctiveness of style that is significant for Cabell's resolution of the dilemma of the clash between new and old. For, in spite of the variousness of what was going on in and around him, Cabell is, if not the most civilized artist produced by the English-speaking world, then certainly among the most civilized. And this brings us to the observations of Toynbee in his *Study of History*:

> If we pass from the general field of manners and customs to the special field of art, we shall find the sense of promiscuity betraying itself, here again, in the alternative forms of vulgarity and barbarism. In one or other of these forms the art of a disintegrating civilization is apt to pay for an abnormally wide and rapid diffusion by forfeiting that distinctiveness of style which is the sign-manuel of fine quality.

So however we examine Cabell's art, whether from the literary, the psychological or the sociological viewpoint, the pieces seem to fit together in a perfectly integrated and harmonious unity from one end to the other—just as with the Parthenon of old.

The last of Cabell's many books is *As I Remember It*. And with this last work as with his first, Cabell was still privileged to be misunderstood by a reviewer. These reminiscences are in two parts. The first part deals with his first wife Priscilla Bradley Cabell, from courtship in 1912 to her death in 1949. This part is a model of lucid, candid and—there is no other word—beautiful exposition. Again there is abundant evidence of the immediate interaction between Cabell's living and his literature.

The second part deals largely with Cabell's contemporaries. A reviewer noted of this part:

> There are also animadversions on other writers whom he once called his friends, and about these the less said the better.

Cabell is indeed remarkably free from nonsense in dealing with his contemporaries and it is evidence of the distinctiveness of his style that he still equates tact with consideration rather than expediency. Here, indeed, are invaluable insights into the private lives and foibles of renowned contemporaries from Mencken and Sinclair Lewis to Hugh Walpole and Ellen Glasgow. The mind at work in *As I Remember It* bestrides the scene like enough to a colossus. The urbanity and humor are as good here as ever and the touch is surer than it sometimes is in the later works. Time is the only arbiter between Cabell and his contemporaries. Here we may note that the sole novel of Cabell's which received a Pulitzer award was the one he completed for Ellen Glasgow in her illness.

Chapter XXVIII, "Discourses upon the Impiety of Art," shows the belief, with only ironical prevarication, that the innate gift is "received from some supernatural Somebody" who is compounded as much of Satan as Jehovah. Here too is, at last, unequivocal evidence concerning the mythologist and his psyche:

> All which reminds me that sincere creative writing, as I understand it, must remain always, not in the least inimical, but indifferent, to popular morals, which it will serve or which it will violate as may best suit the writer's requirements. And by sincere creative writing, I mean writing which develops unfalteringly the writer's innate gifts and his innate predilections, such as they may happen to be, and which thus remains always true to his actual personality.

There is little need, it is hoped, to discuss further the nature of "popular" morals. The point seems to be in the connection between this expressed need for the artist to be true to himself, and

Cabell's observation, in the chapter "An Afterword," that to write and rewrite

> . . . has been to me a demented and bedrugged enjoyment, relished almost sensuously, and yet with an underlying sense of fulfilling my supreme duty, of doing what I was meant for.

To where does this take us? Perhaps back to Jung's statement about nihilism and the metamorphoses of the gods—a metamorphosis which can once again reorientate man in his universe as Eros puts forth his strength to counterbalance Ananke. The bait that will draw toward this metamorphosis is that the enjoyment that went into the writing is there for the reader to take out of it. That fact alone is almost enough to make Cabell unique, betokening, as it does, his refusal to participate in the view that life is awful, at the same time as he refuses to be merely sentimental in his treatment of it. So here, finally, we have verification of T. S. Eliot's requirements as Cabell's ingredients are revealed as wisdom in the metamorphosis of or insight into the gods, pleasure from the nature of the material provided by these gods—and their feminine counterparts—and craftsmanship as expressed in style and construction. The total is imaginative poetry of Miltonic dimensions. It is an epic as distinct from its contemporary literature as, in fact, were the major works of Milton, which were issued against the foreground of Restoration drama. Perhaps that is how they will remember it.

CONCLUSION

Looking back over the full vista of Cabell's works, we see a remarkably ordered, intricate, and beautiful landscape. To begin with, the first writings—the short stories and early novels including those on contemporary life and *The Soul of Melicent*—treat life largely as a challange to youth, although, from the beginning, Cabell has been unusually fair in seeing both sides of every question including that of youth and age. With the major works of the Biography the challenge is directed at mature man over the full range of his dilemma throughout his lifetime; the response to this challenge of life is presented, in depth and breadth, in all its spiritual and—symbolically—physical ramifications. The later writings place the emphasis more on age as Hamlet's Uncle rather than Hamlet receives the bulk of the treatment, or the King of Melphé rather than Cesario, although both sides of the questions are still acknowledged. Toward the end, treatment becomes satiric rather than ironic, the stature of the achievement tends to return to that of the early contemporary novels although in each case, even in *The St. Johns*, the artistic aim is fulfilled even as it becomes less ambitious, as seen even in the last two of Cabell's novels. The prose writings begin, continue and end on the very highest level of human intellectual endeavor and constitute the objective analytical soil from which the art was to flower into magnificent synthesis.

So everything seems most symmetrical. Symmetry is perfection. The pursuit of perfection is a universal impulse retained according to individual strength or weakness—which would appear to be a matter not so much of chance but of constitution. Cabell pursues it both in the form and in the content of his writings; the difficulties of the pursuit, difficulties which, from another point of view, are temptations to abandon it, add doubts to desires, doubts which capture the double nature of good and evil and, in so doing, guarantee the status of classical literature.

Thus we come to the summing up:

> But I at least, who have found human living and this world not wholly admirable, and who have here and there made formal admission of the fact, feel that in honor one ought to acknowledge all courtesies too. With life, then, I, upon the whole, have no personal quarrel; she has mauled, scratched and banged, she has in all ways damaged me; but she has permitted me to do that which I most wanted.

This is the conclusion of all Cabell's books, including *As I Remember It*. He sees life as a pursuit of beauty. Beauty embodies order, harmony, symmetry, and unity not only in the external and tangible but in the ultimately more solid reality of the intangible spirit. The pursuit of integration demands integrity, which needs courage, mostly the courage to face facts, mostly facts concerning self-knowledge. In the end, age must win and man must fail. But this fact does not release him from his obligation. His obligation is never stated, never defined, and it is not known to whom or what it is owed. Yet it fulfills a purpose not entirely contained in individual satisfaction. That which he most wanted was to write perfectly of beautiful happenings, not to throw light upon the universe, not to persuade others to a faith or creed, but to divert himself. In doing so, he has thrown considerable light upon the universe, and stated a creed. His faith, vision, or creed consists of a hope in evolutionary progress at the command of an artist-God, a hope augmented by the keenest of intellectual observation revealed in the interplay of these transformed observations in his art. The philosophical light upon the universe expresses not only that the ways of the artist-God are wonderful but that, ultimately, they are incomprehensible and, either way, are illusions. They have much to do, also, with a small white head known as Misery which moves hither and thither about the world. In expressing these things Cabell has persevered to the ends of thought and limits of imagination while equating his activity with that of mountain goats ranging the heights of idiocy. But it is clear, at least on examination, that his search has been impelled by his feelings—a fact which makes him a poet and brings us, at the last, to "The Sigil of Scoteia."

So many strange things have been written about this sigil that it has seemed worth while actually to see what it says. It contains the final statement which expresses the impulse and destination of all this artist's lifework. It refers not merely to *The Cream of the Jest* but to all his books:

> James Branch Cabell made this book so that he who wills may read the story of man's eternally unsatisfied hunger in search of beauty.
>
> Ettarre stays inaccessible always and her loveliness is his to look on only in his dreams.
>
> All men she must evade at the last and many are the ways of her elusion.

If a man is as great as his defiance of this situation—this predicament called life—then here surely was one who must be numbered among the greatest. Thanks to his persistent defiance, to his continuing to seek, Cabell found for us the key which renders Ettarre a little less inaccessible and thus postpones her elusions. At this dangerously early stage of our evolution, what could man need more? But also, what more could we desire?

The dream *is* the reality—all else is troubled sleep.

LETTER FROM CABELL TO AUTHOR

My Dear Desmond Tarrant:

What you must think of my prolonged silence is a matter that I shudder to reflect on. But you are wrong. The true reason for it is that I have been ill—and for that matter, still am.

In any case, last March I developed a virus infection which gradually and implacably devastated my entire interior for some five months, with the doctors giving me up as done for some three or four times. I did not get rid of this infection until July, and it left me with a host of yet other maladies, a cataloging of which I spare you. It follows that I am still an invalid dosed every day at least twenty times with drugs and injections, of which I do not even know the name and am too listless to inquire about. And all this starting when I had in hand a nearly finished book, which I have but now completed somehow!

What I wanted to say, though, is that I like and admire Towards Jerusalem [proposed title for this study] entirely and enormously. I would delight to see it published. Meanwhile I have noted a very few most minor matters of fact which will have to be corrected in your final draft.—Such as, it occurs to me offhand, crediting me with having composed the epigraph upon the title page of Gallantry, which I really borrowed from somewhere in Walter Pater's works. These tiny flaws, however, I shall check more carefully as soon as may be, if ever I get strong enough.

But chiefly at this instant I want to ask forgiveness for what must have seemed to you my extreme rudeness and inappreciation.

Yours faithfully,
JAMES BRANCH CABELL

8 November, 1955

SELECTED BIBLIOGRAPHY

A bibliography of two volumes, dealing with material by and about Cabell, was published by the University of Virginia Press in 1957. Volume I, by Frances Joan Brewer, has a foreword by Cabell, who observes of this work that Mrs. Brewer

> . . . has listed, not merely everything I have managed to get published, but likewise, to the very best of my knowledge, everything of any least importance concerning me which has ever been printed anywhere—whether it was flavored with approval or with condescension or with frank disgust.

Volume II consists of "Notes on the Cabell Collections at the University of Virginia." It is by Matthew J. Bruccoli, who states, in his introduction, that "this work is basically a listing of all the impressions of all editions of James Branch Cabell's works now in the Alderman Library of the University of Virginia." On the basis of fifty specimen pages (except for *Jurgen*, which was done completely), an indication is given, in this volume, of textual variations in successive editions.

Cabell himself, in a foreword to the revised edition of the I. R. Russell Bibliography, observed of the Biography of Manuel:

> Only in the eighteen volumes which contain the finally revised and co-ordinated text of the Storisende edition can I perceive my own writing in its completed form; and I tend frankly to regard all other books with my name on the cover as uncanonical.

The thoroughness and completeness (except for the English publishers of the later works) of these achievements are surely

283

such as to have made Ben Jonson, who initiated these activities, had he foreseen them, burn the rest of his library down in awed and despairing admiration.

Four critical works written since 1958 are L. D. Rubin's *No Place on Earth* (University of Texas, 1959); *Between Friends*, letters of Cabell and correspondents, edited by Padraic Colum and Margaret Freeman Cabell (Harcourt, Brace, & World, Inc., 1962); J. L. Davis' *James Branch Cabell* (Twayne's U.S. Authors, 1962, and College and University Press, 1964); and A. R. Well's *Jesting Moses* (University of Florida Press, 1962).

All else that seems needed here is to list, in two parts, Cabell's own chief works. Part One lists the works comprising the Biography of Manuel, not in the order in which they were actually written, but in the order required for the historical evolution of Manuel and his descendants from the thirteenth century to the twentieth. Part Two lists the later works, in the order in which they were written, under the collective titles of the successive trilogies. Except where otherwise stated, Cabell was published in America by Edward M. McBride & Co., N.Y., and in England by John Lane, The Bodley Head, London.

PART ONE: THE BIOGRAPHY OF MANUEL

The Storisende Edition of the Works of James Branch Cabell in Eighteen Volumes. New York, 1927–30

1. *Beyond Life* (Critical essays). New York, 1919; London, 1925.
2. *Figures of Earth* (Novel). New York, 1921; London, 1922.
3. *The Silver Stallion* (Novel). New York, 1926; London, 1928.
4. *The Witch-Woman* (A trilogy of fiction (revised) including *The Music from Behind the Moon* (1926), *The Way of Ecben* (1924), and *The White Robe* (1928), New York, Farrar, Straus & Co., 1948.
5. *The Soul of Melicent* (Novel). New York, Frederick A. Stokes & Co., 1913. Revised and renamed *Domnei*, New York, Mc-Bride, 1920.

6. *Chivalry* (Short Stories). New York, Harper & Bros., 1909. Revised, New York, McBride, 1921; London, 1928.
7. *Jurgen* (Novel). New York, 1919; London, 1921.
8. *The Line of Love* (Short Stories). New York, Harper & Bros., 1905. Revised, New York, McBride, 1921; London, 1929.
9. *The High Place* (Novel). New York, 1923; London, 1923.
10. *Gallantry* (Short Stories). New York, Harper & Bros., 1907. Revised New York, McBride, 1922; London, 1928.
11. *Something About Eve* (Novel). New York, 1927; London, 1927.
12. *The Certain Hour* (Short Stories). New York, 1916; England, McBride, Nast & Co.
13. *The Cords of Vanity* (Novel). New York, Doubleday, Page & Co., 1909. Revised, New York, McBride, 1920; London, 1925.
14. *From the Hidden Way* (Poetry). New York, 1916. Revised with five additional poems, New York, 1924.
15. *The Rivet in Grandfather's Neck* (Novel). New York, 1915; England, McBride, Nast, 1915.
16. *The Eagle's Shadow* (Novel). New York, Doubleday, Page & Co., 1904; England, Wm. Heinemann, 1904. Revised, New York, McBride, 1923.
17. *The Cream of the Jest* (Novel). New York, 1917, slightly revised, 1922; London, 1923.
18. *Straws and Prayer Books* (Critical Essays). New York, 1924; London, 1926.

PART TWO: THE LATER WRITINGS

Their Lives and Letters

19. *These Restless Heads* (Fiction and prose reminiscence). New York, 1932.
20. *Special Delivery* (A packet of replies). New York, 1933; London, P. Allen & Co., 1934.
21. *Ladies and Gentlemen* (Reconsiderations). New York, 1934.

The Nightmare Has Triplets

22. *Smirt* (Novel). New York, 1934.
23. *Smith* (Novel). New York, 1935.
24. *Smire* (Novel). New York, Doubleday, Doran & Co., 1937.

Heirs and Assigns

25. *The King Was in His Counting House* (Novel). New York, Toronto, Farrar & Rinehart, 1938; London, John Lane, 1939.
26. *Hamlet Had an Uncle* (Novel). New York, Toronto, Farrar & Rinehart, 1940; London, John Lane, 1940.
27. *The First Gentleman of America* (Novel). New York, Toronto, Farrar & Rinehart, 1942; London, John Lane, entitled *The First American Gentleman*, 1942.

It Happened in Florida

28. *The St. Johns* (History). New York, Toronto, Farrar & Rinehart, 1943.
29. *There Were Two Pirates* (Novel). New York, Farrar, Straus & Co., 1946; London, John Lane, 1947.
30. *The Devil's Own Dear Son* (Novel). New York, Farrar, Straus & Co., 1949; London, John Lane, 1950.

Virginians Are Various

31. *Let Me Lie* (An Ethnological Account). New York, Farrar, Straus & Co., 1947.
32. *Quiet, Please.* (Personal reflections). Gainesville, University of Florida Press, 1952.
33. *As I Remember It.* (Autobiographical recollections). New York, 1955.

INDEX

Index

Norns, the: 110, 112
Noumaria: 161

Obscurity, Cabell's alleged: 37
Observer, The: 193
Odysseus: 226-27, 235
"Of Annual Magic": 40-41
"Olivia's Pottage": 174
Ormskirk, Duke of: *see* John Bulmer
Orton: 257-60
Orts, Simon: 164-69

Paine, Thomas: 222
Pan: 43
Parrington, Vernon Louis: 69, 71
Pater, Walter Horatio: 46, 136, 155, 162, 281
Pathos in Cabell's work: 197-98
Peacock, Thomas Love: 96
Penelope (wife of Odysseus): 226-27, 270, 272
Perion de la Forêt: 102-10, 112
Philippe d'Orleans: 153, 156, 179
Philosophy, Cabell's: 177
Plato: 133
Poe, Edgar Allan: 29
Poetry, Cabell's: 36-44, 163
Poictesme: 15, 19, 22, 43-49, 65, 70, 78-81, 85, 87-89, 92, 102-103, 107, 114, 120, 144-45, 147, 151, 159, 161, 192, 214, 216-17, 227, 236-37, 244, 247, 250-52, 263
Pope, Alexander: 36, 48, 174
"Porcelain Cups": 145, 148
Porter, Mrs. Gene Stratton: 101
Pound, Ezra: 145
Pre-Raphaelites, association of Cabell's work with: 155
Priestley, J. B.: 37
Primitive religion: 6ff.
Prohibition, Cabell's views on: 24
Promethean civilization: 19
Prometheus: 19, 212, 220, 230
Prospero: 212-13, 220
Pulitzer prize: 276
Puysange: *see* Florian de Puysange, Gaston de Puysange, Jean de Puysange
Pyle, Howard: 26

Quetzal: 264
Quiet Please: 271, 273-74

Rabelais: 96, 117
Raleigh, Sir Walter: 222, 228
Rascoe, Burton: 113, 192
"Rat-Trap, The": 120-21, 124
Realism in Cabell's work: 58, 81, 139
Religion: man's use of, 6ff.; Cabell's conception of, 73-77; in *Smire*, 249; *see also* "Christ legend," Christianity, God
Restoration drama: 59, 66-69, 164, 277
Ribaut, Jean: 267
Richmond, Virginia: 20-22, 272
Richmond News: 25
Richmond Times: 22
Rituals, man's use of: 6ff.
Rivet in Grandfather's Neck, The: 27, 33, 36, 49, 236
Rokesle, Lord: 164, 169
Roman gods: 9
Romanticism in Cabell's work: 55ff.
Russell, Bertrand: 115, 117
Russell, I. R.: 160-61

St. Augustine, Florida: 266
St. Johns, The: 209, 267-69, 278
Saraide: 94-95, 97
Sargatanet: 112
Sartre, Jean-Paul: 201
Satire in Cabell's work: 209-10, 251, 278
"Satraps, The": 127
Scepticism in Cabell's work: 68
Scott, Sir Walter: 61
Sesphra of Philistia: 80, 83-84, 87, 140, 157
"Sestina, The": 115-19
Sex in Cabell's work: 180-82
Shakespeare, William: 48-49, 59, 61, 66, 84, 130, 134, 138, 146, 174-75, 216, 225, 230, 234, 263, 274
Shaw, George Bernard: 82, 123, 145, 221, 240
Shelley, Percy Bysshe: 5, 10, 24, 43, 46, 72, 84, 155, 222
Sheridan, Richard Brinsley: 48, 59, 66, 68, 174
Short stories, Cabell's: 46-47; *see also titles of individual works*
Sidney, Sir Philip: 6, 146, 222, 228
Sieur de la Forêt: 253, 255
Sigil of Scoteia, The: 108, 280
Silver Stallion, The: 7, 15, 18-19, 48,

291